A WOMAN'S CRUSADE

ALICE PAUL AND THE BATTLE FOR THE BALLOT

MARY WALTON

St. Martin's Griffin   New York

www.stmartins.com

Library of Congress Cataloging-in-Publication Data
Walton, Mary, 1941–
    A woman's crusade : Alice Paul and the battle for the ballot / Mary Walton.
       p.   cm.
    ISBN 978-0-230-61175-7 (hardback) 978-1-250-11170-8 (paperback)
    1. Paul, Alice, 1885–1977   2. Suffragists—United States—Biography.
3. Women's rights—United States—History.   4. National Woman's Party—History.
I. Title.
    JK1899.P38W35   2010
    324.6'23092—dc22
    [B]
                                                                    2009050149

ISBN 978-1-250-11170-8

St. Martin's Griffin books may be purchased in bulk for promotional, educational, or business use. Please contact your local bookseller or the Macmillan Corporate and Premium Sales Department at (800) 221-7945, extension 5442, or by e-mail at MacmillanSpecialMarkets@macmillan.com.

First St. Martin's Griffin Edition: May 2016

P1

Praise for *A Woman's Crusade*

"Drawing upon press accounts, original papers, and books written by contemporaries of Paul's, Walton is able to give her accounts . . . a colorful immediacy. . . . Walton's book offers lessons in the tenacity, courage, and fierce discipline needed to overcome the obstacles pioneers often face."

—The Philadelphia Inquirer

"Richly endowed with research . . . detailed, absorbing. . . . I value the book for introducing her to the next generation of feminists with a taste for revolution."

—*Vivian Gornick,* Ms Magazine

"Mary Walton has written a passionate history of Alice Paul. All Americans should read this book to learn more about one of our most extraordinary and dynamic leaders."

—*Congresswoman Carolyn B. Maloney*

"Alice Paul used nonviolent protest to win full voting rights for American women; but few Americans know about her. Mary Walton vividly brings Alice Paul to life in this brilliant, important, and highly readable book."

—*Gene Roberts, author of* The Race Beat

ALSO BY MARY WALTON
The Deming Management Method
For Love of Money
Deming Management at Work
Car: A Drama of the American Workplace

To Gene Roberts

CONTENTS

Eight pages of photographs appear between pages 124 and 125.

AUTHOR'S NOTE

Five years ago I was seated at a dinner party next to Gene Roberts, the editor of the *Philadelphia Inquirer* when I was a reporter there in the 1970s and '80s. Roberts is legendary in the newspaper business for his vision and news instincts. Since coauthoring an essay on press and protestors at the White House in 1994, he had been urging writers at loose ends, including myself, to undertake a book about a trailblazing suffragist, a pioneer in nonviolent resistance, who had carried on a David-and-Goliath battle against a president and Congress to win the vote for American women. Her name was Alice Paul and I'd never heard of her. Nor had the others who had rejected the idea. How important could she be?

Roberts is not given to casual chitchat. Hunting for a conversation topic that night, I said, "Tell me about Alice Paul." And for the first time I learned about her in detail. I concluded she was unknown simply because no one had written her story. Before long, I was spooling through reels of microfilm records of her National Woman's Party in the basement of Rutgers University's Alexander Library.

Thanks to an introduction from Alicia Shepard (Thank you, Lisa!), my search for an agent willing to market a book on this seemingly obscure suffragist led me to the doorstep of Gail Ross, who warned me that "women's history doesn't sell." And then she sold it. I am so grateful to have landed with Alessandra Bastagli at Palgrave Macmillan. Her enthusiasm spurred me on, and when the first draft was done, her patient and painstaking editing, so rare these days, and so valuable for a journalist-turned-historian (all those endnotes!), gave shape to the narrative. Copyeditor Jennifer Simington's probing questions brought clarity and structure. Alessandra's helpful and friendly assistant Colleen Lawrie kept me on track and was always available to guide me through the mysteries of photo scans, acquisitions, and Word's track changes feature. Production editor Yasmin Mathew looked after the manuscript in the final stages.

I made one editorial decision along the way that is worth noting here. To preserve historical context, when speaking of African Americans, I use "Negro" and "black," the words employed in the beginning of the twentieth century, with the former by far the most common. "Colored" also appears in quotes from the day. I thank Reverend Gil Caldwell for his counsel on these matters.

Readers will surely find it useful to have a sense of money equivalents. Rather than clutter up the text, I herewith provide a guide, based on calculations by www.measuringworth.com. According to the Consumer Price Index, in 1909 when Alice was periodically receiving money from her mother for living expenses in Europe, $100 was worth $2,441 in 2008 dollars. In 1914, when Alice was paying top organizers $100 a month, the 2008 value was little changed, at $2,222. Although a contribution of $5 might sound like a small amount today, it was actually worth over $110 that same year, a considerable amount for the typical female with no independent income. By 1917, the value of money had slipped substantially; $100 was worth the 2008 equivalent of $1,700. And in 1918, it had slipped even more, to $1,430.

I am grateful to the Radcliffe Institute for Advanced Study for a research grant that defrayed expenses for an expedition to Cambridge to read Alice Paul's diary and youthful correspondence, as well as the papers of several other suffragists that are housed in the Institute's Schlesinger Library, where years ago I had once spent many hours as a student at Harvard. How life does circle.

Few family members remain who knew Alice. Her second cousins once removed, Richard Robbins and Calvin Robbins, shared youthful memories of a serious but welcoming middle-aged woman with a cloud of dark hair, who often attended family gatherings and teared up at family funerals. Richard, a retired librarian and former copyeditor, read every word of the manuscript and saved me from countless errors. Letha Mae Glover, Christopher Henson, and Carol Mullin helped provide a picture of Alice in old age.

The search for information on two of Alice's top lieutenants led me to two helpful keepers of the flame, Dora Lewis's great granddaughter, Dora Townsend, and Lucy Burns's great niece, Janet Burns Campbell.

Paulsdale, the Paul family's "Home Farm" in Mt. Laurel, New Jersey, where Alice grew up, is today the Alice Paul Institute, operated by a group of admirable women who lent a hand to this project every step of the way. Program Director Lucienne Beard and Director Rhonda DiMascio were on board from the beginning. Lucy pointed me in many helpful directions and became a good friend.

Kris Myers generously shared her knowledge of suffrage history. Valerie Buickerood and Dana Dabek-Milstein added their encouragement. No one was too busy to help me run the copier.

Jennifer Krafchik, director of collections for the Sewall-Belmont House & Museum in Washington, D.C., the final headquarters of the National Woman's Party, unpacked the beautiful old banners, opened up photo archives, and provided scans. After Jennifer left on maternity leave, interpretation and education manager Abigail Newkirk took over and was just as helpful.

Christopher Densmore, curator of the Friends Historical Library of Swarthmore College, steered me to relevant materials and took the trouble to find the text of Alice Paul's Ivy Ode, delivered at her graduation, when I couldn't. Dona Laughlin, alumni director of Packer Collegiate Institute, allowed me to research the school archives on Lucy Burns and her sisters and then helped locate Janet Burns Campbell. At the Moorestown Friends School, Beth Stouffer shared materials on the Paul family and the school in Alice's day.

I am indebted for insights and encouragement to the people who read all or portions of the drafts: Peggy Anderson, Lucienne Beard, Kelly Dilworth, Bill Eddins, Emma Edmunds, Antonella Iannarino, Laura Nathanson, Mike Shoup, and Gene Roberts. My husband and live-in editor, Charles Layton, cheerfully read every word at least once and usually twice or more. His interest never faltered. I could not have done this without him.

As the guardian of my offsite auxiliary hard drive, Joyce Klein put up with my constant interruptions to retrieve it for updating. Robert P. J. Cooney Jr., author of the beautiful illustrated history *Winning the Vote,* helped demystify the world of suffrage photo archives and found the best photos first. And all the following people answered questions, provided information and services, and extended comradely help: Joe Adler, Jofie Adler, Bill Barry, Alicia Belmas, John and Rose Boland, Perdita Buchan, Kevin Chambers, Dante Cosentino, M. J. Crowley, Sally Downey, Don Drake, Paul Dunlap, David Gerber, Sarah Heuges, Tina Heuges, Molly Hindman, Erik Landsberg, David Layton, Rebecca Layton, Diane McKernan, Christine McLaughlin, Patsy McLaughlin, Geanna Merola, Connie Ogden, Helen Pike, Donald A. Ritchie, Janice E. Ruth, Andrew Stromberg, and David Walls.

Mary Walton
February 1, 2010

Alice Paul. Courtesy of the Historic National Woman's Party, Sewall-Belmont House and Museum, Washington, D.C.

PROLOGUE

In 1848 when Elizabeth Cady Stanton and her friends organized a woman's rights convention in Seneca Falls, New York, a married woman could not own property. She could not sue or be sued, make a contract or a will, or operate a business in her own name. If she worked, her wages belonged to her husband. In the event of a divorce, the father had custody of their children. Without the money to pay for a private education, a woman who aspired to college was largely out of luck, since the doors of most public universities were closed to her. In no state could she vote, except as a school board member here, a municipal officer there. In the words of the convention's "Declaration of Sentiments," she was "civilly dead."[1]

As the child of a lawyer, Stanton often heard stories of the way discriminatory laws denied married women rights to property and children. When her only brother died, her father's remark cut her to the quick: "Oh my daughter, I wish you were a boy!"[2] In 1850, Stanton met Susan B. Anthony, a Quaker school teacher turned temperance crusader, and the two formed a lifelong partnership in pursuit of equal rights for women.

Led by this remarkable pair, the nineteenth-century women's movement succeeded in eliminating numerous legal barriers to equality. By 1902, when the National American Woman Suffrage Association conducted a survey, a wife could own property in three-quarters of the states and in two-thirds she could keep her paycheck. The doors to most public universities had swung open. The holdouts were largely in the South, a bastion of prejudice against women. In Georgia, husbands no longer had the right to whip their wives, but the state university was one of just four (all in the South) that didn't admit women.

In Alabama, women could not practice law or medicine or serve as ministers. In Louisiana, with the exception of mothers and grandmothers, women, classed with idiots and lunatics, could not be appointed guardians.

Despite advances in family law, in all but nine states and the District of Columbia a father still had sole custody and control of minor children. In almost no state could women be notary publics. And juries with women were rare.[3]

When Anthony died in 1906, four years after Stanton, women had won the ballot in just four states: Wyoming, Utah, Colorado, and Idaho. Because she could not vote, a woman had no voice in the heated national conversation kindled by progressive reforms. Trusts were being busted, tenements cleaned up, political machines ripped apart. But men controlled the agenda. Women had no leverage over elected officials or those who aspired to office.

Voting, it was argued, would distract women from their sacred domestic roles. They would indulge in politics to the exclusion of motherhood and wifely duties. "You are the queens of the domestic kingdom," warned Cardinal James Gibbons of Baltimore, speaking for the Catholic establishment. "Do not stain your garments with the soil of the political arena."[4] Women were said to be uninformed and too emotional to make considered judgments, particularly at a certain time of the month.

In 1908, the *New York Times* polled eight U.S. senators, twenty-two U.S. representatives, and thirty-five college and university presidents on the issue of women's suffrage. Forty-nine percent were in favor, 28 percent were opposed, and the remaining 23 percent were either noncommittal or favored limiting the vote. Highly educated men were less likely than lawmakers to approve of women voting. Eleven of the presidents waffled, delivering so many pros and cons they could not be categorized. Only 14 percent of those polled were squarely in favor of votes for women.[5]

Alston Ellis of Ohio University maintained that, contrary to popular belief, females were no more moral than men. Enfranchising Colorado women had failed in his observation to "purify" politics in the way some had predicted. Worse, "Women, under the recent order of things, are becoming too mannish." Frederick W. Hamilton of Tufts College said the majority of women "do not want the ballot, and probably would not use it if they could." The *Times* concurred, snidely. "While it is not a fact that no American women take an interest in politics, the vast majority never give the subject anything deserving the name of thought."[6]

For southerners obsessed with preventing enfranchised black males from voting, the potential addition of millions of black females to the electorate was a nightmare; moreover, black women were thought to be less easily intimidated than black men. Also hostile were the bosses of the corrupt political machines, who feared that female voters would resist manipulation and favor reform. Manufacturing interests thought it likely that females armed with ballots would battle on behalf of women workers. Protectors of the status quo—the wealthy stakeholders in oil, mining, and the railroads—quietly prodded influential lawmakers to take anti-suffrage stands.[7]

Above all, a powerful liquor establishment stuffed the pockets of politicians with cash and advertised heavily in state after state when the issue arose, certain that the distaff half of the species would overwhelmingly favor prohibition. The malt liquor industry successfully warded off suffrage in a 1912 Wisconsin referendum, convincing voters—all men, of course—that voting women not only would seek to deprive imbibers of a pleasurable birthright, but would also jeopardize the state's economy. Manufacturers and purveyors would suffer, as well as coopers, bottle and cork makers, and the farmers who grew barley and corn.

When convenient, and it was always convenient, the opponents of suffrage hid behind the doctrine of states' rights, which is based on the Tenth Amendment stipulation that those powers not explicitly granted in the U.S. Constitution to the federal government belong by default to the states. Allowing each state to determine its course ensured that in much of the country women would never win the ballot.

Under this onslaught, the suffrage establishment did not die, but it aged and grew weary. Elizabeth Cady Stanton's daughter Harriot Stanton Blatch, returning to the United States from England in 1902, encountered a movement "completely in a rut. . . . It bored its adherents and repelled its opponents."[8]

Then, in the ensuing years, fueled by a potent combination of education, frustration, anger, and courage, a new sisterhood rallied to the cause. The movement had but one goal: a constitutional amendment allowing women the country over to vote. A Massachusetts congressman labeled members "iron-jawed angels."[9] Their leader was Alice Paul, a New Jersey Quaker, who had apprenticed with the British suffragettes. Paul was not only fearless, she was a brilliant tactician, talented fundraiser, and canny publicist. To her side gravitated a cadre of fiercely dedicated women. As Paul launched her campaign in 1913 with a spectacular parade in the nation's capital, she forged a new army of suffragists: college girls from Vassar, Smith, and Bryn Mawr, along with pioneering "new women" from the depths of Greenwich Village, and middle- and upper-class deserters from more conservative suffrage societies. The movement was bankrolled in part by the wealthy Alva Belmont, formerly Alva Vanderbilt, who found suffrage politics more fulfilling than her pampered life at the pinnacle of New York society.

They were not many. Perhaps sixty thousand at their peak. For seven years, they battled with great spirit against skepticism, ridicule, violence, and challenges to their patriotism to bring American women their most fundamental right of citizenship—the vote.

CHAPTER ONE

QUAKER, SOCIAL WORKER, SUFFRAGETTE!

I cannot understand how this all came about. Alice is such a mild-mannered girl.

—*Tacie Paul, Alice Paul's mother*
New York Times, *November 13, 1909*

Alice Paul grew up in a Quaker cocoon. Born January 11, 1885, she was a member of the eighth generation of American Quakers descended from Philip Paul, who fled religious persecution in England in 1685 and settled in what is now Paulsboro, New Jersey. She attended Quaker schools and Quaker meetings in Moorestown, New Jersey, a town settled by Quakers. Late in life, she would tell an interviewer, "I never met anybody who wasn't a Quaker, and I never heard of anybody who wasn't a Quaker, except that the maids we had were always Irish Catholics."[1]

It was those "gay maids," as she called them, whose flights from their third-floor lodgings on their free days to attend dances where music was played—*music!*—suggested suspect pleasures.[2] Elsewhere, young people might gather round the piano in the parlor and croon "After the Ball" or "The Band Played On" or even "A Hot Time in the Old Town." But Alice's parents, William and Tacie Paul, were particularly devout members of the Society of Friends, as

Quakers were formally known. They believed that time was more appropriately devoted to work or silence and that music was quite possibly dangerous.

William Paul's earnings as a bank president and the proceeds from Paulsdale, his modest 167-acre working farm, known to the family as the Home Farm, provided a comfortable life for Alice and her younger sister and two brothers—Helen, Bill, and Parry. At Paulsdale, the family's handsome white stucco home presided from a small knoll over a large, sloping front lawn, where the Paul children hit tennis balls amid grazing sheep. In summer Alice played checkers on the wrap-around verandah and prowled the family's fertile orchard in search of juicy peaches. She read, entranced, the household's leather-bound set of Dickens over and over again, along with every other book in the house and school library.[3]

In a photograph taken with her brother Bill when she was six and he five, Alice is the image of a proper Quaker child. Her unruly black hair has been tamed into a tight bun with a center part in classic Quaker style, and she is simply dressed in a dark long-sleeved blouse under a white cotton jumper. But on mornings when other Quaker girls climbed into family carriages for the mile-long ride to the red-brick schoolhouse in Moorestown, Alice chose an unconventional mode of travel, riding her horse bareback.

In the Friends' school, she would have learned that in 1647 the founder of the faith, George Fox, a handsome twenty-eight-year-old shoemaker's apprentice, had discovered his religious calling while tending sheep with only a Bible as company. In a moment of despair, according to his journal, Fox heard a voice that told him, "There is one, even Christ Jesus, that can speak to thy condition." On hearing the message, Fox wrote, "my heart did leap for joy." He realized that everyone, whether Christian, Muslim, Jew, or pagan, carried within the "inner light" of Jesus Christ.[4]

Fox's first followers called themselves "Children of the Light."

The Friends did not believe in violence, much less war, and they would not pay taxes to support a militia. Once, offered the post of army captain on his release from a prison term, Fox turned it down. He was jailed for an additional six months, one of eight imprisonments. Like Fox, thousands of Quakers went to prison, among them Alice's ancestor Philip Paul. Hundreds died behind bars.

From the outset, Quakers granted women more status than other denominations. Not only were they ministers, they went to jail for their activities just as men did. Fox's wife was the widow Margaret Fell, a Quaker convert who had been married to a judge. After her first husband died and she lost his legal protection, she served several prison terms for her Quaker activities.

In 1827, Quaker harmony was shattered by a bitter schism that divided the faith for more than a century and shaped Alice Paul's upbringing. Her maternal grandparents, William and Alice Parry, threw in with the sect led by a crusading Long Island farmer, Elias Hicks. A religious purist and powerful preacher, Hicks warned that the joys of fine living and elaborate displays of wealth were becoming too common among a thriving Quaker merchant class in cities such as Philadelphia and Baltimore. He found it necessary to remind people that "plainness and simplicity were the true marks of the Lord's people."[5]

Even more alarming to Hicks and his followers—many of them "country" Quakers like the Pauls who lived on farms and in small towns—urban Quakers were strongly influenced by an evangelical movement imported from London. Though Quakerism was firmly rooted in Christianity, the early Friends downplayed biblical history and trusted the inner light to convey Christ's will. The urban revisionists, however, emphasized the primacy of the scriptures and Christ's personification as the Savior.

Quakers had been in the forefront of the Abolition movement. But the Bible-reading evangelicals, known as Orthodox Quakers, would sometimes deal with slaveholders in the course of doing business. For his part, Hicks would neither eat sugar nor rice nor wear cotton clothing, products cultivated by slaves. In Moorestown, the Hicksites had their school, the orthodox theirs, and children of the two sects kept to their respective sides of the street.

Alice's great-grandfather was Charles Stokes, a committed Hicksite active in state politics. Among the visitors to the Stokes household was Lucretia Mott, a Quaker minister, abolitionist, and pioneering suffragist, who helped Elizabeth Cady Stanton organize the 1848 Woman's Rights Convention.

The marriage of Stokes's daughter Alice to William Parry in 1843 merged two distinguished families. Parry, Alice Paul's maternal grandfather, was an illustrious nurseryman, engineer, surveyor, politician, and judge, who had also found time in his busy life to raise money to establish Swarthmore, a Hicksite college.[6] On the northwestern rim of Philadelphia stood Haverford, an all-male Orthodox institution. The Hicksites were more inclined toward educating women than their Orthodox adversaries. Swarthmore was co-ed and Parry's daughter Tacie, Alice's mother, was among the first female students.

Even so, Hicksite Quakers viewed Swarthmore as an experiment "to prove what has never yet been fully proven . . . that it is feasible and desirable to give to woman equal educational facilities with man." It was one thing to provide both sexes with an education, however, and another to trust them with each other. The administration took the *in loco parentis* role to heart and fired the first president for being too soft on issues of moral propriety. His successor, Edward Hicks Magill, was famous for his "100 Rules," of which perhaps the most famous of all was that "Students of the two sexes, except brothers and sisters, shall not walk together on the grounds of the College, nor in the neighborhood, nor to or from the railroad station or the skating grounds. They shall not coast upon the same sled."[7]

Alice entered Swarthmore in 1901 at the age of sixteen. The Quakers at the college spoke the language of the plain people, as Quakers were also known—the "thee" and "thy" that Alice had grown up with and used with family members all her life. But she was free to wear colorful clothing, rather than the monotone dresses and white caps that hung in her mother's closet, and restrictions on music had been relaxed; she and her schoolmates danced, but not with boys.

That year, Alice felt almost giddy with her newfound freedom. On the first page of her freshman diary, housed in a crisp red cover, she wrote, "Had a reception in evening—Old girls to the new. Were presented to all the girls and each freshman received a tiny bouquet. Everyone wore names pinned on. The old girls sang the Swarthmore songs and then we went over to the gym to dance. Danced whole evening and had a glorious time." "Glorious" was a word she often used, sometimes to describe the ice cream and cake celebrations the college hosted. When boxes of food arrived from home, the girls shared in a "feast." Like generations of college girls to come, the slender Alice gained twelve pounds that first year.[8]

In the spring of her freshman year, her father returned from a Florida vacation with a cold that developed into a fatal pneumonia. His death at fifty-two barely caused Alice to break stride. "I was too young for it to be much of a blow to me," she said years afterward. "Life went on just the same." Many teenagers, of course, are devastated by the death of a father. A more likely explanation is that she and her father simply weren't close. He was, she said, "*extremely* busy, terribly busy."[9] It is easy to conclude that the terribly busy William Paul, both bank president and gentleman farmer, and the head of an orderly and disciplined Quaker household, was not an easy person for his daughter to approach. After William's death, things lightened up a bit around the Home Farm. Tacie Paul even bought a piano and allowed Helen to take lessons.

Well before graduation in 1905, Alice lost interest in her major, biology, which she had selected her freshman year only because she knew nothing about it, having studied all the other subjects in high school. Her classmates were mostly young men preparing to be engineers. As graduation loomed, a friendly professor pointed her toward a career in social work.

Until then, the field had largely been the province of volunteers, but in 1898 economist Edward T. Devine and other social work reformers had founded the New York School of Philanthropy to educate a corps of professionals. Armed with a scholarship, Alice moved her belongings into a room in the New York College Settlement on Manhattan's lower east side. A handsome building located at 95 Rivington Street next to a synagogue, it offered a full complement of classes and services for the poor, and also functioned as a place "where educated women might live in order to furnish a common meeting ground for all classes for their mutual benefit and education."[10] By living in such proximity to their underprivileged constituents, the founders reasoned, educated young women would go on to serve them in some capacity.

Stepping out the front door of the settlement house, Alice encountered a foreign city. The surrounding streets were thronged with immigrants, the majority fresh-off-the-boat Jews who had been delivered "from the stench and throb of the steerage to the stench and throb of New York tenements," in the words of novelist Henry Roth.[11] Children spilled from the crowded tenements where large families turned out clothing for the garment trade, living and working in dark three- and four-room apartments with babies underfoot.

On the streets, the noise alone—to Roth "an avalanche of sound"—was a far cry from the cushioned clip-clop of passing horses that had punctuated the quiet of Moorestown. "Countless children . . . countless baby carriages . . . countless mothers. And to the screams, rebukes and bickerings of these, a seemingly endless file of hucksters joined their bawling cries."[12]

The air percolated with Yiddish voices. Signs were in Yiddish and so were the newspapers. The neighborhood was a tinderbox. "Tonight there was a fire opposite us—in the barber's shop," Alice wrote to her mother. "They have fires all the time around here."[13]

On weekdays, Alice pinned on her big black velvet hat and maneuvered north to the relative calm of the School of Philanthropy on 22nd Street to study such courses as "Racial Traits in the Population," "Constructive Social Work" and "The State in Its Relation to Charity."[14]

On evenings and weekends during the winter of 1905–1906, she visited poor families in buildings filled with the pungent odors of unfamiliar dishes. The most she could do for the needy was to steer them toward medical care or a temporary source of food. She also helped out at 95 Rivington, an oasis of order for staff and constituents alike. People trooped in and out of the settlement house all day long for meetings—there were thirty-seven social clubs alone, plus classes in cooking, manual training, dressmaking, and art. For youngsters there was a kindergarten and a popular playground. Small fees were charged so people wouldn't feel like charity cases.

During the summer of 1906, while those who could afford it fled to Newport, Atlantic City, the Catskills, and the Adirondacks, Alice remained behind with the less fortunate, collecting her first salary. The work offered little satisfaction. In those days, before government health care, if a person became ill, "you would try to call up the hospitals and so on that she might be eligible for and get her in and get it for her. Just all day long." By fall, Alice had concluded she didn't want to be a social worker. They "were not doing much good in the world. . . . You couldn't *change* the situation by social work."[15] She spent the next year at the University of Pennsylvania earning her master's degree in what really interested her: sociology, with a minor in political science and economics.

Alice's academic enterprise earned the respect of local Quakers. In early 1907, the community awarded her a scholarship to Woodbrooke, a Friends study center in Birmingham, England, situated on a sculpted eleven-acre estate donated by Quaker candy maker George Cadbury. Before she started classes in the fall, she traveled to Berlin to learn German, a valuable language for the academic she now aspired to become.

Her letters home were filled with keenly observed details about the Germans: the women who smoked, the men, their faces gashed by duel scars, the disgusting table manners. "Most of them shovel their food in with their knives, make a frightful noise while they eat, soak their bread in coffee, etc. till one feels almost sick."[16]

She frequently mentioned Frau Heick, her roommate in her inexpensive Lutheran boardinghouse, who taught her German, but whose life offered lessons as well in the plight of a self-supporting woman. At first, the youthful Alice found the forty-five-year-old frau irritating. She set the alarm for an hour and a half before rising "because she likes to lie in bed and think how nice it is to not have to get up at once. Her neighbors and I object but she snaps our heads off

& pays no attention." As a result "she feels worn out all day—whines & complains without ceasing. She is *most aggravating.*"[17]

Heick had only three students, whom she charged just twelve cents for a lesson. Alice decided to pay twice that amount, for "she is exceedingly poverty stricken it seems. . . . She used to teach school but had to stop when she married & now that she is a widow she can not get back for they take only single women as teachers here. . . . Most peculiar."[18]

Later in the summer, her "eccentric" roommate got a job teaching for a private family from 11 A.M. to 7 P.M. including Sundays for $16 a month. Alice was appalled. "Isn't that frightful pay?"[19]

The frau also answered an advertisement placed by an American man who wanted a "German woman who would walk, drive, play tennis, ride horseback etc. with him. He would pay $15 a month & her expenses." Meanwhile he would be learning German. Alice couldn't imagine "such a ramrod" as the frau playing tennis. She did not have to. "When she went there the court yard was so jammed with women that she couldn't get anywhere near the steps—the steps all the way up to his floor were likewise crowded. Frau Heick said that there were about 600 women there. The poor American was terrified at the bombardment. He sent a servant out to say that he had decided to not engage anyone as it would be an overwhelming task & so the 600 finalists departed."[20]

In England that fall, Alice's schedule was full. Not only was she taking classes at Woodbrooke, volunteering at a small settlement house, playing tennis, and bicycling country roads with new friends, but three times a week she peddled through the gritty coal fog exhaled by a forest of factory smokestacks to the University of Birmingham. She was the first female to enroll in its commerce department. It was there that she happened upon an announcement for a speech by a prominent suffragist.

As Alice Paul watched, entranced, Christabel Pankhurst stepped to the podium in a university hall one December day in 1907, and uttered the opening words of a speech demanding the ballot. Flanked by two other suffragists, Christabel was an English doll come to life, with round rosy cheeks and porcelain skin, a face framed by dark curls, and widely spaced blue eyes that gave her a dreamy look. She was twenty-eight, and had recently earned her law degree.

Her father, Richard Pankhurst, had written the first female enfranchisement bill, introduced in Parliament in 1870. After his death, her mother Emmeline founded the Women's Social and Political Union (WSPU) to carry on the struggle. Unlike other suffrage organizations, the WSPU did not beseech male legislators for the ballot. "Votes for Women" may have been the rallying cry. But the motto was "Deeds, not Words."[21]

Two years before her father's death, Christabel and an accomplice had interrupted a speech at a Liberal Party gathering. When a police officer approached, Christabel deliberately spit in his face, hoping to trigger an arrest that would jolt the suffrage movement into higher gear. Events went as planned. After a week in jail, Christabel emerged a martyr. Suffragists had been going to jail ever since.

Her reputation as a firebrand ensured crowds whenever Christabel appeared, but they were not necessarily friendly. On this December day in 1907, with Alice in the audience, she had barely spoken a word to the predominantly male listeners before a chorus of deep-throated jeers drowned out her words.

This was the first suffrage event Alice Paul had attended since arriving in England. Nothing had prepared her for such rudeness. In the suffrage meetings she had gone to with her mother in the Quaker meetinghouse back home, everyone was essentially in agreement that men and women deserved equal rights. Even those who disagreed wouldn't have dreamed of heckling a speaker.

The university administration rescheduled Christabel's speech and ordered all students to attend. Alice returned, offended by the earlier reception and eager to hear what the suffragist had to say. When Christabel appeared for the second time, Sir Oliver Lodge, a distinguished physicist and the university's administrator, personally took the stage to apologize. This time when she spoke the male students were silent; Alice was able to hear the suffragist's every word.

As she listened, she perhaps felt the stirrings of what Quakers would interpret as a divinely inspired "concern," a word that in their faith has no synonym. Quakerly "concerns" have steered men and women toward such causes as abolition, prison reform, death penalty protests, and anti-war activities.[22]

Alice would never be specific about her sudden conversion to suffrage. Until then, she had navigated England's bumpy political landscape as resolutely as she pedaled her bicycle to classes, veering neither to the left, where socialists and laborites called for a new order, nor the right, where conservatives manned the barricades, and never lifting her eyes to the horizon, where the demands of women were rising like a fiery summer sun.

Did Christabel's words touch her Quaker core where coursed the blood of martyrs? Did she see suddenly that the ballot offered a way out of the female powerlessness she had observed as a social worker? Or did the speaker's message offer a remedy for her own bruised spirit? Or suggest possibilities for an educated young woman unsure of her future?

Decades later, seeking to explain her attraction to the cause, she would remember her indignation at the initial outbreak of insults and jeering, how it had awakened her natural sympathy for the underdog—suffragists in this case—and a desire "to throw in all the strength I can give to help." But it was not until Christabel's second appearance, a singular moment when Alice "understood everything about what the English militants were trying to do," that she became, as she put it, a "heart and soul convert."[23]

The WSPU was seldom out of the news during the winter of 1907. Members marched repeatedly to the House of Commons, seeking an audience. Met by solid lines of uniformed police, the women tried to force their way through, emerging with bruises and torn clothing. The press christened the protestors "suffragettes" to distinguish them from traditional, better-behaved suffragists, the "ette" then as now a disparaging diminutive. The WSPU proudly adopted the label.

In the spring of 1908 the WSPU decided on a more conciliatory approach. Perhaps the obdurate Liberal government could be moved by a massive show of public support. Home Secretary Herbert Gladstone once said that "political dynamics are far more important than political argument." Men had learned to mount large demonstrations in pursuit of their goals. "Of course," Gladstone observed, "it cannot be expected that women can assemble in such masses."[24]

The suffragettes set out to prove him wrong. They announced that on Sunday, June 21, 1908, they would stage the greatest demonstration that London had ever seen. In the ten days before the parade, open-air rallies were held throughout the city, women chalked sidewalks with announcements, and canvassers went door to door and stood on street corners distributing handbills. They thronged the train stations to pass out a million mock railway tickets in the movement's new colors—white (for purity), green (for hope), and purple (for dignity)—advertising the event. The plan called for seven great processions to converge from different directions on London's Hyde Park. Thirty trains were reserved to carry women from seventy different surrounding towns.

Nature delivered perfect weather. Under a radiant blue sky, the seven one-mile-long processions wound through streets thronged with spectators. Women wore white, wrapped themselves in green, white, and purple sashes proclaiming "Votes for Women," and shaded their faces with great swooping hats laden with flowers, bows, and feathers. Men wore summer suits and boaters. In a holiday mood, people sang as they strolled. The processions flowed into the park through different gates, converging on seven speakers' platforms. Watching from an observation post, Sylvia Pankhurst, Christabel's younger sister and one of the organizers, could see not a blade of grass, so thick was the crowd. She thought the colorful mass looked like "a great bed of flowers."[25]

Employed that summer at a settlement house, Alice learned of the parade at the last minute from her supervisor, an ardent suffragist. Just a white-clad droplet in the human wave that washed ashore in Hyde Park, Alice landed at a platform where, in those days before microphones, she was one of the few close enough to actually hear the speaker.

Size estimates of the event varied widely, from 40,000 to an improbable 500,000. But no one questioned that it was the largest suffrage demonstration in British history. The *New York Times* reporter couldn't conceal his surprise that the suffragettes had pulled it off, "displaying totally unexpected genius for organization."[26]

The prime minister was unmoved. Herbert Henry Asquith declared he had nothing new to add to a prior statement that suffrage might at some indefinite time be included in a reform bill.

Nine days after the Hyde Park demonstration, June 30, suffragettes threw their first rock.

In Britain, hurling rocks through windows and assorted other crimes against property had a time-honored history in the annals of protest. But in this case, the action had not been planned by the WSPU. The two women who flung stones through the windows of the prime minister's residence at 10 Downing Street, and were arrested, told Emmeline Pankhurst that they didn't expect her to condone what they had done. They had acted out of frustration after yet another unsuccessful attempt to confront Parliament had resulted in twenty-nine arrests. Emmeline stood by the rock throwers.

That fall, Alice entered the high-powered, left-leaning London School of Economics, founded by Fabian Socialists Beatrice and Sidney Webb, George Bernard Shaw, and Graham Wallas. Almost immediately, Alice began to worry about being left behind academically. Her employment at Peel, a London settlement house, was interfering with her studies.

"I am rather afraid that I won't have any time to read or study as Peel takes so much time & then I'll get the reputation of being stupid which is a disadvantage," she moaned in a "Dear Mamma" letter. "So far I haven't read anything—Peel is a dead place—I spend my time looking after babies & old women." The five-dollar weekly paycheck just covered her boardinghouse rent. And speaking of money, she wrote, "I only have $10 on hand & it will take that to keep me going so I hope thee can spare some."[27]

When her settlement house job ended just before Christmas, Alice avoided taking another in order to leave more time for her studies. She also anted up the twenty-five-cent WSPU membership fee and began to attend weekly meetings. She was pleased when the mail brought "a beautiful letter welcoming me into their ranks and thanking me for my 25 cents."[28] The suffragettes might have been going to jail right and left, but that didn't mean a new member didn't deserve a proper thank-you.

About her daughter's activities for suffrage, Tacie knew only the sketchy details Alice chose to provide, none of them reassuring.

"I walked in the women's suffrage Procession on Sunday & on Saturday," Alice scrawled in a postcard to her mother on July 28, 1908, after she had attended the Hyde Park rally and yet another the following day. "They were quite thrilling. The girl I went with fainted and was carried out by four men."[29]

On January 14, 1909, she reported to her mother that the previous night she "went to a monthly meeting & afterwards to a women's suffrage meeting to welcome Mrs. Pankhurst & Miss Christabel Pankhurst on their release from prison after about 2 months—Over $1000 was taken in the collection though admission had also been charged. This happens at almost every meeting & they are having them constantly. It is wonderful."[30]

Eight days later, in a letter telling Tacie that she had found "a nice boardinghouse for $6, fire and hot baths extra at 12 c a scuttle of coal," she casually informed her mother, "I have joined the 'suffragettes'—the militant party on the woman suffrage question."[31]

Young men appeared fleetingly in her letters, as the occasional companion for dinner or a lecture. If Tacie hoped for more—and what mother didn't?—she was disappointed. Although many girls at Woodbridge found mates—in one letter to her sister Helen, Alice mentioned seven engagements—she herself was not among them.[32]

One day in 1908 a fellow student, an ardent WSPU member, suggested that Alice join her in selling the organization's newspaper, *Votes for Women*.

A pitch for "newsies" in *Votes for Women* promised the opportunity to "bring light and happiness into many lives."[33] Interested readers may have visualized themselves offering the paper to women passersby and perhaps even men, who would smile and produce a coin.

The reality was somewhat different.

In post-Victorian England, where newsies were typically young boys, a certain amount of cheek was required of a well-bred female to don a wooden signboard, sling a pouch full of newspapers over one shoulder, join the common women who worked the streets—prostitutes, flower sellers, and other vendors—and shout out "Votes for Women" loudly enough to override the rumble of horse carts and the noisy new automotive contraptions.

To avoid the stream of pedestrians—and possible arrest for obstruction—newsies were forced to stand in the gutter, amid spit, refuse, and worse. Men hurled sexual insults; sometimes factory workers threw rotten fruits and vegetables.

And what was it about *old* men? "The sex filth which elderly men in particular seemed determined to inflict on us was the most hateful part of my daily experience," wrote one newsie. Months of this treatment, she said, "reduced me to a state of depression from which I sometimes seemed unable to rouse myself."[34]

Just standing on a bustling corner as people streamed by could be a true "acid test" of commitment, wrote another. "The first time I took my place on the 'Island' in Picadilly [*sic*] Circus, near the flower sellers," she said, "I felt as if every eye that looked at me was a dagger piercing me through and I wished the ground would open and swallow me."[35]

Stationed next to the member who had recruited her, Alice was impressed by her companion's boldness and dismayed by her own timidity as she tried to muster the courage to ask people to buy *Votes for Women*. She simply wasn't, she concluded morosely, "very brave by nature."[36]

The post of newsie was an entry-level position for volunteers, but an important one. Newsies were responsible for spreading the news that the dailies wouldn't print, and newspaper sales raised money. Her modesty aside, Alice evidently excelled, for she was soon promoted to street corner speaking—and a new set of terrors. As a student at Swarthmore, Alice had been plagued with a paralyzing fear of public speaking. Her commencement had been almost ruined when she was honored as Ivy Poet, because she had to write and deliver a farewell poem for the class of 1906. Only the coaching of a gifted classmate gave her the confidence to go through with it.

The WSPU started novices off by assigning them to introduce more experienced orators, until they were sufficiently hardened to face crowds sprinkled with hecklers. Before long, Alice could be spotted outdoors and indoors, above-ground on street corners and in parks, belowground in the tubes, delivering im-promptu speeches about current WSPU activities and campaign speeches opposing Liberal candidates.

The campaign against all Liberals, even those who favored suffrage, was Christabel Pankhurst's controversial strategy aimed at nothing less than unseat-ing the present government. Pro-suffrage Liberals were enraged at being tar-geted in such a fashion, but the WSPU reasoned that the threat of losing an election would prompt them to put pressure on their anti-suffrage colleagues.

Tacie Paul did not doubt that her studious daughter was serious about her ed-ucation. Not yet twenty-five, Alice had already earned a bachelor's degree from Swarthmore, a certificate in social work from the New York School of Philan-thropy, and a master's degree in sociology from the University of Pennsylvania. Her first summer abroad, she had studied German in Berlin. She had been at the London School of Economics for a year, mixing it up with distinguished social-ist educators. And now it seemed that what the driven Alice had in mind was to work for a Ph.D. in economics in either Switzerland or Germany in preparation for an academic career.

But Alice was constantly short of funds. Tacie would frequently open her mail and find a laundry list of needs, addressed to "Dear Mamma": "I have used up all my money so please send some. Had to have my teeth fixed & also broke my glasses. Had my little blue dress made into a jumper effect. . . . Please send me the money at once."[37]

Or this, while visiting a wealthy classmate in Amsterdam: "I do hope thee has sent me some money—I wrote on the 12th and so hoped it would come be-fore now. . . . It is awful to be here without any money."[38]

With three younger children to support, Tacie Paul had finally tired of send-ing fifty- and one-hundred-dollar dollops across the Atlantic to a daughter who seemed to have found fulfillment as a perpetual student. By 1908 she thought it was quite time for Alice to leave London and come home to New Jersey.

From Alice's point of view, she was doing her best to scrimp. She made do with last year's suit and hat, argued the dentist down from $13 to $10, bought second-best milk and eggs. At the moment she was living in a tiny apartment in a dilapidated neighborhood where the water supply was a pump downstairs in the courtyard. How could her mother accuse her of profligacy, she wondered, when she had never been given a set budget? "I am sorry thee thinks I have spent too much," she wrote Tacie. "When one has no idea of what one's income is it is impossible to form any idea of what one ought to spend."[39]

Alas, Swarthmore College, her alma mater, had turned her down in the spring of 1909 for the scholarship she had counted on for study abroad the next year and given it instead to Mary Janney, a girl she had considered "not all that bright" when they were together in college. Alice could scarcely bear the thought. She wrote her mother in a huff, "So they must apparently think that I have very little ability if they prefer Mary Janney to me & therefore I will never apply to them again."[40] Her back-up plan, the Ph.D. program at the University of Pennsylvania, fell through as well.

Single women did not have many options. Thanks to her summer in Germany, Alice was reasonably fluent in the language, and she knew girls who were earning money there by teaching English. But doing so would not advance her education. Settlement jobs in England had not altered her views about social work. She felt quite sorry for the people who were hard up and in need of help. But social work was a dead end, a mere palliative.

In the midst of Alice's existential turmoil that spring, a letter arrived bearing the return address of the Women's Social and Political Union. Her volunteer efforts had attracted the notice of the high command. The WSPU was offering her an opportunity to do more for the cause. Much more.

Alice Paul fingered the letter as if it might burst into flames. Would she be willing to join a deputation to Parliament led by Emmeline Pankhurst, the WSPU asked, and, by the way, as she recalled in later years, "it would probably mean that you would be under some danger of being arrested and imprisoned, so you must not accept this invitation unless you were willing to do this."[41]

For more than two years convicted suffragettes had been returning with first-hand stories about the horrors of Holloway Prison, a forbidding structure resembling a Gothic castle, equipped with a gallows and cells for 949 women. Emmeline's middle daughter, Sylvia, had written a graphic account of her own imprisonment. Her description began with the bone-jarring ride in a springless paddywagon commonly called a "Black Maria" that drew cheers as it rattled over stone streets in the poorer sections of London—"They always cheer the prison van."[42]

At Holloway, Sylvia and her fellow prisoners were ordered to undress, then handed a chemise to wear as wardresses searched their bodies and pawed through their hair for concealed items. The prison uniforms were "badly sewn and badly cut, were of coarse calico and harsh woolen stuff."[43] No woman's outfit in those days was complete without a figure-shaping corset, but those the prison supplied were strange-looking garments indeed. The thick wool stockings were black with circular red stripes, and since there were no garters, they slipped down around the ankles. The shoes were heavy and no two seemed to match; their leather laces broke when the wearer tried to tie them. The final article of clothing was a white cotton cap that fastened under the chin. And all the clothes—the dress, the apron, and even the cap—were stamped with a large arrow, black on light colors, white on dark colors.

Furnished with a wooden plank bed and a pillow that was nearly as hard, the cells were cramped, airless, and cold. The inmate's day began with chores: emptying her slops and then using rags to scrub first the cell and its contents, and lastly herself. Breakfast was a gruel of oatmeal and water, and six ounces of bread. The same pallid meal was also dinner every night and lunch three days a week. On the other four days lunch consisted of greasy suet pudding and potatoes, and more bread.

After an 8:30 A.M. trip to chapel, inmates spent the remainder of the day sewing prison linens. Exercise three times a week offered a break and fresh air, but nothing more. "There, all march slowly round in a single file with a distance of three or four yards between each prisoner," Sylvia wrote.[44] Talking was forbidden.

During a confinement in October 1908, Emmeline Pankhurst had demanded the political offender status historically granted to men agitating for reform. She maintained that she should not have to be searched or undress in front of the wardresses. She should be allowed to speak to other prisoners and read books of her own choosing, write, and do her own needlework. All her demands were denied. Her daughter Christabel was also a prisoner at the time. When Emmeline linked arms and spoke with her during an exercise period, she was thrown into solitary confinement for three days.

As Alice considered her response to the WSPU invitation, it was not the well-advertised horrors of Holloway that weighed most heavily on her mind, though she surely must have considered them. Rather, she knew that her friends and family, especially her mother, would consider her arrest a terrible disgrace. She had a momentary thought. She would go under an assumed name! Others had done it. But then she rejected the idea. Quakers did not lie.

Surely Tacie would understand. Both Alice's parents could trace their ancestry back to the seventeenth-century Quakers who settled Pennsylvania and

New Jersey in search of religious freedom. Would prison really be such a dis-grace? And so Alice drafted her answer. But still she hesitated. Letter in hand, she slowly circled the post office. Finally, she summoned all her courage and posted the envelope.

She wouldn't be returning to New Jersey anytime soon.

CHAPTER TWO

"THRILLING TIMES"

Eight P.M. on June 29, 1909. The last streaks of daylight were fading from the pearled London sky. On the steps beneath the arched entrance to Caxton Hall, a favorite venue for suffrage meetings, an all-female drum and fife band played a rousing, high-pitched version of the Marseillaise, the stirring French call to arms. At that signal, a mass of two hundred women, seemingly overdressed in bulky winter outerwear, set out for Parliament several blocks away. Alice Paul moved forward with the others along Victoria Street, which was crowded with thousands of Londoners who had come for a free show.[1]

Ahead, Alice could see Emmeline Pankhurst leading the way, a slender, solitary figure followed by seven other prominent WSPU members. The plan was this: If the group of eight was admitted to the House of Commons, as they had formally requested, the ranks would fall back. If not, everyone would rush the lines of police and attempt to push through.

Posted outside the big wooden doors beneath the jagged spires of the St. Stephen's entrance to Parliament, three thousand uniformed officers in lines six deep stiffened at the clatter of hoofs. A woman on horseback emerged from the gloom to announce the imminent arrival of the delegation. Mounted police stood by.

When Emmeline approached, Chief Inspector Scantlebury greeted her with a terse statement. "The Prime Minister . . . regrets that he is unable to receive the proposed deputation."[2] A physical confrontation was now inevitable. In the vanguard were several distinguished, elderly women who might well be injured in a melee. An immediate arrest would remove them from harm's way. Turning to another inspector, Emmeline struck him lightly upon the cheek. "I know why you have done that," he told her.

"Must I do it again?" she asked.

"Yes," he replied. Two slaps were sufficient provocation. She and her companions were led away.[3]

That was the cue for the rank and file. Egged on by the mob, they hurled themselves, a dozen at a time, against the police lines. Alice described the violence in a letter to her mother a few days afterward. "The police grabbed the suffragettes by the throats & threw them flat on their backs over & over again. The mounted police rode us down again & again."[4]

The women picked themselves up and pressed forward, dodging sharp-edged hoofs—it was clear now why everyone had been counseled to wear thick layers of clothing in late June. This was dangerous business, requiring protection. For an hour the scene replayed itself. Suffragettes charged, police pushed back. A horse and officer fell, knocking a woman to the ground. Having failed to discourage the demonstrators, the men now arrested them.

Just when police thought they had cleared the square, protestors darted from offices that the WSPU had rented for the night. One group smashed windows of government buildings with stones wrapped in petitions, delivering a suffrage message for workers the next morning.

Alice was among those arrested. "The scene was one awful nightmare," she wrote Tacie. "I never shall forget the women as they were brought into the police station, half fainting & their clothes torn to pieces." She marveled "that no one was killed."[5]

As the prisoners milled about the station house, Alice spied a young woman with brilliant red hair and a generous smile who was wearing an American flag pin. Alice Paul, the Quaker from New Jersey, introduced herself to Lucy Burns, a Catholic from Brooklyn. As they perched on a billiard table and exchanged stories, they found they had much in common. Like Alice, Lucy was the daughter of a bank officer and also a college graduate, in her case, from Vassar. She had taught high school English for two years before traveling to Europe to study at the University of Bonn. In a 1908 Vassar class report she wrote that she would be going to Oxford for a summer, "where I expect to work in dignified leisure and think Addison English."[6] But her life took a different turn. She told Alice that day that she had come to England expressly for the demonstration.

In her letter to Tacie, Alice filled ten pages in neat, rounded handwriting with a graphic account of all that had happened. She was most anxious that her mother understand the politics behind the situation. "Mr. Asquith is determined to not see us—he has never received a deputation of women with reference to woman's suffrage since he has been Prime Minister. A bill to give the vote to women on same terms as men has passed the 2nd reading of this House of Commons by a majority of 3 to 1. Some 420 members out of 670 are pledged to support it & the majority of the cabinet are in favor of it."[7]

But Asquith was blocking a final vote. He refused even to receive their petitions but met readily, Alice reported, with "rough hooligans representing the unemployed & representatives on any subject, however trifling as far as practical politics goes, such as vivisection." Her letter seethed with indignation. Asquith "was the one who took illegal action & not we. . . . It seems to be a matter of pride with him never to yield anything to women."[8]

The evening of her arrest had been "very exciting," she told Tacie. But enough was enough. In words her mother must surely have welcomed, "the struggle is getting very grimly & deadly earnest," and she had decided to abandon it. "The best thing for me is to get my degree as quickly as possible." To that end she would do what Tacie so fervently desired. She made one last request for money. "Please send me $100 for my ticket back . . . & I will engage my passage." Should she go to prison, she said, she would come home as soon as she was released.[9]

No sooner had Alice purchased her ticket, however, than she was forced to return it. Her trial was scheduled to take place after the departure date, and she dared not skip it. Alice had also underestimated how difficult it would be to walk out on a righteous cause that offered excitement, satisfaction, and recognition. After the letter describing the confrontation, she no longer wrote Tacie of plans for an immediate return. The young woman who had proclaimed herself a "heart and soul convert" to the cause after hearing Christabel Pankhurst speak some eighteen months earlier was now a true disciple of suffrage's holy family.

Emmeline was its matriarch. Oldest daughter Christabel was the chief strategist, and middle daughter Sylvia, an artist, chronicled the movement in print and pictures. And all the Pankhurst women, including Adela, the youngest daughter, went to jail for their beliefs. Even Emmeline's youngest child Harry, a sickly boy, handed out literature, chalked sidewalks with propaganda, heckled politicians, and spoke on street corners. That the WSPU was an organization with an autocratic leadership but a democratic goal constituted a paradox that did not go unchallenged by members, some of whom resigned for that very reason. But Emmeline's courage and charisma held her movement together. Alice concluded that the WSPU leader was a "genius" for her tactics and the loyalty she inspired.[10]

And Emmeline, it seemed, had taken notice of the slight American girl with luminous blue eyes, a steady gaze, a quiet demeanor, and a streak of boldness. Alice's devotion and conduct were such that every time the suffragettes contemplated a militant action, they now sent Alice another note asking her to take part.

She always said yes.

In 1909, the WSPU was resorting to desperate and ever more creative ways to gain access not only to Parliament but also to meetings of the Liberal Party from which they had been officially barred. All over England, suffragettes "hid in bushes and under platforms, scaled roofs, let themselves down through skylights in order to interrupt meetings with the dreaded call, 'votes for women!'"[11]

When the British postal service boasted that it would deliver anything in the United Kingdom "from a peanut to an elephant," two suffragists applied for delivery as "human letters" to a Mr. Asquith at 10 Downing Street. Carrying placards inscribed "Votes for Women," they were escorted by an express messenger to their destination. On arriving at the prime minister's residence, the bonneted women were met by a bureaucrat in a suit and three helmeted policemen. The bureaucrat told them, "You must be returned."

"But we have been paid for," they protested.

"The post office must deliver you somewhere else, you cannot be received here."

The two women argued that they constituted an official document that required a signature. "You cannot be signed for," the official told them.

"You must be returned; you are dead letters."[12]

During the summer of 1909, a different suffrage group, the Women's Freedom League, stationed members outside the House of Commons and 10 Downing Street to waylay the prime minister. One hundred forty women logged 6,000 hours of picket duty. But the nimble Asquith almost always managed to elude them. Known for his concision, on the rare times the women were able to confront the prime minister, he simply replied, "Don't be silly."[13]

It would have been funny, except—well, the whole chain of events *was* funny to playwright George Bernard Shaw. In July 1909 the Court Theatre presented a private performance of his dramatic sketch titled "Press Cuttings."

The play opens with General Mitchener at his writing-table in the War Office. From the street comes a shrill voice, "Votes for Women."

The general starts convulsively; snatches a revolver from a drawer; and listens in an agony of apprehension. An ORDERLY enters.

ORDERLY: Another one, sir. She's chained herself.

MITCHENER: Chained herself? How? To what? We've taken away the railings and everything that a chain can be passed through.

ORDERLY: We forgot the door-scraper, sir. She lay down on the flags and got the chain through before she started hollerin'.

The woman is brought in. She turns out to be the Prime Minister "BAL-SQUITH" in disguise.

BALSQUITH: It has come to this: that the only way the Prime Minister of England can get from Downing Street to the War Office is by assuming this disguise; shrieking "Votes for Women"; and chaining himself to your door-scraper. They were at the corner in force. They cheered me. Bellachristina herself was there. She shook my hand and told me to say I was a vegetarian, as the diet was better in Holloway for vegetarians.[14]

Bellachristina was, of course, the fetching Christabel Pankhurst.

On June 21, 1909, the week before Alice was arrested at Parliament, Scottish sculptor and suffragette Marion Wallace Dunlop entered the House of Commons with a male companion. As he strode ahead on business, she lingered in historic St. Stephen's Hall amid the life-sized statuary and oil paintings of distinguished MPs, where she furtively pressed an inked block of wood to the stone wall. A policeman spied Dunlop and dragged her away. Left behind was a smudged message, a quote from the 1689 Bill of Rights. "It is the right of the Subject to petition the King, and all commitments and Prosecutions for such petitioning are illegal." Two days later, Dunlop returned to affix the message more clearly. Apprehended once again, she was convicted of defacing the House of Commons and dispatched to Holloway Prison.

The incident would have been just one more prank resulting in one more arrest, except for what happened next. When Dunlop's request for political offender status was turned down, she flatly refused to eat. Prison officials tried to entice her with tasty food, "a fried fish, four slices of bread, three bananas and a cup of hot milk."[15] It came flying out the window of her cell. The fish, the bread, the bananas, the milk, all of it.

Three days passed. Though weaker, Dunlop showed no sign of capitulation. The authorities were stymied. The death of one would provide a martyr for many. After ninety-one hours, on July 9 they released their charge. That same day fourteen suffragettes were arrested; they decided to emulate Dunlop. The next wave of suffrage prisoners followed suit, and their sentences too were shortened. Soon all the suffragettes knew that if arrested, they were expected to hunger strike. But, it seemed, if they refused food they were in no danger of a lengthy incarceration.

When the WSPU put its hunger strikers on display at a mass meeting that summer, a young Indian man made a point of attending. The suffragettes had first come to his attention in 1906 during his trip to London to press for an end to discrimination against his fellow Indians in South Africa, and he had felt a kinship with the women and admired their bravery.

"If even women display such courage," Mahatma Gandhi, already a student of passive resistance, had written back then, "will the Transvaal Indians fail in their duty and be afraid of gaol?"[16]

Now, three years later, Gandhi, too, was a star of the headlines. He had coined the word *Satyagraha*, meaning "non-violent resistance," and led many Indians in South Africa in protests. He himself had been imprisoned. On this visit to London, after meeting with Emmeline Pankhurst, he praised the WSPU for its ability to raise money and organize, while also crusading for the vote. "When we consider the suffering and the courage of these women, how can the *satyagrahi* stand comparison with them?"[17] But Gandhi's enthusiasm waned later that summer when several women shattered the windows of historic Lympne Castle, Asquith's retreat in Kent. Such behavior, he predicted, would cost the suffragettes "whatever sympathy they have."[18]

Tacie Paul must have felt some trepidation when the mail brought a letter with British stamps addressed in her daughter's familiar hand. This time she had only to open the envelope to know something was amiss. Usually Alice wrote on small sheets of paper. But the customary "Dear Mamma" was scribbled on an envelope that had been opened at the seams and flattened. Alice began the undated letter with an explanatory "I haven't any paper with me,"[19] and went on to say that she was confined to bed in the home of two older suffragettes who were looking after her as she recuperated from 126 hours without food.

She had been apprehended at a protest on July 30 where Chancellor of the Exchequer Lloyd George was speaking. Unlike her earlier arrest, when charges were dropped, this time she was convicted and sent to Holloway. When ordered to undress, she and her fellow protestors refused and stood with their backs to the wall, their arms linked. The warden blew a shrill whistle and prison matrons fell upon the women. "They tore off all our clothes & left us with only prison clothes," Alice wrote. "We would not put them on & I sat there for about 2 hours with nothing on. Then they brought me a blanket so I wrapped up in a blanket until I was released." When refused treatment as political prisoners, Alice continued, "we began to destroy as much property as possible. I broke every pane in my window—40 panes they tell me." She was put in a punishment cell, the British version of solitary confinement. After four days without eating, too weak to walk, she was carried on a stretcher to the prison hospital. Just before her release after serving less than a week of a fourteen-day sentence, "they gave me a dose of brandy & sent me home in a cab with a wardress."[20]

The experience seemed to have left her chastened. "I shall *never* go on a hunger strike again, I think," she wrote Tacie.[21]

But she did not swear off protests. In August 1909, she was arrested in Norwich with two other suffragettes for attempting to break into a hall where the speaker, a rising young star in the Liberal firmament, was Winston Churchill. "We were kept in an anteroom of the hall during the meeting with six policemen guarding the three of us. . . . We were charged with having incited the crowd to riot & I, in addition, with having assaulted the police."[22] She suspected the case would be dropped because the government was "at its wits end" and dared not send more hunger strikers to Holloway. Apparently she was right, for soon afterward, Alice set out with Lucy Burns for Scotland to help the great Emmeline Pankhurst herself lay the groundwork for a big fall rally in Edinburgh. Both American girls were thrilled by the assignment.

Six years older than Alice, Lucy was the fourth of eight children. She had the good fortune of having a father who believed in educating his daughters as well as his sons and had the income to do so. The son of a tailor, Edward Burns had started as a bank clerk at age seventeen and worked his way up to vice president. He chose to send Lucy and her sisters to Packer Collegiate Institute in Brooklyn Heights, the best girls' school in Brooklyn's best neighborhood.

During Lucy's years there, Packer was governed by President Truman J. Backus, the enlightened former head of Vassar's English department. The year he arrived, the school's catalogue began to speak of "young women" rather than "young ladies."[23] Under Backus "light gymnastics" were made compulsory and the curriculum was revised to allow the girls to specialize in mathematics, as Lucy did, as well as the humanities. But the liberalism went only so far. Teenage students in the 1890s came to school in high-necked Victorian dresses with swollen leg o'mutton sleeves, and there was a preoccupation, according to an official centennial history, with "female virtue." The novels of Thomas Hardy and the "poetry of Walt Whitman and the wicked Lord Byron" were not considered appropriate fodder for feminine minds.[24]

Like the majority of her college-bound classmates, Lucy moved on to Vassar, class of 1902. She was an active debater and was chosen at graduation to deliver a humorous oration to the incoming seniors. She spent six weeks in the summer of 1903 at Columbia University, "a terrible combination of hot weather hard work," where she made a few "feeble assaults on the German language." The following February she began teaching English at a public high school in Brooklyn. She also coached a basketball team "in a tone of authority and with a wise air."[25]

In 1907 Lucy embarked on two years of studies in Germany. When she arrived in England and encountered the Pankhursts, her entries in the class report became more serious. "I don't mind boldly avowing that my chief interest in life at present is 'Votes for Women;' my one fear, that England will get them before we do."[26]

Unlike Alice, who initially felt torn between her studies and the suffrage movement, Lucy threw in with the Pankhursts immediately. In notes for a never-completed article, she said she attended her first meeting of the suffragettes, "the wild women of Westminster," and "was amazed at the quality of the meeting. In short I came to scoff, and remained to sell papers on the street, take part in deputations, get carried off to jail, and eventually became an organizer for the Women's Social and Political Union in Edinburgh."[27]

If Alice had been brought up on stories of Quaker resisters, Lucy's childhood was steeped in tales of Catholic martyrdom. Now she had the opportunity to prove her own mettle. During one of the WSPU's many protests in 1909, reported the *Brooklyn Daily Eagle*, "Miss Burns smacked the chief inspector in the face and knocked his cap off."[28] Lucy was fined forty shillings. She also admitted throwing ink bottles through panes of glass in police headquarters and to disorderly conduct.

The people in Lucy's circle expressed astonishment at her behavior. "All this has distressed her friends and relatives and they have been unable to account for her prominence in the militant suffragette agitation," the *Daily Eagle* reported.[29]

Her former Packer classmates may have been less surprised than some. In the mock epitaphs for each graduate, the one penned for Lucy had reflected a personality untamed by Packer's genteel culture. "I ought to have my way in everything, and what's more, I will too."[30]

Alice and Lucy's trip to Scotland in mid-August 1909 was memorable on several accounts, not the least of which was the mode of travel. Alice, who would never master a car, was fascinated to see that Pankhurst was being driven about by a woman. It was unusual enough for a female to take the wheel, but to be a chauffeur was rare indeed.[31]

Sometimes it must have sounded to Tacie as if Alice was romping merrily through the United Kingdom. "We had thrilling times here last night," she wrote after one arrest. On learning that punishment was less rigorously applied in Scotland than in England, she merrily flaunted the law. Warned in Glasgow that they would be pursued if they failed to appear in court, she and the rest of her crew skipped town anyway. "It would be a big expense for them to hunt all over Scotland for us & besides they hate to send Suffragettes to prison."[32]

In Glasgow on August 20, Alice and Lucy had orders to interrupt a speech by Colonial Secretary Lord Crewe in St. Andrew's Hall. The night before, with a boost from Lucy, Alice scaled a fence and climbed a scaffolding to reach the roof, where the pair planned to spend the night in readiness for the morrow. Before she could follow, Lucy was frightened off by the approach of a stranger. Alice was on her own. A heavy rain began to fall. When dawn lightened the sky, a workman atop a neighboring building spied her slight, sodden figure and summoned police. They climbed up to the roof and found Alice, according to one newspaper, calmly eating chocolate. Soaked through and shivering, she descended to the cheers of a small crowd that thought the audacious suffragette charming. The informant apologized when he learned of her mission, saying he had thought she needed help.[33]

More arrests followed. Tacie was beside herself with anxiety and let Alice know it. Alice wrote back, "Thy last letter was doleful. There is no reason to worry about one. I am perfectly well."[34]

But she wasn't perfectly well. She and Lucy emerged from another hunger strike so weak that they were taken in by a wealthy WSPU supporter to recover. Her estate was "a big sort of park and it is one mile from her front gate to her front door," Alice wrote her mother afterward, making it sound as if her convalescence were a holiday.[35]

The Scots, not among the British crown's most loyal subjects, treated the spunky suffragettes like heroes. Dundee's women hosted a banquet attended by the mayor, followed by a meeting where a school board member and a clergyman sang their praises. One of the men presented Alice and Lucy with huge bouquets. And a WSPU lieutenant awarded both with the medal struck for members who had gone to jail. It was a brooch in the image of a prison gate.

When Alice returned to London in late fall, prison authorities had initiated a new policy toward hunger strikers. No longer would they be released after a few days, to emerge pale and ill, rousing the sympathy of an indignant public. Instead, food would be forced into their bodies through the nose, mouth, and even, at least once late in the struggle, the rectum.[36]

In this heightened atmosphere, Alice took on an assignment that once again, if she were caught, meant almost certain arrest.

Police knew that the annual Lord Mayor's banquet on November 9, 1909, in Guildhall, the seat of city government, would be a tempting target for suffragettes. The presence of one cabinet member was enough to warrant a maneuver of one sort or another, and *all* the cabinet members were invited.

Throughout the day, the police kept a watchful eye on comings and goings, checking the roof and various nooks and crannies. One surveillance tactic was to stick a hatpin into dark corners in hopes of pricking a hidden suffragette. For all their vigilance, they missed two young women dressed as charwomen and toting buckets and brushes, who had arrived at 8 A.M. armed with the password, "kitchen." Climbing up to the balcony that overlooked the hall where the guests would dine that evening, Alice Paul and Amelia Brown found a hiding place and remained there throughout the day. One officer making the rounds came so close his cape touched Alice's hair.

That evening, Lucy Burns, clad in an evening gown, blended with the dignitaries entering the medieval hall. When Winston Churchill arrived with his wife, Lucy waved a tiny banner in his face. "How can you dine here while women are starving in prison?" she asked the startled cabinet member.[37] Police quickly removed her from the building.

Just as Asquith began to speak, Amelia took off her shoe, reached over, and smashed a window. Both she and Alice cried, "Votes for women." Asquith halted. The band played.[38]

The pair was arrested and sentenced to a month of hard labor. Following WSPU protocol, Alice refused to eat or wear prison clothing and so remained in bed. Twice daily she was plucked from her cell, wrapped in blankets, and taken to a chair in another cell. A heavy woman, who she was certain must be Holloway's largest matron, straddled her across the waist and leaned forward, pinning her shoulders down. Two other matrons sat on either side holding down her arms. Behind her stood a doctor, as she would later relate, who "pulled my head back till it was parallel with the ground. He held it in this position by means of a towel drawn tightly around the throat & when I tried to move he drew the towel so tight that it compressed the windpipe & made it almost impossible to breathe. With his other hand he held my chin in a rigid position."[39]

A second doctor pushed one end of a five-foot-long tube into her nostril so hard that it felt as if he were driving a stake into the ground. Once the tube had reached her stomach, a funnel was positioned at the top and milk and liquid food poured through.

In subsequent feedings, more often than not, the tube would not reach its destination on the first try. In those cases the doctor pulled it out, smeared it with thick grease and tried the other nostril. Three times the tube went astray and poked out through her mouth. Alice clamped her teeth down tightly, leaving the team no alternative but to pry her mouth open. "While the tube is going through the nasal passage it is exceedingly painful & only less so as it is being withdrawn. I never went through it without the tears streaming down my face."[40]

Once she managed to free her hands and snatch the tube, tearing it with her teeth. Another time her flailing arms broke a jug. After seeing how Alice struggled, the team tied sheets around her chest and her abdomen, which made breathing even more difficult.

After the first feeding, she was taken back to her cell with blood streaming down her face. When the same thing happened twice more, the doctors used a smaller tube. But her nostrils grew inflamed and the feeding episodes became even more painful. They were always accompanied by throat spasms and a feeling of nausea that was "not pleasant."[41]

When she was sentenced to a month's hard labor for the Guildhall incident, Alice had asked her fellow suffragettes not to disclose that she was an American, hoping to keep the news from reaching U.S. papers. But thanks to an Associated Press dispatch, her detention was common knowledge the day it happened; by November 19, reports that she was being "pump-fed" had appeared in newspapers everywhere. One dispatch quoted a former inmate who said Alice's anguished screams could be heard throughout the prison.

Some American newspapers couldn't contain their glee at the jailing of "the window smashing suffragettes." In a report that was more fancy than fact, readers of the *Fort Wayne News* were treated to a story about "a sassy little suffragette from the States who journey [*sic*] all the way to England in short skirts and shorter hair to proclaim the cause of suffering womankind. When the English people paid little attention to her rather lurid line of conversation, being accustomed to a home line just as lurid, Alice proceeds to tip over the statuary and spit on the police. She was put in jail and reliable reports are to the effect that she will have to suspend her Christmas stocking from a steel slat in a six by four cell."[42]

When the big city newsmen from Philadelphia and New York made their way to the Home Farm for an interview with the mother of the infamous suffragette, Tacie Paul professed puzzlement at her older daughter's notoriety. "I cannot understand how all this came about," she told the fellow from the *New York Times*. "Alice is such a mild-mannered girl."[43]

Admirers, both family and strangers, wrote Tacie of their support. "Suffragettes all over regard her as a *heroine*," said a nephew. "I myself being a *man* do not agree with their views on the voting question, but I rather admire Alice's pluck and determination than otherwise." Marshall D. Swisher, a Philadelphia music publisher, predicted that, "while strenuous methods may be criticized, those brave women will command consideration *now*, and ultimately win a victory." In an apparent reference to their Quaker heritage, Tacie's brother-in-law, Mickle Paul, wrote, "It is cause for pride to find that there is yet the spirit of progress—independent thought—& individual responsibility—that marked the family in earlier days—still in the head & heart of one of its members."[44]

Tacie might have confessed to a trusted confidante that not one of her four children was turning out quite as she had hoped. Helen, four years younger than Alice, was emotionally fragile, easily swayed and easily hurt. She had followed her older sister to Swarthmore, only to suffer rejection by the college's sororities. When in 1908 she begged to transfer to Wellesley, Tacie resisted. Swarthmore was her alma mater as well. Alice took Helen's side, writing sternly that "I should think thee would consider her happiness more than a sentimental feeling of loyalty to the College."[45] Tacie yielded.

Her son William, a year younger than Alice, was drawn to farming, a blessing since someone was needed to oversee the family's homestead. But young Bill had only a perfunctory interest in his father's principal business, banking, and visitors found him withdrawn and reclusive. He loved to hunt and his dogs were his closest companions. Alice confided to her sister Helen that she thought Bill "so morose" that he might benefit from seeing a "mental specialist."[46]

With Parry, who was still a teenager, Alice had assumed the role of a sage older sister. She advised her mother against his studying Latin. "There is no profession in which it is necessary. . . . I'm sorry I did,"[47] she wrote in 1907. Two years later, she was still mulling over his language studies. Better French than German, she wrote Tacie, because it was much easier.[48]

Tacie had come to lean on Alice for advice. She was a headstrong girl, but until now, she had been the sensible one.

As November 1909 drew to a close, while Alice was still in prison, Emmeline Pankhurst was winding up a six-week speaking tour of the United States to raise money for the treatment of her son Harry, who had contracted polio. Wherever she went, audiences were surprised to encounter not a stereotypical harridan who shrilly denounced male oppressors but a beautiful and eloquent woman, age fifty-one, whose speeches were laced with humor.

"Mrs. Pankhurst is quite unlike the cartoon type of suffragette," wrote the reporter for the *Syracuse Post-Standard*, clearly charmed. "She is one of those women whose portraits do not do her justice. She looks far younger than her most recent photograph indicates, her hair might well be the envy of many a girl in her 'teens, she has large, brown, expressive eyes. She doesn't rant. Her lecture was given in quiet, conversational tones of a low, pleasant voice that could be heard in every part of the house."[49]

In two final speeches in New York City, Emmeline brought up the subject of the jailed Alice, "a woman whose only offense was proclaiming at a public banquet, 'Votes for Women.'"[50]

"I think her case is a great object lesson to the American women," she told a crowd at the Hudson Theatre on November 28. Why, she wondered, had not President Taft intervened. She challenged the audience. "What are you American women going to do about it?"[51]

Poor Tacie was, in fact, trying to do something about it.

Well before Emmeline spoke in New York, Tacie had both cabled and written the American embassy in London asking that it intervene on her daughter's behalf. She received a personal reply from Ambassador Whitelaw Reid telling her that he had conducted an inquiry and was satisfied that justice had been served. "It appears that Miss Paul was convicted of breaking a window at the Guild Hall during a public dinner by throwing a stone through it, which nearly fell on the head of a Member of Parliament, and with otherwise interrupting the proceedings. She was given a fair and open trial and awarded the same punishment which has been repeatedly awarded to English subjects for similar offences."[52]

Alice would always deny having thrown a rock on that occasion.

With no recourse but to await her daughter's release, Tacie pleaded with Christabel Pankhurst. "I am so worried and anxious about her, and so afraid she will not come home I thought you might be able to persuade her to do so."[53]

Christabel assured Tacie that when Alice left prison, "She will be most tenderly cared for." And she pledged that the WSPU would "dissuade her most strongly from taking any further militant action for a long time to come. She is so unselfish, and has so much courage that she is always eager to take part in the most dangerous and difficult work." But Christabel would not encourage Alice to leave England as Tacie asked. The American suffragette was "much beloved by the members of our Union, and we hope that she may be able to remain in this country for a long time." She added, prophetically, "The experience she is gaining here would qualify her to take a very prominent part in winning the enfranchisement of American women."[54]

In fact, Alice had been steadily rising in the Pankhursts' estimation. Before her arrest she was a featured speaker on the WSPU roster and doubtless could have remained in England and worked for the Pankhursts, as Lucy Burns would do for the next two years. Alice had grown to love England. But she missed her family. And she hadn't abandoned her academic aspirations.

Released on December 9 after a month in prison, Alice learned that her forced feeding had made headlines in America and immediately cabled her mother that she was coming home. She followed up with a letter saying she was "sorry thee was so worried." She had thought Tacie knew nothing of her imprisonment, let alone the feeding. "Thee ought not to believe anything that appears in the papers," Alice wrote her mother. "It is pure imagination to talk about the prison resounding with my screams." In fact, she said, "I was well all the time. I gained 2½ pounds in prison. . . . The officials in prison were very kind. I had something to read. It was not at all bad. I can't see why you were so excited."[55]

It was more than two weeks before she could bring herself to confess the truth—she didn't want to relive the terrible experience—and then she wrote her mother about everything—the pain, the fear, the nausea. The part about the screams had been true. "I never went through it without the tears streaming down my face & often moaned from beginning to end & sometimes cried aloud."[56]

Alice explained her motive in terms she thought her mother might accept. The suffragettes had decided a year earlier "to resist prison—passively by taking no food & also by refusing to obey any of the regulations, with the purpose of making the situation more acute & consequently bringing it to an end sooner." It is, she added, "simply a policy of passive resistance & as a Quaker thee ought to approve of that."

Finally, in the words her mother had been waiting to hear for six months, she relayed her departure date. After two and a half years in England, seven arrests, and three jail terms, she would sail on January 5, 1910, from Liverpool. Tacie was not to tell any newspapers. "I hope I will never have to see my name in the paper again."[57]

Her ship experienced a stormy crossing and arrived four days late, on January 20. Alice was the last person to disembark. Looking small and frail in a heavy winter suit and large hat, but very happy, she descended the gangplank to the dock, where Tacie and Alice's younger brother, Parry, were waiting to greet her.

Along with a handful of reporters.

CHAPTER THREE

PHILADELPHIA STORY

Alice gave her first American interviews dockside and others when reporters trailed her to Moorestown. She obliged them with details of the forced feeding, which she said was "something like vivisection," in all a "trying ordeal, but if it ever becomes necessary for me to face it again I shall do so without hesitation."[1] England, Alice told the press, was "too conservative. . . . To make them wake up over there you just have to stand on your head or do some other foolish thing to attract attention."[2]

As much as she had looked forward to the comforts of the Home Farm—the big house overlooking a lawn frosted with snow, and within, the warmth of generous fires and a mother's care—in the early months of 1910 following her well-publicized return Alice was pulled away frequently by people eager to put her on display. In New York, where rival suffrage societies competed for money and members, Harriot Stanton Blatch moved quickly to co-opt the notorious American suffragette.

The younger daughter of suffrage pioneer Elizabeth Cady Stanton, Harriot, forty-four, had lived in England for twenty years with her husband, Harry, an English businessman, and had known Emmeline Pankhurst in socialist circles. Since her return to the United States in 1902, she had been working to breathe new life into the old cause. A member of the New York chapter of the Women's Trade Union League since its organization in 1904, she believed the vote would help working women "as nothing else could." In 1907 she formed the Equality League of Self-Supporting Women, "open to any woman who earns her own living, from a cook to a mining engineer."[3]

When Harriot invited Alice to speak on February 17, 1910, Alice could scarcely say no. While Alice was serving her last jail term, Harriot had pressed for her release. And perhaps she foresaw a way in which the older woman with the distinguished pedigree could be helpful.

Alice spoke easily of her experiences and took questions from an audience that filled most of the nine hundred seats in the Great Hall of Cooper Union, a free college in lower Manhattan for working-class children and women and a suitable venue for a militant suffragist, having once housed the offices of Susan B. Anthony. In the more intimate surroundings of the League's New York headquarters, she also confronted a cadre of avid reporters.

The scribes gathered around Alice in a semicircle. Keen to tell their readers "Precisely How It Feels To Be Bound and Then Forcibly Fed," as one headline would trumpet, they asked questions about the exact size of the feeding tube and whether she was tied or physically held down.[4] They were not so much interested in what Alice had to say about the righteousness of the suffrage cause.

Wrote one of those sensation-seekers, "Miss Paul sat with both hands in her muff, a little figure in a queer shade of green velvet, a genteel sort of a necklace, brown hair, nose glasses, low shoes and lisle thread stockings." The writer sounded almost disappointed that his subject looked "more like a perfectly good Sunday school teacher than a rampant suffragette."[5]

No matter that she still dreaded public speaking, and had vowed to return to academia, in the weeks after her arrival, Alice seemed unable to turn down an opportunity to defend the British militants. In addition to Blatch's forums, she spoke to at least three suffrage organizations in Philadelphia. But the invitation that surely provoked the most anxiety came from the people of Moorestown, who had known her since childhood.

On February 10, 1910, she stood before five hundred men and women in muted Quaker dress, packed into the auditorium of her alma mater, the Moorestown Friends High School. She was the headliner in an evening of entertainment, the final act of three after a piano solo and a short story reading.

In her talk, Alice compared the British suffragettes to the principled American abolitionists, whose legions had included so many Friends. The suffragettes injured no one, she said, according to a faithfully rendered account in the *Friends' Intelligencer,* an organ of the Hicksite community. They themselves were the only ones who suffered harm. She defended breaking windows as a recognized form of protest in Great Britain, and noted that only public buildings were targeted— ones, after all, that the women themselves had helped pay for with taxes. Alice's discourse, said the *Intelligencer*, was "clear, concise and convincing. She speaks earnestly and rapidly, but without heat or bitterness."[6]

When she had finished, Alice was asked pointedly about the "legitimacy and Christian nature of window smashing." Alice replied forthrightly that "she attached no particular sanctity to a twenty-five cent window-pane, that she herself had broken forty-eight, and that she endorsed it because it was a means to an end long recognized in England, if somewhat incomprehensible to Americans."[7]

In another speech to Quakers that year, Alice scolded her listeners. "As we look at the placid, comfortable attitude with which Friends regard the social ills about them, it seems indeed a far cry to the aggressive vigor with which the early Friends challenged the evils of their time."[8]

Quakers, she said, had forgotten "the spirit of democracy," particularly where women were concerned. As evidence, she quoted a female Friend who took pains to dress and speak in Quakerly fashion but responded to the "needs of a certain reform movement" with a question: "What sort of people are taking this up— what is their social caste—are they *ladies?*"[9]

In April, when members of the National American Woman Suffrage Associa- tion—widely known as the "National"—gathered for their annual convention in Washington, Alice was among the speakers. The ballroom of the Arlington Hotel was jammed, and men and women waiting outside were turned away. No doubt some were eager to learn of Alice's experiences. But most had come to hear the president of the United States.

The very fact that William Howard Taft had agreed to deliver the welcome on April 14, 1910, the first sitting president to speak to the nation's largest suf- frage organization, was cause for elation. He was known to oppose votes for women. But surely he would offer greetings and extend his best wishes for a suc- cessful convention. That alone would bolster the cause.

And that was precisely what had riled opponents of suffrage. New York Sen. Elihu Root, a rabid "anti" and, like Taft, a Republican, had written the president in high dudgeon that with his appearance the suffragists could now represent themselves as "having secured your sympathy."[10] Root asked that Taft make it clear that such was not the case.

As the hour came and went for Taft to appear, the audience grew restless. Where *was* the president? Finally, Anna Howard Shaw, an ordained Methodist minister and president of the National, began the meeting. She was well into her annual address when Taft sailed in, accompanied by his retinue. His immense bulk—he was the stoutest president in history, weighing more than 350 pounds at one point—made his entrance particularly imposing. He was so large that the White House bathtub was replaced after he became stuck more than once.

Members of the audience rose to their feet as Taft navigated past, a wide-beamed steamboat with a curled mustache stuck to its prow. Their white handkerchiefs fanned the air like the wings of tethered doves as they offered their warmest welcome, the "Chautauqua salute," originated by women in another place and time to cheer a deaf performer.

Halting in mid-speech, Shaw greeted the president warmly. Taft did not, however, deliver the gracious welcome that the women had hoped for.

The president said that at the age of sixteen, under the influence of his pro-suffrage father and the writings of John Stuart Mill, a believer in woman suffrage, he, too, had strongly favored votes for women. But he had since modified his views.

Taft could have stopped there, and been only slightly reviled. Instead, he went on: "The theory that Hottentots or any other uneducated, altogether unintelligent class is fitted for self-government at once or to take part in government is a theory that I wholly dissent from."[11]

Perhaps the nation's highest elected official did not notice the consternation among his listeners as they took in words that seemed to suggest that women were no better than "Hottentots"—a derogatory term for a South African tribe, and a synonym for ignorance. It also carried unpleasant sexual connotations: Hottentot women were said to have outsized breasts, genitalia, and, especially, buttocks.

But the ship of state sailed blithely on. The danger in granting suffrage, Taft suggested, was that "it may be exercised by that part of the class less desirable as political constituents and be neglected by many of those who are intelligent and patriotic and would be most desirable as members of the electorate."[12]

Listeners took a moment to digest this mouthful. The "less desirable" females from the lower classes, he seemed to be saying, *would* vote, while the "most desirable" would neglect to do so. The most desirable would include, presumably, the intelligent and patriotic women in this very room.

Air deliberately forced between clenched teeth is audible. When carried out in unison, the result is a hissing that is anything but friendly. At this point just such a sound erupted. "Oh, my children," chided Anna Shaw. An official history attempted to whitewash the incident, suggesting that the noise may not have been hissing at all, but rather exclamations of "hush" as people moved chairs to get a better view.[13]

But the hissing was real. A listener told the *Washington Post* that "it came simultaneously from all parts of the hall. One could easily overhear words of disapproval such as 'He knew more when he was 16 than he does now.'"[14]

Decades later, as an old woman whose memory was fading on many points, Alice Paul would still remember how "unperturbed" Taft appeared by the expression of disapproval coming from hundreds of women.[15]

The truth was that in 1910, when women could vote in only four states, all in the thinly populated West, the political risk to a president who insulted the female half of the nation's population was negligible.

Taft responded to the hissing with a smile. "Now, my dear ladies, you must show yourselves equal to self government by exercising, in listening to opposing arguments, that degree of restraint without which self-government is impossible."[16]

The president had managed to insult them again! He was saying that unless they learned some self-control, they did not deserve the right to vote. When the president shook hands with Dr. Shaw and abandoned the platform, women once again rose to their feet in a farewell gesture. Except, of course, some who did not.

But it was not Taft who was castigated for his remarks. In an era of civility, when raised voices were a sign of bad breeding, and women especially were the custodians of etiquette, the hissing was viewed as a shameful lapse in manners. One hyperbolic newspaper report contended that everyone—suffragists and anti-suffragists alike—agreed that the behavior that day "will prove the hardest blow the suffrage cause has yet suffered in America."[17]

The distraught Dr. Shaw labeled the outburst one of the "saddest hours" she had ever known at a convention. The diplomatic response was clearly an apology, or at least something that *sounded* like one. With only one dissenting vote, and it was said to have been cast in error by a non-member, the National passed a resolution the following day thanking Taft for his historic appearance and dispatched it to the White House with a letter that expressed "deep sorrow" and "regret" for the interruption and also disclaimed all responsibility. "Hissing" was not mentioned. By return post, Taft thanked the women and said he hoped the incident would soon be forgotten.[18]

By then the president's Hottentot speech had been reported around the country.

Alice was fooling herself if she truly believed she could be contented with the life of a scholar. Not only did she focus on women's rights in her doctoral dissertation, *Outline of the Legal Position of Women in Pennsylvania 1911*, but also, during the summer of 1911, she commanded Philadelphia's first campaign of open-air meetings.

For help, she turned to Lucy Burns, home from England on a family visit. The pair had forged a close bond during their time together in the service of the Pankhursts, but they were never destined to be best friends. It was always "Miss Paul" and "Miss Burns" when they corresponded, with none of the flowery language that often characterized close female relationships. But beginning that summer and for the next eight years, they worked as a team without apparent disagreement over goals or tactics. At times they seemed interchangeable. When one was absent, the other filled in seamlessly.

To veterans Alice and Lucy, a street corner meeting was the mildest form of agitation. But Philadelphia suffragists had not previously attempted anything so bold. As they set out on July 25, 1911, they had not secured a police permit, likely on Alice's advice. If they applied and were refused, they wouldn't dare hold the meeting. But if they went ahead with no permit, and the meeting took place without incident, the authorities would have no grounds to turn down future requests. It was a small risk and one that seemed worth taking. And so seven women, including Alice and Lucy, hopped aboard a trolley headed for a working-class neighborhood. Five of them were worried.

As they approached the targeted intersection, Caroline Katzenstein spied a policeman and panicked. "I am frank to confess that I seemed to develop a sort of *Jack and the Beanstalk* complex," she wrote later, "because the policeman on the beat near our corner appeared to grow taller and taller and bigger and bigger the closer we got to him. To me he seemed to be not just an arm of the law but the whole body of it!"[19]

Equipped with a horse-drawn cart and a signboard advertising the cause, they quickly attracted an audience of several hundred. The "kindly policeman" stood by but did not interfere. Alice opened the meeting, a second woman spoke, and Lucy closed "with her usual delightful and convincing talk," wrote

Caroline. "The crowd paid remarkable attention, seemed genuinely interested, and asked a number of questions."[20]

Five more meetings that week went just as smoothly. For a time reporters covered the campaign. As their attention faded, however, Alice assigned Caroline and another woman to chalk the sidewalks of Center City during the predawn hours with their slogan "Votes for Women." Philadelphians awoke to a "mysterious defacement of the city's sidewalks," Caroline wrote. The suffragists had literally "chalked up another publicity victory without any raid on our slim treasury."[21]

In the early days of that summer campaign, Lucy and Alice were the chief speakers. "Miss Paul's pale face and frail body made a striking contrast to Miss Burns' ruddy complexion and sturdy frame," Caroline wrote. But Alice knew that reporters would quickly grow tired of the same old faces. She pressed Caroline to speak. The young woman buried her head in her arms, too terrified to say yes. Finally she told Alice, "Miss Paul, I am going through the tortures of the damned."[22]

She got no sympathy from Alice: "We've all done that." Alice suggested that Caroline begin as she herself had debuted in London. "If you only introduce Miss Burns and me, it will give the papers another name to use."[23]

The campaign ended on September 30 with a rally in Independence Square featuring suffrage luminaries, who spoke from five stands to an estimated two thousand people. Alice was among them. Having proved herself as an organizer, she was now more than just a name in the news.

In 1912, when Alice was juggling both studies and suffrage, she and her Ph.D. supervisor, Ellery C. Stowell, an expert in international law, dined in the same boardinghouse. Often, he saw her absorbed in a piece of suffrage literature with little apparent thought of food. Among his students, she stood out, not only because she was one of the few women at Penn but also for "the brilliance of her mind and her capacity for scholarly research." Years later he would recall early evidence of her idealism. "She had a fine taste in dress, but when one of her friends admired the hat she was wearing she gave it to her and went about in a much less becoming substitute. It seemed to be a matter of supreme indifference to her, lost as she was in lifting the low condition of women throughout the world."[24]

When Alice completed her degree, Carl Kelsey, a distinguished sociologist and another of her professors, congratulated her on her examination, "beyond question one of the best I have ever seen." He asked, as if he had a job in mind,

"Do you care to tell me what your plans are for next year, and whether or not you are in line for any position?"[25]

Kelsey perhaps hoped that his star student would remain in academia. But the offers Alice entertained in the spring of 1912 were from suffrage societies. She could have gone to work for the Women's Political Union, a new organization founded by Harriot Blatch, which offered to make her its first paid organizer. Or she could have chosen Ohio, where the state suffrage association guaranteed her a "whirling, rushing campaign." And Philadelphia's Jane Campbell, a member of the National's executive committee, promised her complete independence if she would help out. Campbell wrote, "Everyone says, if we can only 'secure Alice Paul' for the 'open airs,' they will be a success."[26]

Alice turned down all the offers, although she briefly considered one entreaty from the Pennsylvania Woman Suffrage Association. In November Pennsylvania would host the National's convention in Philadelphia. Since 1910, Harriot Blatch had staged ever larger suffrage parades each spring in New York to growing acclaim, and other cities now hastened to follow suit. Given Alice's track record as an organizer, leaders decided she was the perfect choice to put together a parade to welcome delegates.

Evidently Alice was intrigued. Until, that is, the association declared there could be no floats. "If we can't have floats," Dora Lewis, who was in charge of convention arrangements, pleaded with Alice, "we could try and make up for that deprivation by having plenty of music, don't you think?" Banners, she continued, "can be very touching. . . . We *need* the parade, and you are the one person to manage it."[27]

"Touching" wasn't in Alice's vocabulary.

More than the absence of floats, perhaps, it was Alice's other priorities that occupied her attention and convinced her to turn down the assignment, thus ending all talk of a Philadelphia parade. She was carrying on a correspondence that summer with William Parker, a young man who was carving out a career for himself as a bond salesman on Wall Street and also discovering Manhattan's attractions. He was eager to take her to dinner "at a little Hungarian place I know," and perhaps one day she would grace a salon he planned to create "and be amused and warmed by the glow of all the good spirits."[28] Alice kept the letter and perhaps accepted the invitation to dinner. But there is no record of further contact with the friendly young man, or any others. Her mind was elsewhere.

It had taken her less than two years to decide that state suffrage campaigns were a waste of time; the only course that made sense was the passage of a federal constitutional amendment giving the vote to women the country over. Such an amendment had been first proposed in 1878. Section I stated: "The right of citizens of the United States to vote shall not be denied or abridged by the United States or by any State on account of sex." The second section gave Congress "power to enforce this article by appropriate legislation."[29]

What came to be called the Susan B. Anthony amendment, although its provenance was less than clear, had been voted on only once; it was soundly defeated in the U.S. Senate in 1887 and never again debated in either chamber of Congress. Every year thereafter the leaders of the National American Woman Suffrage Association trooped to Washington to expound on its behalf before Senate and House committees. And every year the amendment went nowhere.

Instead, the National put its resources into campaigns to amend state constitutions. But fourteen years had passed with no progress, until 1910, when Washington became only the fifth state to give women the vote. It wasn't for want of trying: Susan B. Anthony herself took part in eight failed campaigns.

Some state laws made it next to impossible to pass such an amendment. At a minimum, a state's two legislative chambers had to approve the wording and then authorize a referendum for the voters—all men, of course. But in thirteen states the amendment could not go to the voters until it had been approved by two successive legislatures. Delaware required a two-thirds majority each time, with absent votes counting against the measure. In rural states, legislatures might meet only every other year, and then only for several months.

Some states required a two-thirds majority of the voters, some three-fourths. Eleven states required a majority of *all* votes cast in the election, not just those cast for the amendment. In seven states, once an amendment failed, it could not be brought up again for periods ranging from four to ten years.[30]

How much more promising it seemed to lobby a constitutional amendment through Congress and then secure ratification by three-quarters—thirty-six—of the state legislatures. Confident that the confrontational tactics employed by England's WSPU could be brought to bear on federal lawmakers, Alice and Lucy decided to volunteer their services to the National on behalf of the Anthony amendment. Since their student days, both Alice and Lucy had received stipends from their families; the pair was willing to work without pay. To be sure, suffragists thus far had not won the vote in England, where an anti-suffrage prime minister and his cabinet ruled Parliament. In the U.S. Congress, the young women reasoned, individual legislators had more freedom.

During the summer of 1912 Alice met with Mary Ware Dennett, the National's salaried secretary and day-to-day administrator. It was clear to Alice that Dennett thought her proposed campaign for a constitutional amendment "rather foolish." However Alice had couched her offer of help, the conservative leadership came away with the distinct impression that Alice advocated "a campaign of 'militancy,'" according to the *History of Woman Suffrage,* the movement's official record. "The idea was coldly received by the suffrage leaders."[31]

Alice also tried to interest Harriot Blatch in a national campaign, but her Women's Political Union was focused on the upcoming 1915 New York referendum. Harriot at least was willing to introduce Alice to Jane Addams, the famed social reformer from Chicago and the National's vice president. Perhaps, Harriot said, Addams could be persuaded to bring Alice and Lucy's proposal to work for a constitutional amendment before the board.

Jane Addams was famous the world over as the founder of Hull House, a run-down mansion in Chicago's old, dirty, crowded, dangerous, pestiferous nineteenth ward that she had bought and stuffed with books, sports, classes, and clubs for impoverished immigrants. Hull House supplied a model for settlement houses springing up in urban slums across America.

She was a foremost Progressive leader, one of the legions dedicated to reshaping a country warped by corporate barons, greedy landlords, payoff-seeking politicos, exploitive industrialists who would work children from dawn to dusk for pennies a day, corner-cutting owners of filthy food factories, and the rest of the powerful riff raff who made life miserable for the working class.

Progressive reformers had not made a priority of woman suffrage, however. But Addams had joined the cause because, without ballots, the constituents who cared most about dangerous housing, contaminated food, filthy neighborhoods, and poor schools were powerless. In 1912 Republicans rejected Teddy Roosevelt and turned to the more conservative Taft as their candidate for president. When Roosevelt decided to run as a Progressive, Addams seconded his nomination and campaigned for his election. She was heartened by the party's pledges for reform, including votes for women.

The Democratic Party took no position on suffrage, nor did its candidate, Woodrow Wilson. When Massachusetts governor Eugene Noble Foss asked Wilson about his position, he replied that he thought it best not "to bring the woman suffrage question into the national campaign."

A devout southerner, Wilson was born in Staunton, Virginia, in 1856 and spent the first twenty-four years of his life in the South—"The only place in the country, the only place in the world, where nothing has to be explained to me." Like a majority of southern males, he was "strongly against" votes for women. [32]

"I believe that the social changes it would involve would not justify the gains that would be accomplished by it," he told a letter writer in 1911. But he hid his personal antipathy behind the more acceptable principle of states' rights. "It is not a national question," he told Foss, "but a state question."[33]

When in 1910 New Jersey Democrats first turned to Wilson, he had been president of Princeton University, his alma mater, since 1902. During his tenure he earned national recognition with an overhaul of the curriculum and reorganization of the faculty. When Wilson boldly attempted to do away with Princeton's elitist eating clubs, however, he ran into a stiff wall of resistance from the alumni. In a battle to control plans for a new graduate school, he lost out to a powerful dean allied with wealthy contributors. A friendly press characterized these failures as efforts to democratize the campus, which added to a growing national reputation.

Wilson accepted the gubernatorial nomination, then publicly repudiated the machine politicians behind the draft, further enhancing his reputation. By 1912 he had established himself as a masterful orator, who was honest, independent and smart with a strong sense of morality, the perfect presidential candidate for a party seeking a little Progressive luster. On the presidential campaign trail, Wilson had often seemed cold and remote, but to his wife and three daughters, and close colleagues, he displayed a warmer side. He spun jokes, danced jigs and loved limericks.

Wilson might have avoided the issue of suffrage altogether during the 1912 campaign, had it not been for Maud Malone.

At the Brooklyn Academy of Music on October 19, just as Wilson launched a well-honed attack on monopolies, a female voice with an Irish lilt interrupted him. "How about votes for women?" Heads craned toward the balcony where a young woman in a purple shirtwaist was on her feet. It was Maud Malone, a city librarian and intrepid suffragist, socialist, and labor activist.

The speaker moved to the front of the stage. "What is it, Madam?" he asked.

"Mr. Wilson," cried Maud, "You just said you were trying to destroy a monopoly, and I ask you what about woman suffrage? The men have a monopoly."

The audience tittered. Wilson answered soberly. "Woman suffrage, madam, is not a question that is dealt with by the National Government at all. I am here only as a representative of the national party."

"I am speaking to you as an American, Mr. Wilson," Maud answered calmly.

The men in the audience hooted as the colloquy continued. Voices erupted around Maud. "Sit down!" "Put her out." "Police!" And, "Why don't you go to your own meeting?"[34]

A three-man police detail dragged an uncooperative Malone out and down a fire exit as the audience cheered her exit. She spent the night in jail and was convicted three weeks later of a misdemeanor.

The Maud Malone incident was a bit of an embarrassment but it had no impact on the campaign. Wilson was easily elected.

Buoyed by suffrage victories in four western states, on November 20 the women of the National were in high spirits as they gathered in Philadelphia for their 1912 convention. Taxi after taxi pulled up at the canopied Broad Street entrance of the turret-topped Hotel Walton, built for the wealthy in the curlicued, high baroque style of New York's palatial Waldorf-Astoria. Liveried doormen ushered the arriving delegates into an extravagantly marbled, paneled, and frescoed lobby where big yellow posters announced the convention and flags shouted "Votes for Women."

Anglo-Saxon and more Protestant than not, often pedigreed, and generally well-off, the convention delegates were anything but a cross-section of American women. To one amazed reporter they looked like a new breed of female as they managed without male assistance to dole out tips and oversee the proper delivery of their baggage. Nowhere to be seen was the suffragist stereotype, "with cuffs, short hair and low heels."[35] These women were stylish, with long hair in clever twists and knots. Their clothing was well-tailored, their hats modish. Some wore the new wool walking suits with gored skirts that promoted freedom of motion.

Even Anna Shaw, habitually clothed in basic black, had evidently decided her appearance could stand a little tinkering. When reporters attempted to talk to her, the National president put them off. It seemed she had another appointment—with a fashion consultant. One woman got so carried away by the elegant attire that she gasped, "Isn't that a beautiful dark-blue velvet suit—the one over there with the violet scarf and a blue hat?" Her companion responded with a reproach: "That is the feminine and not the woman's question."[36]

The suffrage who's who was here in force. Heads turned when Alva Belmont made her entrance in a suit of plum-colored satin trimmed with bands of fur and a lynx neckpiece encircling her throat. Reporters took out their notebooks. The press had followed Alva's dogged climb to the pinnacle of New York society, her scandalous divorce from the impossibly wealthy William K. Vanderbilt, the forced marriage of her beautiful daughter Consuelo to England's Duke of Marlborough, and Alva's second marriage to the also prosperous Oliver Belmont. Now they lusted after each detail of her incarnation as a nouveau suffragist.

After her second husband's death, Alva had undertaken a twilight career as a charitable do-gooder. Much like Alice, she soon concluded that "the uplifting of the slums could, at best, be but ephemeral unless the very conditions which created the slums were overcome."[37] Alva was willing to contribute money, but she wanted to give it to a cause that would be of lasting value to society.

Something like votes for women.

Her great wealth gave her instant access to suffrage's upper tier. Two days after their first meeting in 1909, Anna Shaw crowed to the National's board that she had "got her [Belmont] for a life member of the National Association before leaving." And then the president of the National got to the bottom line. "I think she will help us financially by and by."[38] And so Alva had. Thanks to her largesse the National had moved its headquarters from a corner of the Warren, Ohio, courthouse, in the hometown of treasurer Harriet Upton, to a Fifth Avenue suite of offices. She also underwrote the costs of a press bureau, which ensured her continued presence in the news.

Here, too, fresh from the campaign trail, was Jane Addams. She was first vice president of the National, and its biggest star. "How are you?" arriving delegates had asked as they greeted each other in the Hotel Walton lobby, and in the next breath, "Is Jane Addams coming?"[39]

Harriot Blatch was here, of course. Her mother had been a founding member. Among the younger members present were the beautiful Inez Milholland, always said to be the prettiest suffragist, and the radical socialist Crystal Eastman. Both were lawyers who circulated in Greenwich Village bohemian circles, a breeding ground for a kind of independent female known in the press as "The New Woman."

Inez, the pampered daughter of a wealthy, liberal, self-made businessman, was notorious even before she graduated from Vassar in June 1909. In her junior year, when the college president banned suffrage talks on campus, she pied-piped a group of fellow students to a nearby cemetery. Amid the graves they heard rousing speeches from Harriot Blatch and other feminists. Inez's fame was such that during her senior year the *New York Times* assigned a reporter to visit Vassar in Poughkeepsie, New York, and write a profile. He devoted two columns to the "remarkable girl," who was "the idol of the whole undergraduate body."[40]

In New York City, she had walked picket lines, crusaded for socialism, and denounced corsets. The law schools of Oxford, Cambridge, and Columbia rejected her, but she was admitted to the New York University law school and graduated in 1912. As a newly minted lawyer, she added prison reform to her causes. Her erstwhile lover Max Eastman called her his "Amazon," though when his passion ebbed he dismissed her ungraciously for living "a high-geared metropolitan, function-attending, opera-going, rich girl's life."[41]

As for Alice, her public role was minor—an assignment to speak at an opening day rally of the convention. Her private agenda had been purged of its militancy; it now encompassed one single compelling event in support of a federal amendment.

Who didn't love a parade?

With floats.

On opening day, November 21, 1912, delegates strolled two blocks to the eleven-story Witherspoon building, Philadelphia's first skyscraper. Witherspoon housed the general offices of the United Presbyterian Church of the United States and church business continued during the convention. Rev. Robert E. L. Jarvis, whose arrival coincided with a crush of delegates, was scooped up along with two colleagues in "an unyielding crowd of suffragettes," swept almost off his feet, and jammed into a corner of the elevator. Whimpered one of his companions, "Heavens! Have we come to this?"[42]

A festive mood prevailed among the three hundred women crowded into Witherspoon's main hall. The walls were hung with suffrage cartoons and posters. But a United States map drawn on a big white sheet offered a graphic display of the distance yet to travel before women were truly free.

Anchoring the left-hand side in white were states where full suffrage prevailed: Washington, Oregon, California, Idaho, Wyoming, Colorado, and, thanks to victories that very month, Arizona, Kansas, Oregon, and Michigan. Ten states in all.

Make that nine.

Within hours of hanging the map, the women would learn that their claim to Michigan had been premature. Meanwhile they had met defeat in two other states, Ohio and Wisconsin, where powerful beer and whiskey interests ran one hundred–proof campaigns against suffrage. Enfranchised wives, daughters, and mothers, the liquor people felt certain, would surely vote for Prohibition to prevent their tippling husbands from guzzling their weekly paychecks.

So there had been victories, yes. But stretching eastward was the rest of the country, a vast dark plain of resistance.

At noon on opening day of the convention, eight blocks east of Witherspoon Hall, Alice gazed warily over the upturned faces that ringed the low wooden speaker's platform in Independence Square. The people looked friendly enough, but they knew nothing of her notoriety.

When the ill will surfaced, it came not from the crowd of clerks, shop girls and businessmen but from the woman just a few inches away—the Boston attorney assigned to introduce Alice. In a curiously ungracious dig at the speaker, the woman made it clear that she did not approve of the "militant" methods of the British suffragettes and, by association, of the speaker. Alice let it go.

She had decided to use her brief speaking time to recall another day in this historic square, where the Declaration of Independence was first recited. In 1876, during Philadelphia's celebration of the nation's centennial, a small group of suffragists had asked to present a petition urging votes for women.

"This permission was refused, but led by the redoubtable Susan B. Anthony, the women marched to the square and presented their petition. Then they went to the Chestnut Street sidewalk and held a meeting of their own."[43] That was Susan B. for you. "No" was not an acceptable answer.

Alice felt a special kinship with Anthony, for they were both Quakers and both, if she dared think the term to herself, "militant." It was Anthony who had bullied the Rochester, New York, registrar into registering her and fifteen other women, and then brazenly marched into her polling place and cast her vote in the election of 1872, a crime for which she was promptly arrested. During her trial, she castigated the government—"a hateful oligarchy of sex; the most hateful aristocracy ever established on the face of the globe."[44] Unmoved, the judge pronounced her guilty and leveled a fine of $100. She never paid.

Women still could not cast ballots in Pennsylvania, or in the other twelve colonies that had fought for freedom. "Even the American Indians have been given votes now," Alice Paul said, indignation creeping into her voice. "Why not women?"[45]

As the convention got underway, there were prolonged sessions that revealed divides between West and East as deep as canyons. The two sides of the continent split over how their votes should be tallied and the permanent location of headquarters. Western delegates were unwilling to cede the New York location in perpetuity. The National was also flat broke, driven $5,000 into debt by its magazine, *Woman Voter.*

Alice and Lucy may well have wondered how this fractured organization, in many respects a collection of fiefdoms run by powerful state chairmen, could ever mount an effective national campaign. When delegates could have been debating how best to secure votes for women, they instead spent a full day in angry attacks and counterattacks over whether to take part in partisan politics. The controversy revolved around the venerable Jane Addams.

When she seconded Roosevelt's nomination and joined his campaign, Addams had run afoul of an informal ban on partisan activities that applied to officers of the National. No one seriously believed Addams would be censured, and she wasn't. Nevertheless, the fight occupied the better part of day three. The news stories occupied the better part of the front pages. "Split on Politics Menaces Woman Suffrage Society" was the lead story the next day in the *Philadelphia Inquirer.* And the *Bulletin,* especially, made it appear that the women had lost all sense of decorum. "President Shaw had her hands full in controlling the meeting, as many of the delegates insisted on being heard at the same time, with some of them flinging back and forth accusations that had some bearing on partisan activity in the recent campaign."[46]

But Shaw, the newspaper said, was able to control the outbursts "as well as could be expected, certainly better than any man could have done it."

The convention ended on Tuesday, November 26, the outstanding questions resolved and harmony ostensibly restored. The word "permanent" was removed from the resolution pertaining to the headquarters location. The National decided to hand over the money-losing *Woman Voter* to editor Alice Stone Blackwell, who would endeavor to keep it afloat. Anna Shaw was reelected president, albeit by fewer votes than in the past.

At some point before Shaw gave a closing speech and suffrage delegates stepped aboard trains that would return them to America's four corners, Jane

Addams, her saintly luster restored, lobbied on behalf of Alice Paul and a parade that Alice proposed to organize in Washington on March 3, 1913, the day before Woodrow Wilson's inauguration. (Not until 1936 would presidential inaugurations take place on January 20.)

In 1910, Harriot Blatch had organized America's first major women's suffrage parade in New York City, motivated by her repeated failure to wrest a suffrage measure from the New York legislature. "Mankind," she had concluded, "is moved to action by emotion, not by argument and reason. And what, she decided, "could be more stirring than hundreds of women, carrying banners, marching—marching—marching!"[47]

At first worried that a parade smacked of militancy, Anna Shaw nonetheless took part in the Fifth Avenue march. Sort of. As Harriot noted tartly, "she rode." Harriot disapproved. "Riding in a car did not demonstrate courage; it did not show discipline; it did not give any idea of numbers of 'marchers'." Henceforth, she decided, when parading, women should go by foot, and they should do so properly. To that end, she provided free classes in "the art of walking."[48]

The first parade drew so much attention that she staged a second and a third. In 1912, the event was hailed by the *New York Times* as "the like of which New York never knew before."[49] At least 10,000 people trod north on Fifth Avenue from Washington Square, past sidewalks clogged with spectators. Elderly women were allowed to ride in flower-bedecked carriages.

Her initial misgivings overcome, Shaw enthusiastically strode with the marchers. So, when Alice proposed a parade in Washington, Shaw, said the official *History of Woman Suffrage*, was "favorably inclined."[50] Shaw *loved* parades .

As Alice requested, Shaw appointed her chairman of the National's Congressional Committee, replacing Elizabeth Kent, wife of a California congressman, who had operated with a budget of $10 and spent so little in the previous year that she returned change to the National's treasury. The assignment carried a single condition. The committee, with Lucy Burns as vice-chairman and soon to be number five, would have to raise its own funds for an office, staff, and whatever activities were carried out.

To conventioneers it must have seemed just another minor appointment, but it gave Alice exactly what she wanted: the chance to run her own show.

Not until the 1913 convention would most delegates know even that much about the arrangement. But by then Alice Paul would be a *cause célèbre*.

CHAPTER FOUR

MARCHING WHERE THE MEN MARCH

Alice arrived in Washington in mid-December of 1912, rented a room in a spartan boardinghouse on I Street that catered to Quaker women, and began at once to lay the groundwork for the first suffrage parade in the nation's capital.

She had a vision: a spectacular unfurling of bands, floats, and marchers in multi-hued capes, a melodious, harmonious ribbon of color on monochromatic Pennsylvania Avenue that would announce to the new male president, the incoming male Congress, and the nation's male voters that a distaff cry for equality could not be ignored.

But first, Alice needed money.

An old list of Washington members supplied by the National proved useless. The women Alice contacted had mostly moved or were dead, with one happy exception: Emma Gillett, the founder of the Washington College of Law and one of just four full-time female lawyers practicing in Washington. Not only was Emma "the first person I met who was friendly and interested," but—this was no small matter—she was "still living," Alice said later. Gillett volunteered to serve as treasurer of a rejuvenated Congressional Committee. And she steered Alice to an office at 1420 F Street, next to her own, that was available for $60 a month. Although the space was a gloomy, none-too-warm basement under a real estate firm, F Street itself was the city's principal shopping thoroughfare, and the location was just up the street from "Woodies"—Woodward & Lothrop, Washington's storied department store. The office entrance was just below street level; fashionable females strolling by could not miss it. Alice's predecessor, Elizabeth Kent, volunteered five dollars a month toward rent, emboldening Alice to sign the lease. Elizabeth also introduced the newcomer to prominent suffrage supporters. And then she invited Alice to Christmas dinner.[1]

When in December of 1912 Alice called upon Washington, D.C., Police Superintendent Richard Sylvester to request a permit for a parade, he told her that she was asking for trouble, first by demanding the use of Pennsylvania Avenue, which was just a few paces from the seedy saloons in Washington's Bowery district, and second by demanding to march on March 3, 1913, when the city would be full of men scheduled to take part in the next day's inaugural festivities. Men with time on their hands. Time that they would spend in those very saloons.

Alice was just days short of her twenty-eighth birthday; her weight seldom topped a hundred pounds. Twice her age and bulk, Richard Sylvester cut a commanding figure. His face was fully occupied by a small beard, a bristling handlebar mustache, and a patrician nose. In a 1911 photograph, he poses erect in a dark uniform with epaulets, a stiff collar, and a double row of eighteen brass buttons, the very picture of authority. The visor of his police hat is pulled down firmly, grazing his eyebrows.[2]

He was at the top of his profession. Not only was he the city's chief law enforcement officer, but he was also the president of the International Association of Chiefs of Police, a progressive organization working to purge urban forces of corruption and professionalize the calling. In the eyes of the public, he stood for modern policing.

Even under normal conditions, the Washington police force was spread thin, just 631 men to police a city of 331,069 people occupying sixty square miles. Two parades back to back—Alice's and then the inaugural—would strain Sylvester's resources. To make his point, he confessed that at one recent inauguration, carousers from the Pennsylvania militia had captured a police lieutenant, thrown him on a blanket, and playfully tossed him in the air.[3]

Moreover, because Wilson was only the second Democratic president since the Civil War, and a Virginian by birth, his inauguration would be a magnet for southern Democrats. Alice insisted Sylvester called them "riffraff," and another visitor remembered "roughscuff," although Sylvester would strongly deny using such words.[4]

Alice would not be swayed. As she saw it, on March 3, the city would be overflowing with as many as 150,000 visitors, a huge audience for a suffrage spectacle. Among them would be wives and daughters of the men marching in the inaugural parade—women who might be persuaded to turn out for suffrage. Too, on that date, the trains were offering discount fares, an important consideration. Financially dependent on their husbands, most women had little money to spare. Only March 3 would do.

And Pennsylvania Avenue was incomparable, a broad river of commerce flowing west from the Capitol to the White House and the majestic, columned Treasury Building, with a plaza that constituted a natural stage that would be perfect for a tableau, if she could pull one together.

They *had* to have the Avenue.

That was where the men marched.

Sylvester expressed his reservations when Alice first requested a permit, and at every meeting thereafter, whether she came alone or accompanied by the prominent women who were gravitating to her cause—wives and daughters of congressmen, eminent professionals, and military officers—or whether she sent them in her stead.

Elsie Hill, whose father was a Connecticut congressman, arrived with her mother and informed Sylvester that he was being overly cautious when he warned of a possible disturbance. Having marched in New York suffrage parades, she was certain there would be no trouble "if the police protection was half as good as it was in New York."[5]

As it happened, New York's 1912 parade had not been so easily controlled as Elsie suggested. "At the end of the parade the crush around Carnegie Hall, where the members disbanded, completely overwhelmed the police," the *New York Times* reported. To open a passage, patrolmen "had to charge the crowd repeatedly."[6]

Trying to be helpful, Sylvester offered alternatives. Why not parade on March 5? Many people, perhaps more even than on March 3, would be in town. And why not march on 16th Street, a thoroughfare that was almost half again as wide as Pennsylvania Avenue and lined with handsome homes occupied by well-behaved Washingtonians? On 16th Street, he assured them, they could still "wear their beautiful dresses and have beautiful floats."[7]

In 1913, the concept of marching on Washington was almost unknown.[8] To the American people, the federal government was a remote entity, bottled up in a few buildings in an out-of-the-way spot along the Potomac, and many in the government liked it that way. Not until the following year would Americans in every state vote for their senators, who were previously elected by state legislatures. The framers of the Constitution had deliberately sought to insulate lawmakers from popular pressure.

Sylvester was old enough to recall the only comparable instance when marchers had come to the capital to demonstrate for a cause. It was not an especially happy memory. In 1894 during a severe recession, with unemployment in some sectors approaching 25 percent, Populist businessman Jacob Coxey had herded five hundred scruffy, out-of-work men into the city from points west to pressure the government for jobs. "Coxey's Army" tramped along Pennsylvania Avenue to the Capitol, where Coxey ascended the steps and attempted to read a statement. In a shameful finale, he and other organizers were jailed for trespassing on Capitol grounds.

While Sylvester attended to everyday police matters, Alice was busily recruiting volunteers, furnishing a headquarters, and lining up parade units and continuing to press her choice of date and route. Thanks to the industrious Alice, Sylvester heard from the Chamber of Commerce, the Board of Trade, the Merchant's Association, and other civic organizations, all urging "our right to the Avenue," as she put it to a Pennsylvania friend.[9] The days flew by. Christmas came and went without a decision.

In the last week of December, after more calls, letters, and visits than he cared to count, Sylvester blinked. He announced the women could have their requested date, March 3. But until the route was determined, it was still a parade with nowhere to go.

As Washington prepared to celebrate its final New Year's Eve under a Republican administration, Alice and a quartet of well-bred women appeared in the office of John A. Johnston, one of the three appointed commissioners who governed the city. A retired army general, Johnston's bailiwick was the police department. He was Sylvester's boss.

With Alice were Mrs. Robert La Follette, the wife of a crusading Wisconsin senator; Alice's new friend and supporter, Elizabeth Kent, who was married to a wealthy California congressman; Mrs. Thomas MacDonald, the wife of a prominent physician; and Helen Gardener, a Washington author and colonel's wife.

Johnston seemed, if possible, even cooler toward the parade than Sylvester. The commissioner suggested "some other time of the year and some other place."[10] He recommended that the chairman of the Wilson inaugural committee, William Eustis, be asked for an opinion. Eustis was no friend of suffrage. He had already refused to rent Alice the inaugural grandstands on Pennsylvania Avenue for her parade.

The women left Johnston's office feeling both defeated and humiliated. Gardener later recalled, "All but one said, 'We will give up the Avenue. We can not go on meeting with this kind of thing.'" The holdout was Alice. "Miss Paul did not want to give up on the Avenue. None of us wanted to, but she had the courage to go on."[11]

Publicly she never wavered. But anxiety was keeping Alice awake at night. She confided to a friend that, if they had no other choice, they would march on 16th Street.

A week after the December 31 meeting, Eustis surprised everyone. He announced that he had no objection to a March 3 parade on Pennsylvania Avenue. U.S. Treasury Secretary Franklin MacVeagh granted permission to use the south plaza of the Treasury for an allegorical tableau with "great pleasure."[12] Although it wasn't clear the permission was his to give, or even necessary, House Speaker James Beauchamp "Champ" Clark, whose wife Genevieve was another of Alice's volunteers, said they could form the parade around the Peace Monument at the base of Capitol Hill.

That same week, Sylvester opened the newspapers to discover that the disagreeable Alice Paul had gone public with her quest for Pennsylvania Avenue. The suffragists' plaint appeared in all the newspapers. Alice wrote the National that the *Washington Times* "has printed an editorial stating that there is no reason why we should not have that particular street, since men's processions have already marched there."[13]

On January 9, 1913, Sylvester capitulated. The Congressional Committee could have exactly what had been requested: the entire stretch of the Avenue from the Capitol to Continental Hall on 17th Street, a block past the White

House, where a post-parade rally was planned. The *Washington Post* headlined
the victory: "AVENUE FOR PAGEANT . . . Suffragists Win Permit to Use
Thoroughfare March 3 . . . Purple, Green, and White Banner Unfurled at Headquarters as Token Of Triumph."[14]

A young woman, just twenty-eight years of age, with no experience in organizing parades, pressuring government officials, soliciting money, capturing
publicity, or enlisting volunteers on a mass scale had won her first victory for
suffrage. But the fight had consumed a full month, leaving Alice barely two
months to execute her plans. To fail would give ammunition to anti-suffragists,
condemn the suffragist movement to undoing the damage, and perhaps cost the
battle for the votes a promising leader.

In 1913, no civic celebration was complete without a pageant. Imported from
turn-of-the-century Britain, these elaborate presentations had invaded every
corner of the United States. "In the words of *American Homes and Gardens,*
America was going 'pageant mad.'" Most common were historical reenactments
celebrating the history of a town or city that might feature hundreds of cos-
tumed actors, musicians, and dancers set off by elaborate backdrops. Soon, wrote
historian David Glassberg, "The term stretched to include both the Bryn Mawr
College students' annual May Day fete and the Sing Sing Prison inmates' celebration welcoming back their warden after his acquittal of corruption
charges."[15]

In the back of Alice's mind lurked this question: What if she held a parade
and no one came? Framing the event as a pageant would avoid the inevitable
and perhaps unfavorable comparisons to Harriot Blatch's ever-larger marches
on Fifth Avenue. On the Treasury plaza, a classically themed tableau would enact
the birth of a new era in woman's history. As she saw it, the entire parade would
be a pageant on wheels, each segment a narrative.

She explained to a supporter, "Therefore, while we want, of course, marchers,
above all things, we are endeavoring to make the procession a particularly beautiful one, so that it will be noteworthy on account of its beauty even if we are not
able to make it so on account of its numbers."[16]

"Procession," with all the majesty the word conveyed, was her preferred
word. Alice signed her correspondence, "Chairman Procession Committee."

Alice would not perpetuate a familiar pageant cliché, in which women were
portrayed as pioneer helpmates who only cooked, sewed, sowed, and quilted. As
the procession unspooled onto the Avenue, the public would witness an hom-

age to modern womanhood. Sliding past like pictures in a children's book, the floats would show females breaking through barriers of discrimination, fighting for their places in a man's world. The first sequence would celebrate countries where women had won the vote or were striving for it. Another sequence, the history of woman suffrage in America, would begin with a float, "As it was in 1840." Here, the struggling suffrage pioneers, clad in light purple, would be pitted against "scorners" wearing black. By the fourth float in the chronology, "Today," the women in light purple would have multiplied; their expressions would be jubilant.

There would be floats featuring women farmers, yes, and the usual homemakers, but also, on wheels and on foot, military nurses, college women, lawyers, doctors, social workers, teachers, business women, librarians, writers, artists, actresses, musicians, and wage earners in the nation's offices and factories. Bringing up the rear would be a catchall division, as many women as could be lured to Washington, marching behind state banners.

Given the timing, Alice said, spectators would come away with "the realization that one-half of the people have not participated in choosing the ruler who is being installed."[17]

As the parade took on a life of its own, Alice found it necessary to remind people that it was not an end in itself, but the opening salvo in a campaign for a federal amendment that would halt, once and for all, the tortuous two-steps-forward, one-step-back process by which women were gaining the vote.

Lucy Burns arrived in Washington in early January. Besides Alice and Lucy, the members of the Congressional Committee were Crystal Eastman, a New York socialist who had carried out a highly regarded investigation of industrial accidents that influenced workmen's compensation laws; Mary Beard, the wife of a prominent historian, who had edited the New York journal the *Woman Voter* and worked with female strikers in the garment trades; and Dora Lewis, a Philadelphia widow with a distinguished lineage who admired both Alice and Lucy for the 1911 summer street corner campaign.

In late January, a visiting reporter, finding the large front room of the F Street office thronged with women, drew the inevitable comparison to a "beehive." "Everybody, callers as well as the officers, is busy."[18] At the door, young women sold literature, pins, buttons, and flowers to visitors streaming in. Portraits of suffrage saints—Elizabeth Cady Stanton, Susan B. Anthony, and Lucy Stone—looked down on the worker bees. Four typewriters clattered away.

Alice herself was lodged in a tiny rear office behind a closed door. Winifred Mallon, a reporter from the *Chicago Tribune* bureau across the street who wrote press releases for Alice when off duty, occasionally saw the chairman "as the door to her private office, a retreat about the size of a generously planned coat closet, opened and closed, [revealing] her huddled in her chair before a table piled high with papers—at this time she had no desk—a purple velvet hat pulled closely down over her hair and her hands thrust far into a big black fox muff. The heating arrangements were far from perfect, and she felt . . . the cold acutely." These glimpses provided Mallon with a lasting image of "her thin, finely featured face, the pointed chin nestling into the black fur pulled close around her throat."[19]

Those who met Alice, wrote feminist author Inez Haynes Irwin, encountered "a slender, frail-looking young woman, delicately colored and delicately made. The head, the neck, the long slim arms and the little hands look as though they were cut out of alabaster." Her dark, wavy hair, gathered "into a great dusky bunch on her neck, might be carved from bronze. It looks too heavy for her head."[20]

Her voice, too, was distinctive: "low; musical; it pulsates with a kind of interrogative plaintiveness. When you ask her a question, there ensues, on her part, a moment of a stillness so profound you can almost hear it. I think I have never seen anybody who can keep so still as Alice Paul.... Superficially she seems cold, austere, a little remote. But that is only because the fire of her spirit burns at such a heat that it is still and white. She has the quiet of a spinning top."[21]

And those eyes. Wrote Irwin, they were "big and quiet" and as dark as moss-agates. "When she is silent they are almost opaque. When she talks they light up—rather they glow—in a notable degree of luminosity." Crystal Eastman attributed the young suffragist's persuasive powers to her "great earnest childlike eyes that seem to seize you and hold you to her purpose despite your own desires and intentions."[22]

After the headquarters opened, Alice replaced her table with a hugely symbolic piece of furniture, the desk that had belonged to Susan B. Anthony, contributed by Anthony's secretary when she read that Alice planned to carry on the work of her suffrage predecessor.

The letters flew from Alice's typewriter, dozens a day, fading to a barely legible gray as the ribbon gave out, then resuming in an energetic burst of fresh black ink. On December 28, she wrote to, among others, the National's mouthpiece, the *Woman's Journal,* suggesting a special edition that uniformed newsies could peddle during the parade; a request to Col. Spencer Cosby to use the driveway surrounding the ellipse in conjunction with the Treasury tableau; to a female pastor in Kalamazoo, asking her to organize a section of women clergy, and if that were not possible, could she send a dollar or so?; to M. Goldenberg, a business at Seventh and K Streets, requesting a contribution of one-half dozen towels, a dozen cakes of soap, and "1 small mirror for the wall"; and a note to a contributor enclosing a receipt for one dollar to the headquarters fund.

Meanwhile, Lucy—unlike Alice, a fearless and talented speaker—organized daily suffrage meetings in parlors and on street corners, and took to stumping for the cause. On January 28, a photographer captured the sturdy redhead planted in an automobile, speaking to a gathering of men and women.

After toiling far into the night, Lucy and Alice returned to the I Street boardinghouse where Lucy, too, had taken a room. Alice deliberately kept hers too cold for reading, lest the distraction disrupt her mission. In giving up books, she had foresworn a guilty pleasure—detective stories—and she now avoided bookstores as if they harbored a disease.[23]

Alice was almost incapable of small talk, nor did she cajole or flatter. But inevitably she got her way. One Sunday not long after Alice's arrival in Washington, Eva Evans and her daughter Nina Allender, both government workers, received a stranger "in a slim little dress and a little purple hat," who seemed no bigger—at this point in the story Allender would hold up a forefinger—"than *that.*"[24] Before the small visitor had departed, the mother-daughter pair had agreed both to volunteer for the National and to contribute money. A classically trained artist, Allender was to become the movement's official cartoonist.

Alice recruited everyone. An out-of-town male lawyer stopped into headquarters on business, and Alice put him to work addressing envelopes. An elderly woman painstakingly typed out information with one forefinger, "Because Alice Paul told me to."[25]

One volunteer, offended because Alice had failed to thank her for the work she had done, left in a huff and did not return. When Alice later questioned the woman's absence, she was told the reason. "But she did not do it for me," Alice replied, puzzled. "She did it for suffrage."[26] Nevertheless, expressions of gratitude began to flow more frequently from the chairman's lips.

Having discovered the value of press coverage, Alice quickly became as proficient a publicist as any professional. For reporters making their daily rounds, 1420 F Street was an obligatory stop.

It was news when Hazel Mackaye, sister of a famous dramatist, agreed to direct the tableau on the steps of the Treasury, and news that Flora Wilson, daughter of the secretary of agriculture, had accepted the role of Justice. It was more news when Indian princess Dawn Mist decided to preside over a float and still more when U.S. Representative Richmond Hobson of Alabama, a hero of the Spanish-American War, said he would lead a men's section; and it was especially big news when New Yorker Elizabeth Rogers signed on as a volunteer. Married to a distinguished New York physician, Rogers was the descendant of a signer of the Declaration of Independence; moreover, her brother-in-law was the U.S. secretary of war, Henry Stimson, said to be no fan of woman suffrage.

One day in early February, Elizabeth Kent's car pulled up to the State, War and Navy building next to the White House, and she and Rogers climbed out. Clad in furs, the two distinguished Elizabeths waved their arms to attract a lunch-hour crowd to their position, strategically located under Stimson's nose. Police attempted to disperse the meeting, but the women produced a permit. As the wife of a lieutenant commander sold "Votes for Women" buttons, Rogers advised women, if need be, to defy their husbands and march in the procession. It was a scene clearly designed for newspaper coverage, and it succeeded.[27]

Where once Alice had expressed a desire for a beautiful parade, now the beauty of the participants themselves became a selling point. The *Woman's Journal* would be sold by a "bevy of pretty girls" from Boston. "Attractive Dianas" would ride famous mounts. Dawn Mist was inevitably described as beautiful. Crystal Eastman, in town for streetcorner meetings, "is known as one of the most beautiful women in the movement." Going Eastman one superlative better, New York lawyer Inez Milholland, who had agreed to act as lead herald astride her white horse, "Grey Dawn," was labeled by the press "the most beautiful girl in the suffragette movement." But she had competition. Newspapers wrote that the event had become a beauty contest between her and the also lovely Gladys Hinckley of Washington, who would appear as Joan of Arc "on a milk white steed." Inez had "flashing dark eyes, a mass of dark brown hair and a dazzling smile," while Gladys had "lustrous violet eyes and a Grecian profile." There was even a rumor, emphatically denied by both sides, that "pretty girls" were being offered two dollars apiece by suffragists to march and three dollars by antisuffragists to stay out.[28]

Alice herself was said to be "intrepid and versatile" and "very, very serious minded." But reporters also wrote of her "personal attractions . . . her presense [*sic*] has had a potent effect in securing male as well as female converts." She was "young, wealthy and prepossessing in appearance," and she wore "fetching gowns in subdued shades and demure poke bonnets."[29] In truth, Alice's hallmark was her purple hat.

Washington columnist George Clinton was annoyed by the frivolous descriptions of the event and by the manipulation of his fellow reporters. "The suffragists understand thoroughly the worth of publicity and apparently they also understand the uses of the press agent," he wrote. "They seem to feel that something with circus features is a more potent attraction than a pageant of suffrage solemnities, a fact which makes the advance notice of the March event read somewhat like the unexpurgated forecasting pronouncements of the press agent of the biggest show on earth."[30]

After March 3, an eyewitness weighed in with an incontrovertible truth. "This procession, with its incidental barefoot dancing, was advertised all over the United States as a novelty, a curiosity, a 'woman show,' and every art was used to stir up excitement and furore [*sic*] in regard to it."[31]

When a Mrs. Clifford, a black woman, asked in early January whether "colored women might take part" in the parade, Alice said yes, reasoning that a few Negroes could easily be tucked among friendly women from the North. But Alice became alarmed after a Miss C. L. Hunt, who was white, proposed to run the question by Alice Blackwell, editor of the *Woman's Journal*. And for the next two months she struggled to keep a growing controversy under wraps.[32]

Racist sentiment in Washington had been inflamed by a particularly brutal crime on Christmas Eve. As government clerk Adelaide Grant stepped from a friend's house on C Street near the Capitol, Nathaniel Green pulled her down into an areaway and raped her, after knocking her unconscious with a blow to the jaw.

Green was black and his victim was white. Washington was populated by southerners of both races. The bloodlust triggered by the assault graphically showcased the bigotry in the nation's Capital.

So eager was the judge to see the defendant hang that he refused to accept his guilty plea and instead forced Green to stand trial. Only in that way could Green be subjected to the verdict of a jury, and only a jury could impose the death penalty (and did). And when Green's execution was delayed by appeals, one hundred well-bred women signed a petition demanding that the sentence be carried out immediately.[33]

Alice was certain, she wrote Blackwell in response to Hunt's threatened letter, that many if not a majority of white marchers "will refuse to participate if negroes in any number formed a part of the parade." She insisted that she herself, the
product of a Quaker upbringing, was "predisposed to side with, and not against, the
negro in any question of racial difference" and was in no way prejudiced. But the
racist feelings in Washington were so bitter, she wrote, "as far as I can see we must
have a white procession, or a negro procession, or no procession at all."

Alice's solution was "to say nothing whatever about the question" and "to
keep it out of the newspapers." The *Journal*'s editor agreed to hush it up.[34] But
Mary Ware Dennett, the National's secretary, soon found out about the inquiries.
Alice must not even *think* of turning down an application from colored women,
she wrote. "The suffrage movement stands for enfranchising for [*sic*] every single woman in the United States."[35]

Alice's silence only prompted a stream of inquiries. Confronted with a request on February 15 from a Howard University Negro sorority to march with
the college women, she stalled. "Come to the office," the usually prompt Alice
wrote back after eight days. They would talk it over and "decide on the best place
for your section."[36]

Alice enlisted Mary Beard to work out a solution. The New York socialist
met with a group of black would-be marchers and extended an invitation to
stride alongside the New York City Woman Suffrage Party. Mary Church Ter-
rell, an Oberlin graduate who was active in civil rights for both Negroes and
women, and also a charter member of the NAACP, accepted immediately. But
a more obdurate group felt that "a southern minority was terrorizing the northern majority," Beard reported. They wanted to march where "they belonged."[37]
Where that was Beard didn't say.

The inquiries from Howard continued. Then, four days before the parade,
a panicky telegram arrived from Chicago: "We have application from a colored
woman to march—will Negro women be admitted to the suffrage parade—answer—quick." What the telegram did not say was that the applicant was no
anonymous colored woman but rather Ida Wells-Barnett, the daughter of freed
slaves, a founder of the NAACP, and the author of a national campaign against
lynching. Next came a wire from the National accusing Alice of discrimination,
contrary to their instructions. She was told in so many words, let Negroes
march. The controversy continued up to the day of the parade. Afterward,
Alice's failure to unreservedly welcome black marchers left a permanent stain on
her reputation.[38]

In the final weeks, Alice bounced from one crisis to another. No sooner were the rights to rent the grandstands wrested from a recalcitrant inaugural committee than Dennett objected to the purple, white, and green flag flying outside the F Street headquarters. The same colors were featured on buttons, notepaper, and bouquets. The very colors, to Dennett's dismay, that were flaunted by the British suffragettes. Those would be the same suffragettes, not to be confused with law-abiding suffragists, whose increasingly destructive exploits were much in the news that winter. They had poured acid and black ink into mailboxes, destroying thousands of letters, and set fire to a restaurant pavilion in a London park.

This was no small issue. Anna Shaw declared that she wouldn't march "under the suffragette flag."[39] Better to employ yellow, long considered an American suffrage color, or blue, featured on the National's stationery, or both. Alice obligingly ordered two thousand yellow pennants.

Two weeks before the procession, the National Association Opposed to Woman Suffrage opened a temporary headquarters and announced plans for a big rally. To the delight of reporters, the office of the largely female "antis" was located at 1307 F Street, just down the street from Alice's Congressional Committee.

Both sides immediately claimed fear of reprisals and hired very large watchmen to guard their literature-filled windows. As typewriters pounded out dueling press releases, the *Washington Post* reported that F Street sounded "like a nail factory."[40] When gobs of mud defaced the antis' windows, the women within accused the suffragists. Apoplectic at the suffragists' contention that Abraham Lincoln was a supporter of suffrage, antis dispatched students to the Library of Congress. The students unearthed a quote that suggested his approval was, at best, both qualified and parenthetical, being in fact limited to "whites" and those "who pay taxes or bear arms (by no means excluding females)."

Through this hostile barrage, Alice Paul took the high road. "This is a woman's movement, and we will not attack any woman even with words."[41]

When she wasn't stamping out brush fires, Alice was raising money. The Baltimore suffragists were offering their prize possession: a half-dozen spectacular golden chariots; unfortunately they couldn't afford to transport them to Washington. The bill for costumes was approaching three thousand dollars, while contributions averaged only eight or nine dollars a day.

A feeler from Alva Belmont, a heavy contributor to the National, raised hopes for financial help. It seemed that Alva, sixty years old and top-heavy, was interested in coming to the parade. Were there any provisions for suffragists who could not walk, inquired her assistant? "As a walker Mrs. Belmont is a failure."[42]

Glimpsing dollar signs, Lucy Burns forwarded the letter to a pageant organizer, with a note wondering if Alva might possibly be "made to do" as a figure on a float. She signed it "Greedily."[43] (Another wealthy New York society woman was willing to walk but only in sandals with diamond-encrusted high heels or, alternatively, in no shoes at all.)

In spite of Alice's objections—she just didn't want the thing—a Pennsylvania woman was determined to donate a Liberty Bell float to commemorate liberty and justice. Couldn't she be convinced to instead contribute money for the tableau on the Treasury steps, where Liberty and Justice were two of the characters? Alice asked Dora Lewis. The answer came back: No.

And the press had latched onto a rumor, that a satirical "hobo" float would feature four men in rags with the inscription, "But We Kin Vote." If that were true, wrote an angry Baltimore socialist—Alice denied it—then four or five "of the idle rich, so labeled" should be placed on the float as well. "'Hoboes,'" she said, "were once honest working men, now crushed and ground down by pitiless wheels of industry which revolve for profits for the godless rich."[44]

The cap-and-cape outfits Alice had ordered were not to everyone's taste. The librarians from the Library of Congress were unhappy with their shade of blue. Washington suffragist Elizabeth Hyde wondered if there was a section for "persons who do not care to march in disguise." An Ohio woman announced she would come in chains. Members of the National, Dennett said, would wear blue sashes and carry blue banners, which would make them "quite *blue* enough."[45]

Inez Milholland thought the look she was trying to achieve, "the free woman of the future," could be accomplished "with the blue mantle of freedom, breasted with the torch of knowledge and carrying the trumpet which is to herald the dawn of a new era of heroic endeavor for womanhood." Alice Paul told her that she could wear anything, so long as it was yellow.[46]

Lodging was hard to find for the ever-growing number of participants. Inaugural visitors had booked nearly every hotel room. The enterprising chairman of the housing committee, Anna Kelton Wiley, obtained options on vacant homes and set up "suffrage army dormitories" stuffed with cots. Agnes Ryan, the business manager of the *Woman's Journal,* asked to stay in Alice Paul's boarding house—in Alice's room. Certainly, said the chairman, if Agnes did not object to her "rather crowded and humble quarters." A more sensitive person might have recognized Alice's subtle discouragement, but Agnes proclaimed herself honored "to be taken in by one of your calibre [*sic*]."[47]

In early February a rumor swept Washington that college boys planned to release a thousand mice at intervals along the parade route. If not foiled, predicted the *Washington Post*, the plot would turn the "well-arranged suffrage parade of March 3 from a dignified triumph into a farcical rout."[48]

Suffrage headquarters issued a stiff response. "The idea that any of the women would desert and run for shelter is absurd. All would walk bravely on, merely for the principle of the thing, if for nothing else."[49]

The police superintendent took the mice threat seriously enough to inquire whether the Boy Scouts might help with protection, and Washington's head scoutmaster agreed to supply several hundred lads for guard duty. As time went by, Sylvester was becoming increasingly worried about security for the parade. And so was Alice.

CHAPTER FIVE

"I DID NOT KNOW MEN COULD BE SUCH FIENDS"

Passengers aboard the 9 A.M. train from Manhattan to Newark on February 12, 1913, looked up in irritation at a middle-aged woman in a brown cape, stout boots, and a yellow "Votes for Women" badge who was striding from car to car and back again, unloosing blasts of frigid air as she opened and closed doors. Her companions, also in capes, boots, and badges, remained in their seats, but Ida Craft was determined to begin the group's 260-mile hike from New York to Washington on foot, as advertised.

A month earlier, the group's leader, Rosalie Jones, had informed Alice Paul that she, Rosalie, would be escorting a squad of at least a dozen "Pilgrims" walking from New York to join the March 3 procession. Along the way they would proselytize for suffrage. Very likely Alice was not pleased at this trespass onto her cause, unsolicited and outside her control. But Rosalie, who had just completed a similar trek from New York to Albany, had the blessing of the National and a message from Anna Shaw to the incoming president. Alice was in no position to object.

Heavy-browed and dark-eyed, with a wide smile that displayed small even teeth, Rosalie had, by her own account, fled an upbringing on a two-hundred-year-old Long Island estate that had acclimated her to country walks, drawing-room chatter, and tennis, but not much else. She had jettisoned her "pink tea existence," a reference to that popular upper crust ritual where everything—the linens, the china, the flowers, the cake frosting, and the waitress's cap and apron—was pink, pink, pink. Determined "never to be a society butterfly again," she had taken a turn at raising chickens before joining the suffrage movement.[1]

Christening herself "General Jones" and her followers "The Army of the Hudson," Rosalie proved to be an able commander, holding a shrinking band of numbed and footsore hikers to a rigid schedule as they trudged in freezing weather through New Jersey, Pennsylvania, Delaware, and Maryland.

Occasionally outnumbered by reporters calling themselves "war correspondents," who kept up a steady tattoo in the press, the Pilgrims included a "scout" in a luggage-laden automobile who scooted ahead to arrange lodging and report back on road conditions. Also in the entourage was a yellow wagon packed with twenty thousand suffrage leaflets; the wagon was pulled by Lausanne, a horse purchased just two days before departure for a bargain price of $59.98. To Alice Paul's dismay, men were allowed to tag along.[2] One was a poet by the name of E. S. Lemmon, who wore a contemplative expression and was said to be at work on a masterpiece.

The first day was a template for those that followed. As the Pilgrims set out from Newark accompanied by dozens of well-wishers, the weather turned sharply colder. They tramped south toward Elizabeth, New Jersey, through icy slush, startling horse-drawn wagons on city streets and dodging cows on country roads. Taking up positions in the rear, Rosalie and Ida Craft, the second in command—that would be "Col. Craft"—urged their companions forward.

Stepping out of her farmhouse, a woman handed the hikers freshly boiled eggs to warm their hands. "When they get cold, eat 'em."[3] They got mixed reactions from the men along the way. One farmer bellowed a roadside harangue against suffrage and wagered that not one of the female marchers could cook corned beef and cabbage. But in Elizabeth, a butler from a gentleman's club served them cups of hot bouillon.

Philadelphia newspapers had been closely following the pilgrims' progress, and two thousand people—described as a "dense mob of men and boys"—were waiting when they crossed the Delaware River by ferry into Pennsylvania. (The New York Herald explained the absence of women by saying that Philadelphia females didn't like to go out on Sunday afternoons.) Some of the onlookers jeered rudely and tugged at the Pilgrims' capes.

A hundred miles into their journey, in Leiperville, Pennsylvania, boys threw snowballs and stones while older males laughed. One marcher's toe had poked through her shoe; another discarded her painful boots for high heels, which disintegrated in a day. But Rosalie was elated to see welcoming placards in suffrage yellow pasted to the front of every cottage. That is, until she learned the truth from a small boy. "Tain't suffrage, it's mumps. Nearly everybody in town is down with 'em and the doctor made us put up those yellow signs."[4]

By Wilmington, Delaware, Lausanne was suffering from a bone spavin, split tendons, and sprung front knees. Like her human counterparts, she continued on nevertheless. Ida Craft fell to the rear, her feet bleeding and so swollen she couldn't lace her boots. At one point, she disappeared altogether. A searcher found her miles behind, leaning for support against a road sign reading "Slow down to ten miles an hour." She picked up her staff and marched on. South of Havre de Grace, Maryland, a drenching rain turned the road into a quicksand of red clay. The yellow wagon sank to its wheel hubs, and the baggage car got stuck and caught fire.

When they reached Maryland, Rosalie led the main body into Baltimore ahead of schedule, leaving Ida and others stranded and full of apologies to the disappointed populace of tiny Overlea, which had gone all out in preparing a welcome. By the time Ida caught up, the two leaders were not speaking.

Closing in on Washington, the breach healed, their spirits rising, the Pilgrims were met on February 27 by Alice Paul, who stopped them short. "I have come for the letter you are carrying," she announced.[5] It seemed that the National had told Alice that the Congressional Committee, not the Pilgrims, was to deliver Shaw's message to Wilson: a request to include suffrage in his inaugural address. Rosalie angrily handed over the envelope she had carried through snow, rain, and mud and announced she would have nothing to do with the activities planned for the Pilgrims' official welcome.

As soon as she learned of the impasse, Mary Ware Dennett, the National's secretary, immediately claimed a misunderstanding and declared that the presentation to Wilson was to include the Pilgrims. Rosalie wasn't mollified.

Confusion when Rosalie and her troop arrived in Washington the next day made matters worse. The Pilgrims waited in vain at Fifteenth and H Streets for a promised band and official escort, then gave up and entered the city on Maryland Avenue. After pausing for an emotional moment at the sight of the Capitol's sun-burnished dome, the Pilgrims turned onto Pennsylvania Avenue. There the Washington suffragists, who had been stationed elsewhere, caught up. Alice and two companions drove a car to the head of the ad hoc procession, while others fell in behind the thirteen front-row hikers who had walked each blistering step of the way.

Word had traveled faster than the now-famous Pilgrims, and thousands of enthusiastic Washingtonians swarmed into their path. The few policemen on hand were unable to restrain the crowd. Reported the *Washington Post*, "Incoming Presidents have not received more clamorous applause than did the company of brown-clad women, huddled in a little group forced to fight their way through veritable walls of shouting humanity for more than a mile of their historic hike." The paper detected a certain "lack of enthusiasm displayed by the local suffragists, whom the pilgrims declared to be jealous of the attention they were attracting."[6]

What worried Alice at the moment was neither the accusation of jealousy (although she took time to deny it) nor the ill feelings over the message. Rather it was the way an unruly mob of thousands seemed to materialize out of the thin winter air.

Two weeks earlier, Alice had asked the district commissioners for a "sufficient military force" to protect the March 3 procession.[7] The commissioners passed her request along to the secretary of war, whose assistant promptly vetoed it. Not "practicable," he said.[8] Alice set aside her fears. But now, alarmed by the rowdy turnout for the Pilgrims, she wondered if the police superintendent had been right all along. What if, in fact, he couldn't protect the marchers? The Congressional Committee had expected twenty-five hundred; it now appeared there might be twice that many.

Two days before the parade, Alice sought with renewed urgency to obtain reinforcements. President Taft's office referred her to the secretary of war. Stimson responded that his hands were legally tied unless local authorities asked for help. But Sylvester was now telling everyone that security was not a problem. Special officers deputized for the occasion would swell the police detail to 575, considerably more than the 367 who would patrol the inaugural parade. Still not satisfied, Alice appealed to the governor of New York to deploy the inaugural contingent of the New York militia. He refused.

On the morning of Alice's parade, the red, white, and blue bunting draped across buildings in preparation for the next day's inaugural celebration gave Pennsylvania Avenue a mood both patriotic and festive. An air of expectation hung over the city. The suffrage event had commanded headlines for weeks, prompting speculation that it would outshine festivities for Wilson and his vice president, Thomas Marshall. "The truth is that the women have been, and are, displaying

ten times the 'ginger' and enthusiasm manifested by those who are rather drea-
rily and perfunctorily looking after the inauguration of Wilson and Marshall,"
opined the *Indianapolis Star*.[9]

The temperature was headed for the mid-50s under sunny skies. Newsies in
purple, white, and green sashes were ready with stacks of literature to sell. A
corps of young women from the District Federation of Women's Clubs prepared
to peddle 40,000 sandwiches, 10,000 doughnuts, and 800 pies.

The parade would begin at 3 P.M. and conclude at 5 P.M. By noon, the Avenue was filling with spectators. While marchers and floats assembled on the
side streets, a steady stream of trolleys continued to disgorge residents from all
corners of the District. Only after Congress passed an emergency decree had the
Capital Traction Company agreed to halt streetcar service, and then only for the
parade's duration.

Stimson had been more concerned than he let on to Alice. At 9 A.M. on the
day of the procession, the secretary of war checked in with city commissioner
John Johnston. The commissioner said he didn't anticipate serious trouble, but
would Stimson hold a troop of cavalry in readiness in nearby Ft. Myer, just in
case? Stimson agreed.

Also around 9 A.M., the parade's grand marshal, Mrs. Richard Coke
Burleson, made it a point to speak to Sylvester. Everything was fine, the police
superintendent told her.

Already behind schedule, at twenty-five past three on the afternoon of March
3, the hauntingly beautiful Inez Milholland, her long dark curls held back by a
gold tiara with a single, centered star, her body cloaked in a light blue—not
yellow—cape, nudged her white steed into the center of Pennsylvania Avenue.

Behind her, pulled by two horses, came a cart emblazoned with what was
known forever after as the "Great Demand" banner:

WE DEMAND AN AMENDMENT TO THE CONSTITUTION
OF THE UNITED STATES ENFRANCHISING THE WOMEN OF
THE COUNTRY.

Next came two dozen horse-drawn floats, nine bands, four mounted
brigades, three heralds with trumpets, and at least five thousand women, though
possibly as many as eight thousand—so many, in any case, that the organizers lost
count. In caps and capes from dark to light blue came the social workers, teach-

ers, business women, and librarians; in three shades of rose, the artists, actresses, and musicians. On and on, a glorious cavalcade of color.

To those who had worked with Alice, the elaborate, orderly sequence was a triumph of determination over adversity, for no part of it had come easily, from housing and costuming so many women, to renting grandstands, to dealing with the racial politics of both Washington and the suffrage movement, albeit tardily, by tucking a troop from Howard University behind the all-white college brigades, to placating the band of brown-cloaked Pilgrims who had tramped down from New York to a clouded welcome and were now bringing up the rear, their sulfurous mood lifted. She had also managed to satisfy the high command of the National, which had first given her the assignment and then second-guessed her smallest decisions. Shaw and other officers marched in the vanguard. And she had done it all while fending off nasty attacks from anti-suffragists.

As the procession eased forward, a relay of vigorous trumpet blasts sounded at intervals along the Avenue. A mile west, on the Treasury's wide, white marble steps, a hundred women and girls dressed in filmy white gowns and sandals stood motionless. Hearing the final trumpet note, they commenced a balletic tableau set to stirring music in which allegorical figures—Liberty, Justice, Charity, Hope, and Peace—descended one by one to the plaza where the robed figure of "Columbia" was waiting.

The climax of the dance was timed to coincide with the arrival of the parade's front lines, forty-five minutes into the march. At the appointed time Columbia and her companions stood poised to review the "new crusade" of women. But there were no marchers in sight. The scantily clad performers gazed anxiously toward the Capitol, their bare toes growing numb with the cold. Pennsylvania Avenue was clogged with spectators standing shoulder to shoulder, curb to curb, as far as they could see. An hour passed.

Something had gone terribly wrong.

The suffrage procession had been under way for fifteen minutes when the special train carrying Woodrow Wilson and his entourage from Princeton huffed into Union Station.

Despite his setbacks there, Wilson loved Princeton. On the day of his departure for Washington, the president-elect joined in as students serenaded him with a lusty rendition of their alma mater, "Old Nassau," and other college songs. An observant reporter noted that Wilson had recently had a large mole removed from the center of his forehead, "distinctly improving his appearance."[10]

One railcar was stuffed with newsmen intent on ferreting out the names of Wilson's new cabinet members. Eight others carried 560 Princetonians. On detraining, the college men placed their hats over their hearts and formed a corridor through which the president-elect strode solemnly with his family, members of the inaugural committee, and other dignitaries. But the president's arrival went largely unnoticed by the public.

"Where are the people?" he is said to have asked.

"On the Avenue watching the suffragists parade."[11]

Or perhaps this exchange is merely a legend that made its way unsourced into several suffrage histories. It may well be that no one wanted to be the bad news messenger who informed Wilson that he had been upstaged by a phalanx of females.

Sylvester, heading up the security detail, took a moment to inquire about the suffrage parade just a few blocks from the station and was told that "The Avenue is just packed."[12] The suffragists, his informant said, would have difficulty getting through. The superintendent now decided he had no choice but to ask for help from the cavalry. He placed the call to Fort Myer, then guided Wilson and his entourage to the Shoreham Hotel at Fifteenth and H streets on a roundabout route that skirted the Avenue, where a disaster was taking place.

Earlier that morning, police had strung half-inch steel cables anchored by heavy stanchions along the sidewalks to hold back the crowd. But at the first sound of trumpets, spectators streamed under and over them, and spilled into the center of the Avenue. The parade stuttered to a halt.

Just four blocks into the route, on horseback behind the two flag bearers, the grand marshal Burleson found herself and her six mounted aides completely surrounded by a "horrible howling mob."[13] Most were men, and many were drunk.

A few paces ahead, she could see thirteen police cars in a "V" formation, like flying geese, trailed by a troop of mounted police, driving the length of the Avenue in an effort to forge a path for the parade through the river of bodies. So slowly was the line moving that Commissioner Johnston stepped out of his car on the left flank of the wedge from time to time to instruct police on how to force back the crowd with their batons: tap the heads of people in the third or fourth row, he said, and tell them to move back.

No sooner had the wedge passed, however, than people poured into its wake, swallowing up the police troop. Desperate, Burleson looked around for help. She made out several officers on horseback. "They seemed to be doing absolutely nothing, simply standing there on their horses." She also saw an alarming sight: Inez Milholland astride her white steed, "a figure solitary and alone struggling with this mass of humanity."[14]

Inez charged the crowd on Grey Dawn, trying to create an opening. Suddenly three cars pulled up on Burleson's flank. Seated in one were Alice Paul and Lucy Burns; they took up a position on one side, while the two other vehicles, driven by pageant director Glenna Smith Tinnin and her assistant Patricia Street, maneuvered in front. As the cars plowed a human furrow, Burleson was able to inch forward, a few steps at a time.

At one point Alice, wearing the black academic gown in which she had planned to march with the college women, jumped from her vehicle and strode forward, pushing people back with her outstretched hands. Equipped with a megaphone, Street halted her car, stood on the running board, and barked orders to clear the way.

Farther back in the procession, the orderly rows of four women were squeezed to three abreast, then two, then single file. Men snatched banners, tugged at women's clothing and sometimes the women themselves, and tried to climb the floats. They hurled lighted cigarettes and matches, reached out their canes to dislodge women's hats, pinched and spit and shouted insults delicately described as "barnyard language" by their targets. To the marching men they yelled, "Henpecko."[15] A man grabbed a woman on a float by her foot. A drunk toppled into the path of the Massachusetts delegation.

Even more shocking to the women was the conduct of their protectors. Policemen "just stood by and laughed" as a bystander slapped Nora Blatch de Forest, Harriot Blatch's daughter, leaving a red mark on her face that lasted the rest of the day. One woman claimed to have seen a policeman jerk down the barrier at 15th Street, allowing the crowd to tumble forward. And Sarah Brown heard mounted police indulge "in all manner of smutty conversation as to the nature and quality of our undergarments."[16]

Seated high on a platform on the press float, titled "Forming Public Opinion," Helen Gardener could see a space six feet wide behind the front lines of the crowd, plenty of room for the police to push back the wall of people, had they tried. She worried that the horses or the float itself would run someone down. Grooms tried to open a path. As spectators snatched the newspapers and magazines that decorated the float, the men in uniform looked amused.[17]

Marching with the Connecticut contingent, Helena Hill Weed watched eighteen or twenty young men in the crowd link arms as if to charge forward.

They froze as the voice of a pretty young woman rang out. "Girls, get out your hatpins; they are going to rush us."[18]

When Helena asked a policeman to help, he folded his arms and told her, "I can do nothing with this crowd, and I ain't agoing to try."[19] To her astonishment, he began to pick his teeth.

A Philadelphia newspaperman sought police protection as he attempted to take photographs. Instead police ejected him from the street, saying, "You ought to be ashamed to give them space in your paper."[20]

An elderly woman tried to push aside a drunken man with a German accent whose mouth was filled with chewing tobacco. He unloosed a brown stream that struck her face. Witnessing the incident, Patricia Street complained to a police officer. "There would be nothing like this if you would stay at home," he told her. She hit the German "and would have hit the policeman too, if I could."[21] Instead the officer grabbed her, ripping her coat, and again told her to go home.

The Pilgrims drew cheers, but also hoots. Someone pulled down their American flag and tripped one of their male marchers.

Among the guests of honor assigned a grandstand seat was the celebrated Helen Keller, a committed socialist and fan of Emmeline Pankhurst. "I am a militant suffragist because I believe suffrage will lead to socialism," she explained to the *New York Times*, "and to me socialism is the ideal cause."[22] Caught up in a crowd that she could neither see nor hear, Keller gave up on her efforts to reach a grandstand and fled with her companion.

Waiting in a reviewing stand near the White House, Mrs. William Howard Taft, her daughter Helen, and other White House guests grew so disgusted at the rude clamor of men gathered at their feet that they left before the procession arrived.

Some four hundred Boy Scouts stationed along the Avenue to thwart mice-toting pranksters instead wielded their staffs to press back the hordes. Their performance was one of the few high notes. A male marcher wrote that the Boy Scouts were "active and determined." Jeannette Gallinger was watching from a stand near Ninth Street. "You could see the little fellows were red in the face from perspiring."[23]

Setting off from Fort Myer at a fast trot, Lt. Gordon Johnson and his men arrived at the Treasury just as the moving wedge of police cars completed its largely ineffectual run up the Avenue. The steps and plaza of the Treasury were empty. Deeply chilled, the tableau performers had given up waiting and gone inside.

The cavalry brushed aside the Washington police, and charged into the mass of bodies on both sides of the Avenue, turning and wheeling horses to force a retreat. Burleson, who had finally reached 15th Street, met the troop coming from the other direction. She was able to lead the procession the final blocks with some semblance of its glory and dignity restored.

As the ranks went forward, two thousand yellow pennants fluttered gaily in the breeze. Baltimore's six golden chariots, freshly gilded and transported free by the Pennsylvania Railroad, clattered by.

In addition to the Howard University women, a "large delegation of dusky suffragettes" from West Virginia had fallen into line.[24] But where was Ida Wells-Barnett? That very morning, the leader of the Illinois delegation told the distinguished Negro leader to join a unit of black women, claiming that the order had come from the National. Tears rolled down Wells-Barnett's face. "I shall not march at all unless I can march under the Illinois banner," she declared.[25] Furious at the discrimination, two of her white companions said they would accompany her in a Negro formation. But when the time came to muster, Ida was nowhere to be found. Not until the state contingent was halfway through the route, did she join the parade, boldly stepping into the ranks of the white women from Illinois.

And here, bringing up the rear to loud applause, were the Pilgrims in their trail-worn brown capes, looking happy at last. Braving the cold, the tableau performers emerged from the Treasury building to greet their sisters.

But nothing could undo the damage. Although no suffragists were reported seriously harmed, the *Post* put the number of injured parade-goers at more than one hundred. Among them were two dozen confirmed wounds or fractures, eight cases of drunkenness, and fourteen of hysteria or fainting.

Sylvester's national reputation would never be the same.

And the enemy had a face. Dr. Nellie Mark, marching with fifty other professionals from Maryland, concluded angrily, "I did not know men could be such fiends."[26]

Around the country, people read jumbled accounts of what had happened. The number of marchers was pegged at five thousand, seven thousand, eight thousand. The crowd estimates ran from one hundred thousand to three hundred thousand. Nor did newspapers agree on what had happened.

Basing accounts on the official program, a number of papers reported on the parade as if all had gone as planned. Pennsylvanians reading the *New Castle*

News were told on March 3, too early for a reporter to have witnessed the parade, that "It was a wonderful, impressive demonstration and when the women in gorgeous costumes swept along in almost perfect military order, with their pennants and banners snapping in the breeze, it brought a tumult of cheers and hand claps from women spectators in which thousands of men joined spontaneously." Reported the *Fort Wayne News* on the same day, "Society leaders in hundreds from all cities trudged sturdily beside humble housewives." In this fabricated account, Inez Milholland frequently sounded her trumpet, "as the procession slowly swept up Pennsylvania avenue" and proceeded without incident to Continental Hall.

The following day, less precipitous newspapers told a different story. Five thousand women, the *Washington Post* said, "practically fought their way foot by foot up Pennsylvania avenue. . . . No inauguration has ever produced such scenes, which in many instances amounted to little less than riots." The mounted police, the paper said, "seemed powerless to stem the tide of humanity."

"Police Must Face Charges. Failed to Protect Suffrage Parade Against Hoodlums. Scene Was Shameful," bannered the *Fort Wayne Sentinel*.

"From beginning to end the police mismanagement was the worst in the world," said the *Chicago Tribune*. "To say that Maj. Sylvester, superintendent of police, is being criticized here would be putting the thing mildly."

What had been planned as a celebratory post-parade rally at the DAR's Continental Hall turned into an "indignation" meeting. "Never was I so ashamed of our national capital before," declared Anna Shaw, holding forth to an angry audience. "The women in the parade showed wonderful dignity and self-respect by keeping cool in the midst of insult and lewd remarks."[27] Carrie Chapman Catt, president of the International Suffrage Association, called for a congressional investigation. A resolution condemning the police conduct passed without dissent.

Several women were notably absent from the meeting. Although she had been offered a place on a float or a seat in a grandstand, Alva Belmont had not come after all. Scheduled speaker Helen Keller was too rattled to attend. And Alice Paul, of all people, was not there.

Worried, reporter Winifred Mallon tracked her down at the F Street headquarters. Flags and banners were heaped on the floor and tables piled high with fliers. "Through the wreck came Alice Paul," Mallon remembered years later, "the long black robes of her doctor's gown swinging from her slender shoulders, and her thin, wonderfully expressive hands in her flowing sleeves." For the first time, Mallon saw Alice without her little purple hat. "She had taken off the mortar board, and for the first time I saw the masses of her brown hair piled carelessly high on her head.

"Her face was whiter than ever, and her eyes darker and larger. She stopped by a table, under a swinging electric light bulb, and waited for me."

As the reporter began to sputter about the disgraceful police conduct, Alice cut her off. "It was meant to happen," she said.

You don't mean, Mallon said, that the police acted on purpose?

Alice told the reporter how she had walked into the crowd and pushed people back. "That was all there was to it. The police could have stopped the disorder instantly. They had only to be determined about it."[28]

Rank-and-file marcher Mary Foster was astonished at what happened after the parade. The suffragists were angry, then suddenly they weren't.

One of Washington's many young "government girls," Foster had fled the family farm in Ohio in search of a more stimulating life. She was working for the Post Office and attending art classes when she decided to volunteer at the F Street headquarters. On the day of the parade she marched with other art students.

As the procession came under siege, her section shrank to a single file. "We struggled along with lumps in our throats, fighting back tears. We thought all was lost."

That evening at Continental Hall Foster discovered otherwise. "To our great surprise, these leaders were jubilant! We learned that what had happened was not a catastrophe, but an unlooked-for blessing. It would promote the cause of suffrage far more than any beautiful parade could do."[29]

In a letter afterward, Anna Shaw lavished praise upon Alice for the "splendid work that you did in getting up the parade. . . . Too much credit cannot be given to you and Miss Burns and the others who are responsible for all this." She added, "While it may seem to you that the work of all these months was lost in the fact that the parade as a spectacular display was destroyed, nevertheless I think it has done more for suffrage and will do more for suffrage in the end than the parade itself would have done."[30]

Alice agreed with Shaw. "This mistreatment by the police was probably the best thing that could ever have happened to us," she wrote a supporter a week after the procession, when protests and testimonials were pouring in, "as it aroused a great deal of public indignation and sympathy."[31]

The day of Wilson's inauguration, the U.S. Senate approved a resolution to investigate police conduct during the parade. For eleven days in March and two in April a Senate subcommittee heard graphic accounts of the violence and the failure of the police to act. The final report concluded that traffic could have been better handled, but "There is not sufficient proof upon which to single out any particular individual for reproof or condemnation."[32]

CHAPTER SIX

THE SPLIT

For the last two decades of Susan B. Anthony's life, from 1888 to 1906, Dr. Anna Howard Shaw had been her trusted helpmate, her "bonnet holder" as Shaw put it. She fully expected to succeed the suffrage saint at the helm of the National American Woman Suffrage Association. When in 1900 Anthony instead anointed Carrie Chapman Catt, Shaw stepped aside gracefully. In 1904, however, Catt resigned and the bonnet holder received Anthony's blessing at last. By the time Shaw turned sixty-six in 1913, many members of the National thought she should make way for a successor. But the National's president showed not the slightest inclination to do so.

No one questioned Shaw's bona fides. Yoked together like workhorses, she and "Aunt Susan" had pounded through the closing years of the nineteenth century in hot pursuit of the vote.

"Many days, and in all kinds of weather, we rode forty and fifty miles in uncovered wagons," Shaw wrote of the 1890 South Dakota campaign. "Many nights we shared a one-room cabin with all the members of the family." Often water was scarce and even the best was brackish. "The more we drank the thirstier we became, and when the water was made into tea it tasted worse than when it was clear. A bath was the rarest of luxuries." Heating the water presented another unpleasant problem. "The only available fuel was buffalo manure, of which the odor permeated all our food."[1]

Shaw was no stranger to the rigors of frontier life. She had spent her adolescence on a farm carved from the Michigan forest, helping out during her father's frequent absences. At age twelve, she hoisted a shovel and dug the family well.

Largely self-educated, at fifteen Shaw became a teacher of pioneer children. At twenty-three, she blazed a trail of another sort by entering high school. At twenty-seven, drawn to the ministry, she enrolled in Boston University School of Theology, the only woman in a class with forty-two males.

After four years serving Methodist congregations, the call of God diminished in volume, and Shaw entered medical school. Both pastor and physician, she could claim the honorific "Doctor" on two grounds. (She was always *Dr. Shaw*.)

Her credentials served her well in suffrage circles, but by far her greatest asset was her oratory. Shaw's strong contralto emanated from a personage just five feet tall and round as a plum. Reporters likened her voice to a mountain stream or the pealing of a bell. She used neither text nor notes, and leavened her speeches with anecdotes and humor. Her style was forceful, and she was fast on her feet.

On one occasion a young woman opposed to suffrage bolstered her case with a raft of statistics. She asserted that figures didn't lie. "Well they don't," conceded Shaw, "but some liars figure."[2]

Though formidable in many ways, Shaw was a poor administrator, and many were jealous of her authority.[3] Unsalaried, she spent much of the time on the road, earning her living through speeches. Beginning in 1910, and at every convention thereafter, dissidents plotted to unseat her. In 1912, they schemed to elect Jane Addams, but the distinguished social-work pioneer refused to run against Shaw.

As the 1913 convention approached, it was not surprising that the aging president was glancing over her shoulder for signs of trouble.

She did not have to look far.

In the aftermath of the parade, Alice Paul could scarcely make a move without also making the papers. On March 8, she appeared before the Senate committee that was investigating the disorder. "Miss Alice Paul Testifies That Superintendent of Police Warned her of Riffraff." On March 12 Alice was "heading the 'prosecution'" and obtaining "additional evidence."[4]

On March 17, the story of the hour was Alice's first visit with Woodrow Wilson. Her agenda contained just one item: a federal suffrage amendment. She had faith that Wilson, elected on a progressive platform that would fine-tune democracy, could be persuaded by reason. And her request was so reason-able. Would the president include a call for suffrage in his message to the new Congress?

Five chairs placed in a row awaited Alice and her companions as they en-tered the White House. A sixth faced them. Later they would consider this stu-dent-and-teacher arrangement "most amusing," but at that moment, nervous about the meeting, they didn't give it much thought.[5]

This was their first close look at the nation's most powerful official. He was a thin man, just under six feet tall, with a long, narrow face dominated by a high forehead and jutting jaw. When not smiling, his features took on a stern expression, heightened by thin lips and cold blue-gray eyes behind rimless glasses.

When his visitors announced their mission, the president replied that he had no opinion on woman suffrage, that he had never given the subject any thought, but that his priorities at the moment were his campaign pledges: cur-rency revision and tariff reform.

"But Mr. President," Alice protested, "do you not understand that the Ad-ministration has no right to legislate for currency, tariff, and any other reform without first getting the consent of women to these reforms?"

Wilson looked blank. "Get the consent of women?"[6]

Twice more that month, Alice descended on the White House with groups of suffragists. Twice more Wilson explained that he had other priorities.

Thrice rebuffed by Wilson, Alice turned to the east end of the Avenue, where Congress was back in session. Just a month after the inaugural demon-stration, on April 3, 1913, 531 women dressed in white—two from every state and one each from each congressional district—retraced the parade route in re-verse. Preceded by two bands, yellow pennants waving vigorously, the marchers followed their state flags down the Avenue to the Capitol, where a welcoming party of friendly senators and representatives was waiting. The marchers filled a box with petitions addressed to every member of Congress. The demonstration was "far less elaborate" than the March 3 parade, the *New York Times* said, but, because it was the largest suffrage delegation to confront Congress, and had pro-ceeded smoothly, it was "in some respects more impressive."[7]

That same day, the federal suffrage amendment was introduced in both houses by two Republicans, Sen. Joseph Bristow of Kansas and Rep. Frank Mon-dell of Wyoming, both from states where women had the vote. In the Senate, the Bristow-Mondell amendment was immediately referred to the Woman Suffrage

Committee. In a small sign of progress cheered by suffragists, the committee had emerged just two weeks earlier from legislative limbo, where it had languished as an inactive minority committee.

As Alice made one well-publicized move after another, Anna Shaw, the National's leader, worried that she was not keeping up. A few weeks after the parade, she wrote to Alice and Lucy: "I do not want you to feel for a moment that we are finding fault, only we feel if there could be consultation we could work together and know what each is doing." Secretary Mary Ware Dennett was more blunt, expressing deep concern about "the lack of satisfactory working connections between Washington and Headquarters."[8]

Shaw summoned Alice and Lucy to a meeting at the house she had built in Moylan, Pennsylvania. The house was Shaw's reward to herself, a dormered creekside refuge in the gently rolling countryside not far from Swarthmore. How far she had come from a three-hundred-acre patch in the Michigan woods and the hardscrabble life of a pioneer. And how different her upbringing had been from that of Alice and Lucy, two easterners from well-to-do families whose combined ages did not equal her own. They had been raised in comfort, educated at fine schools, and only recently come to suffrage, a commitment they could afford to make thanks to the largesse of their parents.

Whatever Shaw and other leaders of the National who were present in Moylan had to say seemed not to have had the intended effect. In mid-April, in her first report since December, Alice stunned the leadership with the news that she had formed a membership organization, the "Congressional Union," to push for a federal amendment. Each state would have a Union chairman, supported by a team of volunteers. Shaw was instantly suspicious that Alice's organization would rival the National for funds and steal its members. She sent word through her longtime friend Dora Lewis—a Paul loyalist—that the Union wasn't "to have anything official" to do with the National's Congressional Committee. Nor was it to use the National's letterhead.[9]

In May 1913, the National officers got word that Alice was planning to start a weekly newspaper. Once again they had not been consulted. "How about your plans for the newspaper?" Dennett wrote Alice. "You have'nt [sic] written me anything about it."[10] Alice promised the newspaper would focus only on the federal amendment, not state issues.

As much as Shaw and Dennett might resent Alice's unilateral moves, at the moment they were in a bind. In November, the National would hold its convention in Washington. According to custom, local suffrage societies underwrote the costs and made arrangements. For purely practical reasons, they needed Alice.

To help with the campaign, Alice reached out in the spring of 1913 to her Swarthmore schoolmate Mabel Vernon, who was teaching high school German in a Philadelphia suburb. Mabel had struck her first small blow for suffrage while still in college, when, without seeking permission, she replaced the battered frame on the portrait of suffrage pioneer Lucretia Mott that hung in the girls' parlor.

Agitating for suffrage required speakers, and Mabel had the gift, as Alice well knew. A decade earlier they had competed in Swarthmore's public speaking contest. Both made the finals, but Mabel won first prize with a speech about racial equality, and Alice won nothing. Just before graduation, Alice learned she had been awarded a senior class honor, the designation as "Ivy Poet." It carried with it the obligation to write a poem. That was not so difficult, but then she faced "the awful problem" of the recitation. She turned to Mabel for help. Her friend rehearsed her over and over. When at last Alice reached the point "where probably people could hear me . . . I gave my little Ivy poem."[11]

The final stanza concluded:

And when we are far from each other,
May our ivy between us watch still—
Keep our hearts ever loyal to classmates,
In a friendship that time shall not chill.[12]

Hoping that time had not chilled their relationship, in April 1913 Alice entreated Mabel to give up her job and join her in Washington. She told her airily, "There are plenty of people to teach school."[13]

Mabel did as Alice asked. For the next five years she would be Alice's most trusted organizer, the only one who addressed her as "Alice" and not "Miss Paul." She was small and wiry, with blue eyes, blonde curls, and a happy disposition. She was "not beautiful in the conventional sense, her nose a little long, her mouth a little large, but her radiant vitality left that impression," said another organizer, remembering her years later. "*What a wonderful face*, you thought."[14]

On June 13, the Senate Committee on Woman Suffrage issued its first favorable report on the federal amendment in twenty-one years. Naysayers warned that the measure stood no chance of passage. Alice's response was to announce yet another demonstration: On July 21 hundreds of cars crammed with suffragists from around the country would descend on Hyattsville, Maryland, gathering publicity and signatures as they traveled, and then bear down in formation on the Capitol.

It was an ambitious plan—*too* ambitious, protested Mary Garrett Hay, head of the New York City Woman Suffrage Party. She, Hay, would never be able to get anyone to come. New York women had paraded in March; they didn't like to do the same thing twice, it was too hot, vehicles were too expensive, and everyone, including herself, would be on vacation.

But in the end, people did come—five hundred in all. On July 31, some sixty gaily decorated cars set out from a baseball park in Hyattsville. Marchers trailed behind in the mud left by a heavy rainstorm the day before. Alice was in the lead, followed by officers of the National. From the District line to the Capitol, they were escorted by a substantial force of police on horses and bicycles. Police Superintendent Sylvester was taking no chances.

Six miles later, their filmy summer dresses aflutter, the women wafted like butterflies up the steps of the Capitol and into the elegant Marble Room just off the Senate chamber. From the paneled ceiling supported by towering white Corinthian columns hung a seemingly endless row of chandeliers, a repetition reflected in tall mirrors. More typically occupied by senators in their leisure moments, the room's dignified hush was shattered by feminine voices demanding that their cards be taken to their senators. After delivering petitions bearing eighty thousand signatures, they listened to the first suffrage debate in either house since 1887.

It was an important moment. Twenty-one senators spoke in favor of the amendment. Alice was delighted. She wrote a supporter, "The prospect of the passage of our measure grows brighter every day."[15]

By late summer 1913, the once-fraught relationship between Alice and the National seemed almost harmonious. Dennett congratulated Alice "on the wonderful success of the Senate demonstration" and invited Lucy to lecture at a "suffrage school," a series of workshops that Carrie Catt was organizing. Most extraordinary, Anna Shaw not only invited Lucy to speak at the next convention but offered what was perhaps the greatest honor of all. "What is more, I mean to have you give it the first night, when I give my annual address."

She added in a motherly tone, "I think of you and dear Miss Paul almost constantly. You are two valiant soldiers and I am glad you are in the army."[16]

The honeymoon lasted only until fall, when Alice skipped a board meeting with the single-word apology, "Sorry." Lucy failed to show up for the suffrage

school, and Alice invited Shaw to a meeting with Wilson, then neglected to in-
form her when the appointment was cancelled. Shaw wrote reproachfully, "I had
my grip all packed on Monday waiting for a telegram that would summon me
to leave on the night train."[17]

In the two months before the National's convention, there was scarcely a civil
exchange between Washington and New York. Alice strongly objected when Shaw
wanted to invite Wilson to offer the official welcome. She foresaw conflict with her
own efforts to arrange a meeting between the president and the National bigwigs.
Faced with two invitations, he would almost certainly choose the less threatening—the welcome. Shaw invited the president anyway, but he declined.

The convention would conclude with the National's annual trek to Capitol
Hill to voice the customary plea for a federal suffrage amendment. The year before, speaking to the House Judiciary Committee, suffrage historian Ida Husted
Harper had noted that forty-three years of entreaties had "been so absolutely
barren of results that in the past nineteen years, the committees have made no
report whatever, either favorable or unfavorable."[18] No one expected a different
reception this year.

When Alice began lining up speakers for the congressional appearance,
Shaw insisted the selection should be hers alone. Finally, Alice had had enough.
"I did not know that you were expecting to do the Congressional Work," she
replied tartly, "but since you wish to undertake it we will, of course, gladly hand
it over to you."[19]

Across the ocean, Emmeline Pankhurst was about to add fuel to the simmer-
ing conflict between Alice and the National.

When that January Parliament refused yet again to consider the franchise,
Emmeline called for "guerrilla warfare." Until then, the militant suffragettes had
targeted only government-owned property—buildings and mailboxes. Now they
hurled stones through shop windows, slashed the cushions of train seats, and
stopped up keyholes with lead pellets. Proclaiming "no votes, no golf," they
singed cherished greens with acid. They cut telegraph and telephone wires and
blew up fuse boxes, burned down the orchid house at Kew Gardens, and smashed
a jewel case at the Tower of London. The violence persuaded many women to
resign and the public turned against the Pankhurst shock troops. But that was
part of the WSPU plan. Emmeline declared, "We shall never get this question
settled until we make it intolerable for most people in this country. . . . We have
tried everything else."[20]

When suffragettes set off a bomb in the partially completed home of Lloyd George, chancellor of the exchequer, Emmeline was arrested, charged with incitement to violence, and sentenced to three years in prison. Under a quirky new law nicknamed the "Cat and Mouse Act," prisoners weak from hunger striking were released until they were well enough to continue serving their sentences. Several times over the next few months, Emmeline was turned loose, only to be thrown back in Holloway.

When, in fall 1913, temporarily free as a "mouse," the WSPU leader announced a fundraising sweep through America, Shaw denounced the British leader, telling a *New York Times* reporter, "I honor Mrs. Pankhurst as a woman, while I disapprove of her methods." Furthermore, whatever money Pankhurst collected would be at the expense of American suffragists, who needed "every penny that can be raised."[21]

Both Alice and Lucy were fiercely loyal to Emmeline, in Lucy's words, "one of the most splendid champions of women now living."[22] Risking Shaw's almost certain disapproval, not only did they book halls and accommodations for their mentor, but they researched immigration law and lawyers in the event that Emmeline was detained by U.S. authorities. When that in fact happened—the reason given was "moral turpitude"—Alva Belmont provided legal counsel. Such was the public outcry that Wilson ordered Emmeline's release.

That the woman identified as Emmeline's "travelling companion" aboard ship was Rheta Childe Dorr would also have annoyed Shaw. Dorr, a prominent journalist, was the editor-to-be of Alice's forthcoming newspaper, the *Suffragist.* But Dorr had postponed the launch in order to write a series of magazine articles that were later published as Pankhurst's autobiography, *My Own Story.* Dorr was still in England in October, when she had promised to return.

In Dorr's absence, Alice and Lucy went ahead with the newspaper. Shaw opened the November 15 debut issue and found still more to upset her. On the cover was a caricature of Woodrow Wilson, a smirk on his face as he considered "the next great question" to follow recent legislative successes. The portrayal of the president, Shaw said, made her "sick at heart."[23]

Next, Lucy got in trouble. To advertise a mass meeting of support for seventy-three women from Wilson's home state of New Jersey who were in town to see the president, she scrawled "Votes for Women" on a sidewalk across from the White House. She stopped when a policeman told her it was against the law.

The next day, reporters got wind that a warrant had been issued for her arrest. A scribe from the hometown *Brooklyn Daily Eagle* found Lucy at her desk in the F Street headquarters. Between bursts of laughter, Lucy admitted her guilt. Clearly she thought nothing of it. "In New York and other cities writing on the sidewalk is not prohibited."[24]

Militancy was on the mind of every reporter. Just a few days earlier, British suffragettes had blown up the cactus greenhouse in a Manchester park, destroying a $50,000 collection; set fire to an elegant mansion; and burned down the pavilion at a bowling and tennis club in London.

Was chalking the sidewalk a form of militancy? the reporter felt obliged to ask. Lucy replied gravely, "It is a form of economical advertising."[25]

Shaw instructed Lucy "to immediately plead ignorance of the law and pay whatever fine there is upon it," and thereafter to behave. "I know some people think it is cowardice and all that sort of thing to take the present attitude," she added stiffly, "but it requires a good deal more courage to work steadily and steadfastly for forty or fifty years to gain an end, than it does to do a [*sic*] impulsive rash thing and lose it."[26]

The National's president was also irritated with the New Jersey delegation for having barged in on Wilson unannounced. They had waited over a weekend for an appointment, but even with a New Jersey Democrat, Rep. Walter McCoy, interceding on their behalf, no response came from the president's office. At 10 A.M. on Monday, November 17, Alice telephoned the White House to say they were on their way.

McCoy phoned Alice to protest. It was too late, she told him. "The delegation has already started." Indeed. At that very moment the women were trotting in double file along 15th Street and Pennsylvania Avenue, past the Treasury and up to the doors of the White House, where Wilson met with them after all.[27]

Shaw insisted their peremptory visit was "in violation of all the ordinary methods."[28]

Lucy pled guilty, as Shaw had asked, and paid a one-dollar fine. She wrote the older woman a placating letter. "I do not feel that Miss Paul or I have had a militant spirit in conducting our work." Things were going so well with the president and Congress that "We have no occasion for it." She reassured Shaw that Alice could be trusted, that she had "a very calculating and cautious temperament."

Lucy conceded in the letter that the Wilson cartoon was unfortunate. Neither she nor Alice had seen it before it went into print. If they were guilty of anything, it was undertaking so much work that "we do not sufficiently control the details of it."[29]

But Shaw found it increasingly difficult to contain her resentment of these Washington youngsters. She knew that people like Dora Lewis, once loyal to Shaw, and also Crystal Eastman, who had led the suffrage campaign in Wisconsin, were now squarely in their court. Even Mary Garrett Hay, head of the important New York City Woman Suffrage Party, and best friends with Carrie Chapman Catt, credited the pair with having "accomplished more in a National way than has been accomplished in a long time."[30]

Anna Shaw was accustomed to being the center of attention at the National's gatherings. But when the 1913 convention opened, it was Alice who held court in the hotel lobby. Suspicious by nature, Shaw was certain the young suffragist was up to no good. She complained that Alice was seen "talking to reporters and to other people, trying to create discord, even when the Convention was in session."[31]

Among committee reports, none could rival Alice's: three parades, three congressional hearings, a petition with two hundred thousand signatures that prompted the first Senate debate in twenty-six years, three summer campaigns, eight theater rallies, and an average of a half-dozen street meetings daily, plus the launching of the *Suffragist.*

After giving Alice three cheers, the delegates considered her future. Unlike the 1912 convention in Philadelphia, when the National's dirty linen was spread across seven city newspapers, the reporters from Washington's three hundred news outlets were kept in the dark. The National had closed its doors to the press.

Even so, with a record 456 delegates clumped together, there were inevitable hints that something titillatingly terrible was happening and that whatever it was once again involved the National's newest star. Confirmation came in the form of a denial. Rumors of a split "were stilled," the *Washington Post* reported, when the National president announced "it is certain that Miss Alice Paul and Miss Lucy Burns will remain on the congressional committee."[32]

In the end, the closest thing to a record was an undated letter that Shaw penned in late January to the state presidents and executive board members.

The membership of the National was confused, she said, by the overlap between the Congressional Committee and the new dues-paying organization with a similar name that shared officers and office space. When former president Carrie Catt pressed Alice Paul to separate the financial reports of the Congressional Committee and the Congressional Union, Alice had replied, according to Shaw, that "it was impossible for her to comply."[33] In the end the conflict focused on money. The National had raised just $42,723 in 1913, while Alice's fundraising pulled in $27,378. Henceforth the National wanted the funds Alice raised funneled through its treasury; Alice refused.

Apparently it was a bitter confrontation. One member of the National felt "mingled grief and indignation" at the "deliberateness" of the attack on Alice by the leaders. She was so disturbed that she joined the Congressional Union immediately afterward.[34]

In the days following the convention, Shaw offered a compromise. Lucy could chair a reconstituted Congressional Committee; Alice could remain as one of its members. The Congressional Union would agree not to send organizers across state lines to work for the federal amendment.

When both Lucy and Alice rejected the conditions, Shaw appointed an entirely new Congressional Committee. Mary Ware Dennett ordered Alice to turn over her files and any equipment the old committee had purchased, including typewriters and desks.

Any chance of reconciliation evaporated during a January 11, 1914, Congressional Union meeting at Elizabeth Kent's elegant Washington townhouse. It was the one-year anniversary of Alice's federal campaign, and also her twenty-ninth birthday. She was always well turned out in clothes that flattered her slim body, and for this occasion she had made sure that her sister Helen shipped a favorite dress from Moorestown. Kent presented Alice with a silver loving cup "in affectionate recognition of her wisdom, her devotion and her courage." In an unusual display of emotion, according to the *Suffragist*, the usually contained Miss Paul "rather brokenly" thanked the assemblage for the gift.[35]

To the four hundred supporters who crowded into the double drawing rooms, Alice announced a daring tactic: If the Democratic Party, "the party in power . . . refused to heed the call of the women for enfranchisement, then, in those congressional districts where the political situation is acute, and a few votes one way or the other will decide the issue, our policy will be to use every legitimate means to defeat the Democratic candidate for Congress at the Congressional elections in November."[36] The principle echoed Christabel Pankhurst's strategy for defeating Britain's Liberal Party. It would apply only in those states where women voted.

"Party in power" became the shorthand for the new hard-line approach. The gathering at Elizabeth Kent's raised more than nine thousand dollars for the effort. But shock set in among some Union members when they realized they would be opposing even pro-suffrage Democrats in order to weaken the party as a whole. Antoinette Funk, a Chicago lawyer and second-in-command of the reconstituted Congressional Committee, protested that it was "suicide for the suffrage movement" to go after legislators such as Sen. Charles Thomas of Colorado, chairman of the committee on woman suffrage and "one of the closest friends and supporters," just because he was a Democrat. The National, Funk pledged, would mount "a countermovement on the part of thousands of women in our organization who will go to the support of such men."[37]

Alice argued that women who voted out a pro-suffrage Democrat would vote in a pro-suffrage Republican—the only kind there were in states where women had the ballot—without a net loss in congressional votes. It would have no impact in states where women didn't vote, but perhaps it would send a message where they did. It was a radical plan that would govern her strategy for the next two elections.

Alice was bone weary. After the Kent fundraiser, she headed for the Home Farm, where she planned to take to her bed and engage in that forbidden pleasure— reading. En route, she stopped at Dora Lewis's four-story brick Philadelphia townhouse, where she penned one last appeal to Shaw.

"I need hardly add that we all regret deeply your hostility toward us. We are utterly at loss to understand what we have done of which you disapprove and hope that sometime you will be willing to give us an opportunity of clearing up whatever misunderstanding exists."[38]

Given the note's snippy tone, it is little wonder the National's president wasn't mollified. The next month, the National's executive council turned down the Union's application for auxiliary status.

Less than a year had passed since eight thousand or so suffragists had gathered at the foot of Pennsylvania Avenue, fused by a slender, little-known Quaker into a grand and moving display of unity. Shaw and other leaders had marched in the vanguard. Now the National, which claimed two million members, was the enemy.

Alice was on her own.

CHAPTER SEVEN

SUMMER OF DISCONTENT

The convention that dislodged Alice also pushed Alva Belmont over the edge.

The National's preoccupation with rules and bylaws—much of the 1913 convention was devoted to a mind-numbing revision of the constitution—was wearing her down. Moreover, she did not feel appreciated. For the second year in a row she had stormed out after offering a resolution that flopped.

Alva's disenchantment was not lost on Alice. There was much to draw them together. Though separated in age by three decades, both were relative newcomers to the movement. Both revered the Pankhursts and thought the American movement needed a stiffer spine. Like Alice, Alva recognized the value of publicity. She was seldom out of the newspapers. She also had an appreciation for spirited young women. The beautiful socialist lawyer Inez Milholland was her closest suffrage buddy. For Anna Shaw, an alliance between Alva and Alice at the expense of the National would be a bad dream come true.

Early in January 1914, Crystal Eastman, a charter member of Alice's original Congressional Committee, conspired with fellow member Mary Beard to reel Alva into the Congressional Union. Both knew Belmont from New York suffrage circles. Mary was married to the prominent Columbia historian Charles Beard and was a historian in her own right. In later years they would work together, but she also had her own mission, to expose the way historical accounts overlooked the contributions of women.

Crystal had been drafted by Lucy Burns, who had been a year ahead of her at Vassar. In addition to authoring a groundbreaking study of workplace accidents, which earned her the first female appointment to a New York state commission, Crystal was the sister of Max Eastman, founder of a men's suffrage society and editor of the left-leaning *The Masses*.

She lived in Greenwich Village, a fertile breeding ground for activists of all stripes. Here in large numbers dwelled "The New Woman," a female who was smart, educated or at least informed, outspoken, and independent. They were professionals: teachers, nurses, lawyers, social workers, librarians. Or they were artists, performers, and writers—novelists, poets, journalists.

In the Village, they took up residence in apartments carved out of once-grand homes, and sometimes even dared to cohabit with men—or share romance with other women. There they could bob their hair, shed their corsets, smoke in public, and engage in discourse. Everybody knew everybody and everybody talked about Margaret Sanger and birth control, free love, Freud and the new practice of psychoanalysis, free sprit Isadora Duncan and her freeform dance, rhymeless poetry, and the new fractured art from the Continent. Add to the list Alice Paul and suffrage politics.

Crystal regularly joined several dozen women over Saturday lunch in what was perhaps the first female consciousness-raising group, Heterodoxy. "All could talk; all could argue; all could listen," wrote member Inez Haynes Irwin, who like Crystal and as many as a dozen other Heterodites would eventually rotate into Alice's orbit.[1]

Her sights set on Alva, Crystal reported to Lucy that her target was "quite keen about the C.U. She wants to undermine the National—perhaps that's her chief reason for wanting to back us." She didn't think Alva "would want to interfere or dictate. She just doesn't want to be made a baby of—to be used just for money and not for work or advice." It would be enough, chimed in Beard, to organize an advisory committee with Alva as a member, and ask "her opinion now and then."[2]

Lucy Burns was not convinced. When Belmont requested a visit from Alice, Lucy suggested that Crystal go along. This would ease the introduction and also "keep Crystal from being too positive." The meeting went well. Afterward, Alva sent Alice a check for five thousand dollars with a note. "I so thoroughly endorse the work of the Union as you so ably mapped it out to me that it is a great pleasure to me to be able to send you this amount. Believe me."[3]

Following the 1913 convention, only a close reader of the *Suffragist* might have realized that the National had ousted the Congressional Union. The news that the National had appointed a new Congressional Committee, and that the

Union would operate as a separate body, was buried in an account of the Kent fundraiser. A straightforward announcement of the rupture would have struck Alice as unseemly; she did not wish to appear at odds with sister suffragists. When a new Union press secretary was quoted as saying the National was "lacking in political wisdom," Alice warned her never to do it again. "It puts a bad spirit through all our work and can do us nothing but harm."[4]

The National showed no such restraint. One woman complained to a supporter of Alice's that the National was sending her so many "long screeds" denouncing the Union that she didn't have time to read them.[5]

When the Union invited suffragists to a fundraising ball that Alice was counting on to pay rent on headquarters, Ruth McCormick, who had replaced Alice as head of the Congressional Committee, told her society friends not to help. McCormick was the daughter of legendary Ohio politico Mark Hanna, and had inherited considerable influence. One ball organizer moaned that her opposition cost the Union "several valuable allies."[6] Proving she could do more than give money, Alva Belmont took over as the ball's chairman and tapped her society contacts to make the ball a success.

In New York, the National's attacks forced newspapers to choose sides. Mary Beard complained in March that it was "hard to get editorials in the sympathetic New York papers because the National is right here and editors know their scalps would come off."[7]

These, however, were minor annoyances compared to what happened next. In an effort to undermine the Congressional Union, the National offered a bizarre counterproposal to the long-standing federal amendment. Drafted by McCormick and named for its sponsor, Sen. John Franklin Shafroth of Colorado, the new version required a state to hold a suffrage referendum if petitioned by 8 percent of the electorate.

As with any proposed constitutional amendment, it would first have to be passed by a two-thirds majority in both houses of Congress and ratified by the legislatures of thirty-six states. Then there would be the added step of a popular vote in every state. In effect it was the state-by-state approach in camouflage. Harriot Blatch called it a nightmare.[8]

To sharpen the distinction between the two amendments, the Union began referring to theirs, heretofore known as the Bristol-Mondell amendment, as the Susan B. Anthony amendment.

When the National's Antoinette Funk tried to explain the complicated Shafroth measure to the Senate Judiciary Committee, she was met with puzzled requests to repeat what she had said. Even its author acknowledged that the amendment was a tough sell. "When first described to women, it usually aroused opposition," said Ruth McCormick. Then "gradually, if the discussion continues long enough, they favor it." She searched for, and found, an analogy. "It reminds me a good deal of the first time you taste an olive."[9]

Seeking to deal the Union a death blow, the National simultaneously pressed for an immediate Senate vote on the Anthony amendment, knowing full well that it did not have enough support to pass. Alice begged Sen. Charles Thomas, chairman of the Woman Suffrage Committee, not to schedule a vote. He did so anyway on March 19, 1914, with predictable results. Thirty-five senators voted in favor to thirty-four against. It was the first time since 1887 that the Senate had voted on suffrage and represented a marked improvement from that first vote, when there were sixteen ayes, thirty-four noes, and twenty-six non-votes from senators who hadn't managed to show up. But it was still eleven votes short of the required two-thirds majority. Shafroth introduced his amendment the following day.

Alice wrote a bitter note to the National's Harriet Upton in Ohio, no friend of Anna Shaw. "We knew and every member of the Senate knew that it would be lost if voted on yesterday. The Congressional committee, however, insisted upon such action and by this demand of theirs gave the Democratic leaders the opportunity of killing the bill and seeming, at the same moment, to be following the wishes of suffragists. . . . We reintroduced our measure this morning and will not accept any other as a substitute."[10] As a practical matter, however, once a bill had been defeated, it was rarely voted on in the same Congress.

Rheta Childe Dorr's failure to appear in October 1913, when she had promised to help launch the *Suffragist,* undoubtedly soured her relationship with Alice. In December, she was still in England working on Emmeline Pankhurst's memoir. On December 15, Alice wrote a colleague, "We have no idea as to when she will return." In January 1914, Rheta was shivering in a frigid room in Paris, working on the Pankhurst project and despairing of news from Washington. The Union's press secretary, Jessie Stubbs, stepped in as the *Suffragist*'s acting editor, freeing Alice and Lucy from their newspaper duties. Columbia educated, the daughter of a journalist and the widow of a doctor, Stubbs had come to Washington from Chicago in July 1913 for the car pilgrimage and stayed on to take charge of the Congressional Union press bureau.

When Dorr finally returned to the United States on February 2, 1914, and took up her editor's pen at the *Suffragist,* Alice demanded much. Rheta should read the *Congressional Record* daily, contact specified writers for stories, and, of course, get the paper out on time. By focusing on the Union's push for federal action, the eight-page weekly newspaper would become, Alice hoped, the "backbone of our work."[11]

In mid-February, Alice checked into the Woman's Hospital in Philadelphia to combat fatigue that had set in after the 1913 convention. With time on her hands, she waited impatiently each week for the latest issue of her cherished *Suffragist*.

On Tuesday, March 3, she wrote business manager Elizabeth Harris, the "*Suffragist* has not yet reached Philadelphia." She wrote again the next day when it still had not arrived. "It should be out on Thursday and reach all nearby cities so people can read it on Sunday." Once, from the Home Farm, Alice complained that the paper "did not arrive till Monday noon. . . . Mine was rolled in a tight roll so that I took a considerable time and expenditure of effort before it was straightened out enough to be readable. Unless a person were anxious to read the paper I think she would not bother to iron it out."[12]

When she returned to Washington in mid-March, Alice set about taking care of business. On April 21, Rheta discovered that Alice had held back the editorial page. The journalist wrote out her resignation on the spot. "Nobody," she protested, "has a right to lay hands on a single piece of copy without the editor's permission, much less edit, erase or change without consulting the editor." Six weeks later the business manager resigned, citing a wide difference in "ideas as to the proper business management of 'The Suffragist.'"[13]

Although the work of putting out the paper now fell on her shoulders, Alice seemed not at all displeased. She wrote Alva Belmont that the Union would be saving money on both salaries and rent.[14]

It had been too many months since women had rallied for suffrage. Lest the public lose sight of the cause—a *federal* amendment—Alice announced coast-to-coast demonstrations on May 2, 1914.

The 1913 pre-inauguration parade had brought suffrage to Washington. Now, on a single day in 1914, suffrage spirit would blossom in the heartland. When Alice dispatched a half-dozen Union organizers to various cities to whip up enthusiasm, however, Anna Shaw charged that these forays were attempts on Alice's part to raid the National's membership. The National nevertheless jumped on board the May 2 bandwagon. Confused suffrage societies weren't sure which group to follow or whether to endorse the Anthony or Shafroth amendment.

In New York, Blatch joined forces with Belmont and invited Alice to speak at a Carnegie Hall meeting. The invitation, more like a demand, gave Alice the usual case of jitters. But Blatch was too influential to ignore. Lucy Burns reported to Mary Beard that she had persuaded her colleague to attend "with great difficulty." She added, "It seems to me that she ought to be seen at such a large and important meeting in New York City."[15]

Alice was distinctly put out and confided in Beard as well. "Miss Burns says she will not go to New York at all unless I do as she seems to think that Mrs. Blatch will not like it. I do not agree with her at all, but since she refused to go alone, there is absolutely nothing for me to do but go also."[16]

Cities large and small welcomed the chance to demonstrate their enthusiasm for the ballot. On May 2, in Chicago, five thousand women in white dresses and bonnets crowned with ten blue stars marched through the streets. In Grafton, Vermont, little girls in yellow crepe-paper tunics and boys in yellow neckties formed a procession, singing, "Hurrah, hurrah, we're suffragettes you see. So we'll shout the chorus from Grafton to the sea." In conservative St. Paul, Minnesota, Mrs. George M. Kenyon wrote Alice that the demonstration so far exceeded expectations that "we are walking on air. . . . Women who had hardly dared come out for Suffrage, on account of their husbands, or friends or relatives, marched with us."[17]

In Alice's hometown, where her sister Helen was in charge of the rally, plunging temperatures forced it to move from outdoors into the Grange Hall. Helen reported: "Place was packed. Parry came home. We made a huge banner and put it across the street as they do at elections."[18]

A week later in Washington, the Congressional Union staged yet another procession to the Capitol, this time to deliver the resolutions in favor of the Anthony amendment from around the country. After all the vitriol, the National's new Congressional Committee asked to participate, with one reservation. Marching "does not mean that we have abandoned our support of the Shafroth Resolution," said Vice-chairman Antoinette Funk.[19]

It was the last time the National would extend an olive branch.

Although Alice viewed state campaigns as a diversion from the battle for the federal amendment, she made an exception for Nevada, where an ally was fighting hard for the vote. Like Alice and Lucy, Anne Martin was the daughter of a banker and had her own income. During a two-year sojourn in England, she too had thrown in with Emmeline Parkhurst. A Nevada native, she loved the outdoors and could ride, play tennis, golf, and climb. In March Alice agreed to lend her Mabel Vernon, fresh from six months campaigning for suffrage in her home state of Delaware.

In recruiting her Swarthmore classmate, Alice had chosen well. Not only was Mabel dependable, loyal, and so quietly persuasive that people readily agreed to do what she asked, but she was also an exceptional fundraiser.

She almost always wore white for her appearances, with white shoes and stockings, her dress impeccably laundered and ironed—she liked to iron—and a hat designed on an angle, one side higher than the other. At a typical rally, Mabel followed the national headliners. She would face the audience, her head tilted, one foot forward. Then she would make her pitch and ask for a thousand dollars. A plant in the audience would volunteer the money. Next, recalled fellow organizer Hazel Hunkins, "She'd say, 'Now the next thousand.' . . . Before long she'd have $5,000, sometimes $10,000. Then we small-fry would go up and down the aisles to collect silver by the bushel. I never saw a woman bleed an audience as Mabel did."[20]

Everyone wanted Mabel. "Miss Vernon's loss to us was very great," complained Mary R. de Vou, a leader of the Delaware Equal Suffrage Association. Alice reminded de Vou that the state had failed to cover Mabel's salary and expenses during her six-month stay, running up a deficit of five hundred dollars.[21]

Now that Mabel was gone, perhaps Delaware would properly "appreciate her while she is alive instead of waiting until after her death," Alice snickered in a note to Dora Lewis. But Lewis wasn't happy either. She had thought Mabel would be helping out in Pennsylvania. Just because that state had hired a summer replacement, she wrote back to Alice, "does not let you out of giving us Mabel Vernon in the autumn."[22]

Anne Martin quickly bonded with Mabel; the pair formed an enduring friendship. Of one early meeting, attended by two hundred, Martin wrote that the Union organizer held the audience "in the hollow of her hand"; she commended her "sturdy honesty and reliability."[23]

In 1914, Nevada had roughly eighty thousand inhabitants, most of them men drawn to the state by mining jobs or cheap farmland. Through Mabel's colorful dispatches, readers of the *Suffragist* could experience the rigors of barnstorming the West.

In May she spent a day "in a diminutive tin box on wheels run by a horrible smelling gasoline engine, traveling or rather bumping one hundred miles from the main line of railroad across an apparently endless desert with nothing to be seen except an occasional ranch and the mountains looming in the distance." A fellow traveler took one look at the train and sought a refund, saying "what he needed was not a ticket but a can opener."[24]

Mabel disembarked at 3:30 A.M. in one town that consisted of a train station, one house, and one saloon. She wrote, "From this place I had to drive in an automobile in company with two squaws about ten miles across the desert to reach a town where two hundred people dwell. . . . Yet the people in all these small towns must be reached if Nevada is to win next November."[25]

She spoke in camps where miners came down from the hills and farmers drove in from the fields. In hopefully named Goldfield, a large crowd of men listened to a group of suffragists for almost two hours in a cold, biting wind. They were so enthusiastic, wrote Mabel, that when the women drove away, the men took off their hats and cried out, "Three cheers for the suffragists."[26]

In June 1914, Alice told Martin that Mabel could stay till July. In July, Martin begged to keep her till September, saying that without her Nevada would lose the campaign. Alice relented. Mabel could remain until September 1, but after that Alice had to have Mabel back.

During the summer of 1914, Alice and Lucy were locked in tense combat with the House Rules Committee. Weighted with southern Democrats, in January it had defeated the proposal for a standing suffrage committee like the one in the Senate. Now Rules was sitting on the Anthony amendment, refusing to schedule it for a House vote.

Her droll sense of humor on display, Lucy Burns described the committee's dilemma in the *Suffragist:* "It was difficult for them to vote against it and it seemed to be difficult for them to vote for it. They apparently decided that the best policy for them to pursue was to take no action at all, so they hit upon the happy expedient of holding no meetings whatever."[27]

When finally the committee did meet in a closed session on August 28, it quickly reported a special rule for an unrelated administration measure and then adjourned. Suffrage was dead in both the House and the Senate for the remainder of 1914. And as far as Alice and Lucy were concerned, there was only one direction in which to point a finger.

Democrats had a lock on both houses of Congress, and many supported suffrage. But the Virginia-born president and the powerful Democratic legislators from the cotton and tobacco states who controlled key committees had no reason to court people who could not cast ballots. The only women with political power lived in nine western states.

In readiness for a new strategy targeting Democrats, Alva Belmont threw open the doors to Marble House, her summer seaside "cottage" in fashionable Newport, Rhode Island, on August 29, 1914, for the Congressional Union's advisory council. To Alice's disappointment, socialist Mary Beard had refused to set foot in an edifice with a ballroom slathered in gold and a sixteenth-century Tintoretto fastened to one ceiling. Doing so felt wrong and would shatter her credibility in labor circles. Her loyalty to the Union was "steadfast," she insisted, "but I can't do the Newport stunt."[28]

Lucy Burns set the stage with a speech listing the ways that the president and House and Senate Democrats had failed suffrage. Alice then asked the press to leave. In this heightened atmosphere, she outlined a bold plan to persuade women voters in the West "to withdraw their support from the Democrats nationally until the Democratic Party nationally ceases to block Suffrage."[29]

"We, of course, are a little body to undertake this—but we have to begin. We have not very much money; there are not many of us to go out against the Democratic Party." Perhaps they could not accomplish much this time, she said, but "by 1916 we will have it organized."[30]

CHAPTER EIGHT

YOUNG WOMEN
GO WEST

Dressed for their mission in dark, ankle-length suits and compact hats, seven smiling young women posed around a large floral bouquet on September 14, 1914, in Washington's Union Station. In a few moments they would board a Chicago-bound railcar draped with purple, white, and gold banners, and from there they would disperse to points west. Alice had hoped for more bodies, two for each of the nine voting states, but candidates for the assignment dropped out one by one. Crystal Eastman had been on the road for ten months and needed time at home. Alva Belmont pleaded fatigue. Sisters Elsie Hill and Helena Hill Weed bowed out, though Elsie promised to handle the Washington press. Mary Beard, Dora Lewis—neither could go.

Alice rarely allowed her worries to show. But she was let down by the rejections. "This has been a discouraging week," she wrote Belmont several days before the scheduled departure.[1] When the departure date arrived, however, she had a plan for covering all the states.

The initial seven women would be supplemented by five others who would come later. Lucy Burns and Rose Winslow, a well-known labor organizer, would set up camp in San Francisco. Doris Stevens and Ruth Noyes would go to Denver. Edna Latimer, president of a chapter of the Just Government League of Maryland (a nest of Congressional Union sympathizers), and fellow member

Lola Trax would open headquarters in Kansas City, Kansas. Press secretary Jessie Stubbs would take charge of Oregon with Virginia Arnold, newly graduated from Columbia. Margaret Whittemore of Detroit, daughter of a Quaker suffragist, and Anna McCue, who had been the summer organizer in Philadelphia, would head for Washington State. Alice would pull Mabel Vernon out of Nevada and send her to Arizona with Jane Pincus, an organizer on loan from the Syracuse branch of the Woman's Political Union. That left only Utah, Wyoming, and Idaho uncovered, heavily Republican states where, she told a Pennsylvania member, "the fight will not have to be such a vigorous one."[2] Alice would worry about them in due time.

In all, twelve young women would be unloosed on a terrain encompassing treeless plains as big and as empty as seas and the tallest mountains they had ever seen. They would alight in cities with short buildings and wide streets where everyone knew everyone else and they knew no one. From those base camps, they would hoist their long skirts and climb aboard a rattletrap train or horse-pulled wagon headed for faraway specks tucked into hills or sprouting on prairies.

Alice armed the little band of anti-Democrats with what she supposed they would need: state maps, a congressional directory, a package of literature, posters and handbills, a Great Demand banner, ten small pennants, ten pieces of regalia, and two banners—all in the Union's signature purple, white, and gold, symbolizing dignity, purity, and intelligence or light. The banners were to garnish the front of the highly visible headquarters the women were to open post haste on the main street of their assigned city. They were also given one hundred membership cards, one hundred subscription blanks to the *Suffragist*, and one hundred copies of the newspaper's current issue.

Their instructions were to call immediately upon all the newspapers in the city (list enclosed), as well as the headquarters of all the political parties, including the Socialists, Progressives, and Prohibitionists. Reports were due weekly, and the women should please include all relevant newspaper clippings from local papers. Also they should find a moment to send Washington a photograph of their activities to accompany the daily press bulletins Elsie Hill would issue.

To comply with a new federal law regulating political campaign finances, every Saturday night the organizers were to post a carefully itemized financial report, accompanied by vouchers and receipts, plus a check for the money they had collected. ("Please try to raise as much money as possible."[3]) At the least, Alice hoped they could cover their expenses.

It was all a lot to ask.

In Kansas City, the Congressional Union flag flew over a storefront bearing the sign of its former occupant, Kansas Tire Supply. Her first week there, Maryland's Edna Latimer shared a podium with Teddy Roosevelt at a rally of three thousand people, and her colleague Lola Trax reported that they had almost more meetings than they could handle. In Seattle, Margaret Whittemore and Anna McCue spoke at four gatherings in a single day, prompting the *Seattle Star* to remark, "They have put on a burst of speed that makes the busiest candidate green with envy."[4]

The *Suffragist* printed cheerful excerpts from letters to the home office, but deliberately omitted the worries. It did not take long, however, for all of the organizers to realize that they were neck-deep in murky political waters full of treacherous currents.

They quickly discovered that the argument for a federal amendment carried little weight where women could already vote and states' rights was a respected principle. Moreover, western women voters were firmly enmeshed in party politics, and those loyalties tended to outweigh sympathy for their disenfranchised eastern sisters. Only Republicans seemed glad to see the suffragists.

Alice had counseled the organizers to remain nonpartisan. She specifically told them not to accept contributions from any political party. But their vigorous attacks on the Democratic Party raised doubts about their motives, especially when delighted Republicans showered the Union women with speaking invitations and other favors. Jessie Stubbs happily said yes to a five-room office suite and furniture from people with close Republican ties, then wondered if she had done the right thing. Democratic women spread the rumor that her campaign was being financed by Republicans, making money difficult to raise.

From Seattle, Anna McCue wrote that she and Whittemore were not only "violently opposed by the Democratic Women's Club," but "there are so many factions in this town and such a feeling between the different parties, splits in the women's clubs and in fact a great deal of petty feeling that one is almost at a loss to proceed."[5]

In Arizona, Jane Pincus lamented that women "aren't particularly interested here in suffrage, they didn't have to work for it, the men gave it to them, so they don't appreciate it." She had heard of only three suffragists in Arizona, and "one has moved away." In Cheyenne, Wyoming, Gertrude Hunter reported, "It is very hard to keep enough courage from one day to another, to work against this blank wall of indifference which is so much more killing than opposition."[6]

They also had to put up with opposition from the National. While Doris Stevens was en route to Colorado, arch enemy Ruth McCormick fired off a telegram to a supporter warning that the Union's emissary was coming "to fight the Democratic party." McCormick offered her assistance "in combating the Union campaign."[7]

Doris, seven years younger than Alice and a 1911 graduate of Oberlin College, had until recently been an organizer for the National's Ohio affiliate. In 1913, she had defied a county suffrage association to put up announcements for an appearance by Emmeline Pankhurst, and then she had dined with the famous suffragette.

As Doris told the story, she had joined ranks with Alice after first marching in the 1913 parade. She returned to Washington in July 1913, intending only to take part in the Congressional Union auto cavalcade to the Capitol. When Alice asked her to help with a hearing the next week, Doris stammered out an excuse. She had plans with friends for a holiday in the mountains.

"Holiday?" asked Alice, as if pronouncing a foreign word. Doris instantly felt ashamed. She stammered out something about not having had one since before college. And then she stayed. "And it was years before I ever mentioned a holiday again."[8]

Unlike some of her less venturesome colleagues, Doris relished combat. She wrote Alice from Colorado, "This promises to be a thrilling fight not only by the Dems but the N.A.W.S.A.—yea verily!" She sensed fear among the "strongly organized bodies of Democratic women. . . . While they try to say we cannot accomplish our aim they are literally scared to death." But she was realistic. Sen. Charles Thomas, a former Colorado governor and current chairman of the Woman Suffrage Committee, was "unbeatable." Even his former Republican opponent favored him.[9]

She also cautioned Alice that "The air is full of hero-worship of Wilson and so is the press."[10] In addition to his legislative victories, the president had staked out a policy of strict neutrality in the European conflict that played well to voters. And just weeks earlier he had lost his wife to Bright's Disease, a kidney disorder, and gained the nation's sympathy.

On the road—well, often there *was* no road—the challenges were daunting. Newly arrived in Wyoming, Gertrude Hunter wired Alice in despair that to cover the state even "superficially with one organizer and time for only largest town on railroad would cost at least five hundred dollars distances so great and sparsely settled." Car travel was cheaper than trains but unreliable. In late October, Gertrude and a companion set out on a thirty-five-mile drive. "We did it every mile through a high wind and torrents of rain with a trail filled with water, going over the prairie, and plowed fields. We did it however with only one blow out, and two very narrow escapes from being completely turned over, getting in at two this morning."[11]

There would be no point, Gertrude said, in sending her a stack of posters to place in storefronts. "These towns . . . cannot use more than four or five. There are seldom more buildings than that." One such "town" (her quotes), where she spoke at a meeting for a Republican candidate, "consists of the station, the post office, general store and a little restaurant. No houses, and only one or two families living there."[12] But that didn't mean the meetings weren't well attended. On that occasion the whiff of excitement was enough to attract 150 people from miles around.

In letter after letter, Alice urged the women to raise money. At one point the Union treasury was down to three dollars. But it was easier to attract an audience than contributions. "I've asked and been refused so many times that I haven't the courage any more," wailed Jane Pincus. Anna McCue wrote, "We are using desperate efforts to extract money from every human being whom we see; Miss Whittemore dragged two innocent people in off the street and persuaded them each to give us one dollar; and one of them was a male Dem."[13]

Among such plaints, stories of success pop out like prairie dogs. Too busy to come earlier, Helena Hill Weed had managed to clear her schedule and was now in Boise, where she debuted to a rapt audience of hotel chambermaids. "Many of them have worked in the east under bad conditions before they came out here, but they had never stopped to think that they, by the use of their vote out here, could help the women back east."[14]

Edna Latimer received a rousing welcome in Vermillion, Kansas, where a "Ladies Band of thirty pieces greeted me." Local suffragists marched her up the street to a concert and then to a women's meeting at which a "very prominent Democratic woman" told her she had "flopped over to the other side," and now opposed the party. Latimer spoke at three meetings. "Practically a thousand people in Marshall County were reached in one day."[15]

In Dodge City, Kansas, after finishing up a speech at the Dreamland Theatre at 9:30 P.M., Latimer and Trax learned four hundred people had been waiting for two hours in a schoolhouse in a prairie town some distance away. "Trying to find the trail," they lost their way in the dark and arrived two hours later. Much to their surprise, wrote Latimer, the audience was still there. "We found whole families that had come from miles." Almost every desk had a baby asleep atop a pillow. "After the meeting was over the women rose in a body to thank us for coming. They said that they were more than willing to help their eastern sisters."[16]

Male Democrats didn't know what to make of these lady spoilers. Democratic bigwigs in Utah invited Elsie Lancaster to headquarters, then grilled her for two and a half hours about her intentions. The *Ogden Standard* had a field day with the story, reporting that "W. R. Wallace, Democratic generalissimo, and his gang of political manikins [*sic*]" kept her "under fire of cross questioning and denunciation" in a "vain endeavor to have her bring to an immediate close her campaign against the Democratic nominees for the United States senate and congress."[17]

Lancaster held her ground even after Wallace threatened to tell the Associated Press that she was "working for [Republican] Senator Smoot, the Mormon church, the liquor interest and against the Democratic party in Utah." Undaunted, Lancaster declared, "I am going to stay here until the end of the campaign and fight against the Democratic nominees whose party has broken faith with the people and with the womanhood of this country."[18]

Back east the campaign was creating waves. A Kansas congressman demanded the removal of Trax and Latimer from his district. Colorado's Sen. Thomas wrote an angry letter to the Union. And in October, Alice heard from Mickle Paul, the uncle who had been so proud of her courage in England. Her home front militancy was too much for him. "Why defeat known friends for the benefit of known enemies? I have pride in thy success—believe thee is earnest & sincere, yet in this manifesto of opposition to all Democrats I believe thee has erred."[19]

Alice shrugged off the criticism. She feasted on the clippings sent by organizers. "Democratic papers in Wyoming," Alice wrote Jane Pincus, "have become almost profane in denouncing our activities." Oregon papers were irate over "Stubbs madness." A Wyoming paper "says we are proposing to 'prostitute religion, charity, society itself to the ambitions of a place and plunder hunting politician [*sic*].'

"So altogether everything is going well."[20]

For her wandering charges, isolated and spurned, dedicated but armed with meager resources, Alice was a lifeline, ready with advice and support drawn from her own experience. She counseled the earnest Gertrude Hunter not to be "the least bit discouraged because the important people, club women and so on are not interested. They never are, you know."[21]

It reminded her of when she arrived in Washington in the waning days of 1912. "We were told that no one would give any money; that no one was interested in suffrage because this was a Congressional and Diplomatic city; with no industrial or commercial population; that parades, open-air speaking, or demonstrations of any kind, would alienate the few who were interested, and so on. But we paid no attention to the big and important people, and began on large and rousing demonstrations, appealing for help to the ordinary middle class person of no position or influence. Invariably they respond."[22]

Hunter told Alice her letters were "the most cheering things that come to me in this campaign." Ten days later she seemed to have taken Alice's counsel to heart. She wrote about a meeting in "Granite Canon [*sic*]" that was "the most encouraging thing yet." Hunter delivered a fifteen-minute speech which even the Democratic women praised. "We had a dance immediately after, and I danced with the voters (male) until one-thirty in the morning, when we were all taken to a railroad station in a lumber wagon and four-horse team." She got home at 2:30 A.M. "I sold twenty *Suffragists* and could have disposed of more if I had had them with me."[23]

As the Colorado election returns trickled in on November 3, 1914, Doris Stevens sent a joyful telegram to headquarters. It appeared that Charles Thomas had lost his Senate race. In the final count, however, she was crushed to learn he had squeaked through. Doris also claimed credit for the defeat of Harry Hunter Seldomridge, the Democratic congressman from Colorado Springs. It was the one clear victory on a day of muddled results.

In Oregon, Chamberlain sailed to victory. In Arizona, Democrats made a clean sweep. "I can't say that I shall be sorry to leave," wrote Jane Pincus. "The Socialists have really been the only ones to show any great amount of kindness."[24]

It was a fact that most of the men the Union organizers opposed were elected. Indeed, the Democrats gained three seats in the nine campaign states. But after studying the results, Scripps Howard reporter Gilson Gardner reached the conclusion that "the figures show greatly reduced majorities for the democrats who were successful, and almost universal defeat for the democratic candidates who tried to wrest from the republicans and progressives the seats which the latter held." Gardner was not an impartial observer. His wife Matilda was one of Alice's most loyal followers, and he wrote frequently in favor of suffrage. But he was a respected journalist, and his analysis was based on comparisons with margins in past elections.[25]

Women the country over celebrated victories for suffrage in Nevada and Montana, raising the number of states where they could vote to eleven. But suffrage lost in five other states: the two Dakotas, Nebraska, Missouri, and Ohio.

The five losses clearly demonstrated the difficulty in fighting for the ballot state by state, and gave Alice hope that the setbacks would "swing many people into the federal work."[26]

CHAPTER NINE

FIELD TRIP

The galleries were packed on January 12, 1915, for the first-ever vote on the Anthony amendment in the House of Representatives. No one expected it to pass, but everyone wanted to hear the debate. At last all sides would know where they stood. Suffragists in white with tri-colored sashes sat to the left of the Speaker's desk, filling the galleries with a wave of color. Alice had a front-row seat; Shaw and fellow members of the National sat in the private gallery of House Speaker Champ Clark. On the other side were the antis, clutching red roses, their symbol. Separating the hostile camps was a gallery occupied, a newspaper noted, by "plain American men who already have the ballot."[1]

During the six-hour debate, the Speaker was forced to gavel for silence more than once when a particularly outrageous remark, floating up from the floor, triggered a vigorous protest from the females in the galleries. Rep. Thomas Heflin, an Alabama Democrat, confessed to this concern: "Most women now control one vote. As I told a blushing suffragette the other day, if you are given the franchise you'll control two votes in every household—and that's too many."[2]

Rep. Stanley Bowdle of Ohio, an outgoing Democrat, offered another dubious tribute: "The women of this smart capital are beautiful. Their beauty is disturbing to business; their feet are beautiful; their ankles are beautiful, but here I must pause—for they are not interested in the state."[3] Beautiful but offended women responded with hisses.

The vote went against the amendment 204 to 174.

Not long after the vote, Alice decided to resign from her leadership post in the Congressional Union in order to raise money, "the part of the work that must be pushed."[4]

Alice's choice to replace her as chairman was Edith Houghton Hooker, the head of Maryland's Just Government League, which had severed ties with the National and allied with Alice. To Alice's dismay, Hooker wouldn't cooperate. "Mrs. Hooker absolutely refuses to be Chairman of the Union in spite of the most fervent appeal and argument on my part," Alice complained to Matilda Gardner. "In fact no one seems to want to undertake it, so I really do not know just what to do."[5]

So Alice did what she had wanted to do anyway. For much of 1915, she left Lucy in Washington running the Union and editing the *Suffragist*, while she took to the road to raise money.

The Union leader had grown into a world-class rainmaker. "The easiest way to collect money is to aim at a definite sum and take a very short period in which to get it," she instructed Margaret Whittemore, a Union organizer who was in charge of opening a booth to proselytize for suffrage at the 1915 Panama-Pacific International Exposition, a world's fair on 625 extravagantly landscaped acres overlooking San Francisco Bay. Continued Alice, "For instance, we had to meet a printer's bill of three hundred dollars last Monday and in a few hours we collected the whole amount by telephone."[6]

For Expo furnishings, Margaret was to "beg or borrow" whatever was needed, as Alice had done for Washington headquarters. Rather than sell literature, which would require hiring a cashier and buying a cash register, she was to give it away, then ask for donations. When Margaret wanted a telephone, Alice advised her to wait. "Once an expense is incurred," she told her, "it is next to impossible to get anyone to donate for it." Margaret was also to make a show of using the public telephone. When people saw that she was "greatly inconvenienced by the lack of a phone, it is quite likely that a great many people would be willing to give each a dollar."[7]

Elsewhere in the summer and fall of 1915, Union members across the country dutifully embarked on a campaign to confront the 531 members of Congress during an extended recess that year. For many if not most lawmakers, it was the first time they had been waylaid by suffragists on their home turf. If they were Democrats, memories of last year's hostile party-in-power campaign were as fresh as a newly laid egg, and just as raw.

Representative Carl Hayden, born in a small Arizona town that bore the family name, and just three years into a long congressional career, flatly refused to have anything to do with the Union. He labeled the 1914 anti-Democrat campaign "political treachery without parallel in the history of the suffrage movement."[8]

Republicans were not necessarily friendlier. In Connecticut, Mary Beard and her husband, Charles, led seven cars filled with women up to the door of Republican Rep. James P. Glynn. Glynn insisted that suffrage "was a state matter and the majority of women did not want it," Mary reported.[9] The state's Republican senator, Frank B. Brandegee, refused even to see them.

Overshadowing all other suffrage events that year were four important state campaigns in the Northeast. Victories in the country's two most populated states, New York and Pennsylvania, plus New Jersey and Massachusetts, would roughly triple the number of American women with the ballot.

Suffrage supporters—men and women alike—in those battleground states turned out by the thousands in an unprecedented and well-organized effort to win the vote. In a show of dedication matched only by the opposition, they swarmed over cities and small towns, knocking on doors, speaking on street corners, holding outdoor rallies and indoor meetings.[10]

In Pennsylvania, a "Women's Liberty Bell," moored to a wagon with its clapper chained, traveled from "bell meeting" to "bell meeting." When the electorate gave women the vote, the clapper would be freed to peal victory. Backyard gardens bloomed with massed blossoms in suffrage yellow. Pittsburgh suffragists held bake sales to fatten coffers.

New Jersey suffragists' hopes soared when Woodrow Wilson announced on October 6, thirteen days before the referendum, that he would vote "yes." Thomas A. Edison endorsed suffrage, pronouncing women "more moral" than men and also "more honest."[11] The state chairman, Lillian Feickert, predicted victory by at least twenty-five thousand votes.

In Boston's biggest suffrage parade to date sixteen thousand people marched on October 16. In New York, on October 23, thirty-five thousand supporters flowed like lava up Fifth Avenue.

At a Manhattan training school, a male speaking coach told novice activists that their approach was all wrong. "Too many of your speakers by voice and manner give men the impression that they are attacking them. Don't forget that we have the power to grant you the ballot and that you are asking for it."[12]

Even though four state victories could produce a more tractable Congress, the Union took no part. Alice had other priorities than misguided state campaigns, as she saw them, chiefly raising money and boosting the Union. From Wisconsin, she wrote Lucy "that most of the leading suffragists lived in small villages—a day's journey from the other suffragists. . . . I had, therefore to go to them." She collected only $200. But in a rare burst of exuberance she concluded, "I have never had a happier time or a more delightful trip than in Wisconsin."[13]

In Denver, the Union's Ella St. Clair Thompson was struggling to rebuild an organization that had fallen apart since the 1914 election. Headquarters was under the thumb of a highly partisan Progressive who entertained her friends there, "and they only chit-chat. . . . The place lacks *tone*. . . . There is absolutely *no* activity." Moreover, "The Congressional Union is hated as no other organization ever has been." With Alice's permission she moved the office to Colorado Springs, where she hoped Alice would stop on her way west, and bring Alva with her. "The people are *clamorous* for you and for Mrs. Belmont."[14]

But Alva wasn't going anywhere, not even to San Francisco in September for a convention of women voters, organized by the Union in connection with the Expo, that she was supposed to chair. Earlier that year, her society counterpart Mamie Fish had suffered a fatal stroke. Mamie was sixty-two, two years younger than Alva. "I am afraid Mrs. Fish's sudden death from over-exertion has made us women of the same age a little nervous," she wrote Lucy in June 1915. Her doctor told her it would be foolish to undertake a long journey.[15]

Alice steamed into Colorado in August, recruited six women for a state committee, and collected $124 in several hours, enough to pay an organizer for a month. She and Thompson managed to pull together a state convention out of the dregs of the 1914 organization. One hundred fifty women paraded in cars to see their congressman.

Alice moved on to Boise. Idaho's senior senator, the influential Republican William Borah, was elsewhere, but she wasn't surprised. The heat surpassed Washington at its worst, she wrote Lucy. "One has the feeling of burning sand in one's throat and eyes and nose—as though one were in a dust storm all the time. I don't wonder that Borah left the city."[16]

By September 7, Alice had reached California, where she was putting the finishing details on a scheme that would rivet the nation.

Mabel Vernon had warned Sara Bard Field about Alice. Sara lived in California and she had never met the Congressional Union leader. "She's no bigger than a wisp of hay," Mabel told Sara while they were working together during the 1914 Nevada campaign, "but she has the most deep and beautiful violet-blue eyes, and when they look at you and ask you to do something, you could no more refuse."[17]

And now, Sara was staring into those violet-blue eyes and listening to a most extraordinary request, if "request" was the word for the stunt that Alice had decided that Sara was to carry out in the name of suffrage.

Sara had been a volunteer at the Expo booth, a favorite destination for female fair-goers, who gravitated to its comfortable sofa and chairs or rendezvoused there with friends. Daily attendance averaged four hundred, and once there, many paid dues to join the Union, and many more signed a petition in favor of the federal amendment.

As mid-September approached, and the Expo neared its end, Alice envisioned a bold coast-to-coast journey. An "envoy" from the enfranchised West, a *voting* woman beating the drum for national suffrage, would pilot an automobile across desert, mountains, and prairie. Along the way, she would give speeches and interviews, curry favor with politicians, and gather more signatures. This transcontinental odyssey would arouse a tidal wave of enthusiasm for the federal amendment that would pound ashore on the steps of the U.S. Capitol precisely on December 6, 1914, the opening day of the 64th session of Congress.

At the moment there was no volunteer and no automobile, but Alice was sure that somehow they would appear. And of course, as if preordained, Maria Kindberg and Ingebord Kindstedt, two Swedish sympathizers from Rhode Island, materialized with a shiny new Overland touring car that they intended to drive from San Francisco to the East Coast. Yes, they would happily take an envoy with them.

And that envoy, Alice had decided, fastening those violet-blue eyes upon Sara, was to be a smallish, sweet-natured former preacher's wife and mother of two.

Sara was devoted to suffrage, but perhaps not *that* devoted.

Roads had scarcely improved since 1909 when Alice Huyler Ramsey and three other women drove a Maxwell "30" from New York to San Francisco, a 3,800-mile publicity stunt for the Maxwell-Briscoe Motor Company. Ramsey chronicled the trip in her journal, *Veil, Duster, and Tire Iron.* The few good roads were crushed stone bound into macadam, but more often they were dirt, even in the East. Occasional stretches of limestone provided a firm surface but raised voluminous clouds of dust. In the West, roads were sometimes no more than the faint impression of wagon wheels through thick prairie grass. Worse, they were "mere horse trails."[18] Marked by crude red, white, and blue signs stuck to telegraph poles, the Lincoln Highway was just beginning to inch across the country.

Ramsey and her companions had been trailed for much of their fifty-nine-day journey by a company team that repaired broken axles and a dozen flat tires. Sara and her two Swedish sidekicks would be on their own with a tool kit.

"But Alice, do you realize that automobiles have to be serviced?" Sara whimpered. "I hear that service stations across the country are very scarce, and you have to have a great deal of mechanical knowledge in case the car has some accident."[19]

Alice had a notably unfeminist response. "Oh, well, if that happens I'm sure some good man will come along that'll help you."[20]

Sara tried a different tack. "I'm starting a new book, Alice. I was going to stay home this fall to continue."

"But now you're doing this work."

That was Alice, Sara reminisced years later. "That was her way of answering you. The book—what was the book? There was this great work to be done."[21]

Sara might have known she would end up saying yes. "You went into her office knowing you were going to refuse what she asked and you came out having said you'd do it."[22]

Sara said she would do it.

The plan Alice had outlined called for Sara to travel with another young woman, Frances Joliffe, a society maiden turned actress turned drama critic, as well as with the Swedes. Frances had campaigned for Wilson in 1912. Since then she had become a suffrage starlet.

The trailblazing journey appealed, perhaps, to her sense of drama. While on a visit to Lawrence, Massachusetts, to cover a strike in the textile mills, Frances had been evicted from a hotel rathskeller for smoking a cigarette. She then strolled into the lobby, planted herself front and center, drew out a silver case, lit a gold-tipped cigarette, and began to blow "ringlets into the air." Unnerved, the proprietor asked her what she was doing.

"Why smoking, of course."

If she continued, she would have to leave, he told her. According to a reporter, "Miss Joliffe, in utter disgust, threw her lighted cigarette upon the floor and ground it under her dainty heel."[23]

Sara was less flamboyant, but her commitment to suffrage ran deeper. Raised in a religious household, her marriage to a Baptist minister had ended in 1914. They shared the care of their two children. While she was in Nevada awaiting her divorce, she campaigned for suffrage and met Mabel Vernon, who recruited her for the Union. Sara was self-effacing and often in poor health. But she was not easily intimidated by important men.

During the Expo, Sara confronted William Jennings Bryan, the famed Populist leader and erstwhile presidential candidate who had recently resigned as secretary of state. She invited him to speak to the Union. He replied, "I would never move one inch to speak for a body of women that had opposed the Democratic Party."[24]

House Speaker Champ Clark, a Missouri Democrat married to a suffragist, was more gracious when Sara asked for his support. But he pointed to the defeat of suffrage in his home state of Missouri as evidence the voters didn't want it.

The Panama-Pacific Exposition was particularly beautiful at night. Hundreds of searchlights played over the eleven domed "palaces" that housed the exhibitions. Strands of light filtered through graceful arches and illuminated artfully landscaped courts. Every World's Fair required an attention-getting centerpiece. At this exposition, it was a 435-foot tower encrusted with multi-colored fragments of cut glass. Illuminated from within in red, the "Tower of Jewels" shimmered in the sunlight and glittered at night as spotlights danced across its surface. The Expo not only celebrated the completion of the Panama Canal, but it also marked the rebirth of San Francisco after the devastating 1906 earthquake that set the city ablaze.

Against this dramatic backdrop, on September 16 Congressional Union members gathered onstage in their traditional colors for the closing ceremony of the Union's three-day convention. Alva Belmont had decided at the last minute to come west after all; she presided over a luncheon for 600 and donned a purple, white, and gold gown with matching jewels for a ball that drew 2,500.

A special issue of the San Francisco *Bulletin* written by Union suffragists and edited by Belmont commemorated the finale. Allowing for hyperbole, it was nevertheless a moving sight, testimony to Alice's flare for pageantry. The Palace of Education, home of the Union booth, "was softly and naturally lit except for the giant tower gate flaming aloft in the white light, focused on it as on some brilliant altar. Far below, like a brilliant flower bed, filling the terraced stage from end to end, glowed the huge chorus of women which was one of the features of the evening."[25]

The Great Demand banner hung side by side with the Stars and Stripes. Three thousand female voices lifted in song. First, the "March of the Women," a stirring anthem written for England's WSPU, and then the "Song of the Free Women," with words by Sara Field set to the strains of the Marseillaise. As the words hung in the air, Sara and Frances appeared onstage.

"We are going through the states where women are enslaved in the factories and the mills," cried Frances, "where they work long, back-aching hours, and cannot register their protest in any way. We are only two women, but we go armed with the fighting strength of four millions to do our best to help set other women free."[26]

As the lights grew faint, the Expo gates swung open to reveal the shiny new Overland car with Maria Kindberg at the wheel and Ingebord Kindstedt at her side. Sara and Frances climbed in behind the two sturdy Swedes. The large vehicle eased forward and disappeared into the darkness. With the entourage went a precious cargo: a petition measuring 18,333 feet, inscribed with half a million women's signatures.[27]

For Frances, however, there would be no passage through "states where women are enslaved," et cetera. In Sacramento she dropped out with vague references to her health. She promised to rejoin the expedition in its final weeks.

Sara was suddenly on her own with two strangers. Thankfully, Alice had tapped Mabel Vernon to precede the car by train, making arrangements for lodging, meetings, and interviews in the long string of towns and cities that linked the two coasts.

They had no map. "It hadn't occurred to Alice to start us out with a map how to get across the country," Sara said, as she recalled the trip decades later.[28] But it's questionable how much a map would have helped. In those days the traveler's bible was a set of "Blue Books" that gave mileage between towns and detailed instructions on where to turn and which fork in the road to choose. The Blue Books, however, covered only the distance between the East Coast and the Missouri River, and even then there were pitfalls. En route to Cleveland, Alice Ramsey had lost her way following a direction that said, "at 11.6 miles, yellow house and barn on rt. Turn left." She was watching the odometer carefully, but saw no such house. A woman told her she had missed the turn a mile back.

"By the green house?" Ramsey asked her.

"That's right."

"But the Blue Book says to turn by a yellow house."

The woman laughed. The owner had changed the color. "He's agin' automobiles. So he said, 'Now you watch! We'll have some fun with them automobile drivers.'"[29]

Sara knew that Lucy Burns was expecting regular dispatches for the *Suffragist*. But it was hard to compose after a taxing day bumping over a primitive road followed by a speech at an evening meeting. "If you *could* see how I write these awful scrawls, you would expect them to be awfuller and scrawlier than they are," she moaned in one missive. "We're stopping at impossible little towns now where I can't get a bath or a stamped envelope and have to write by an oil lamp which smells badly and burns worse—you know the sort where the wick gets tipsy. If you turn the thing up so you can see to write, the one side of the wick smokes the chimney. If you then turn the wick down so it won't smoke the lamp sputters and goes out."[30]

When she penned her first letter on September 28, she was in tiny Fallon, Nevada, on the edge of the desert, nine days and 380 miles into the trip. They had crossed over "meadowland, green, luxurious rolling hill country, steep mountain grades, across the walls of the Sierra and now through bare but beautiful dessert [*sic*]." In Sacramento—she did not mention Frances's defection—Rep. Charles Curry, a Republican, "declared himself wholly in favor of the Amendment." In Reno, the Nevada Civic League hosted a reception at which she and Anne Martin spoke. "The meeting which was largely attended caught the C.U. spirit."

She closed: "At noon to-day we left for the most trying and perilous part of our journey. We are traveling across some 600 miles of barren land known as the Great American Dessert [*sic*]."[31]

The women would have heard the stories. Going astray in the desert was as terrifying as being adrift in the ocean aboard a tiny sailboat. Apprehensive, the suffrage trio paid a man twenty dollars to drive them across the desolate expanse. After he lost his way, they vowed never again to depend on a male guide.

Sometimes traveling ahead, sometimes hopping into the Overland, Mabel Vernon had baggage on her hands and finances on her mind. From Colorado Springs on October 15, she wrote Alice that her bank account was $20 overdrawn and she had to draw another $80 to go on. Had the Union deposited money? She wrote that the envoy, too, was worried about funds. Sara, with two children to help support, couldn't find time to churn out the newspaper stories she planned to peddle and was threatening to abandon the trip. Mabel was "terrified."[32] How was she going to hold the team together for two more months?

She dropped Minneapolis from the itinerary, "first because of the conditions of roads and secondly because the whole party insists they must have more days of rest." Per Sara's request, she asked that someone else do the advance work in Chicago. Sara wanted Mabel at her side in the "big places."[33]

When they reached Missouri, they stepped across the invisible line from suffrage to non-suffrage states. Women allied with the National wouldn't help organize a procession. And Democratic Sen. James Reed refused to see a delegation. When Mabel threatened to hold a meeting "under his windows," he changed his mind. But what he said was useless, she reported—just "several sentences in such a low and indistinct manner" as to be inaudible. The mayor of Kansas City, Missouri, gave them a pro-forma welcome, but "rather coolly" refused to state his convictions.[34]

Evidently Mabel felt Alice didn't appreciate what she was going through. "The reason I tell you these things is because I want you to have some understanding of our little difficulties. . . . When the newspaper accounts sound . . . smooth and thrilling it all seems to have come off easily."[35]

The next day Mabel discovered the "dear Swedes" had departed for the next destination taking her only copy of the itinerary. Now she wasn't sure when she had to be in Ohio. And she couldn't stop fretting about money. It had been impossible to take up collections in Utah and Colorado. "I wish I were of a more pushing nature."[36]

Mabel shared another worry in a letter to Doris Stevens. Newspapers referred to the 18,333-foot petition with 500,000 signatures. But they had only 4,000 names in their possession. When Doris was in charge of the Expo booth, did they ever count the number?

After receiving Mabel's letter, Doris wrote Alice that she had never known where the press got the figure, but she thought "4,000 is probably much nearer the total than half a million."[37] Mabel and Sara feverishly began to collect signatures.

Mud was a constant hazard for those drivers daring—or foolish—enough to attempt the continental crossing. Lying in wait for Sara and the Swedes during a driving rain on the night of October 20 was a slimy pit as big as the Overland. They plunged in at 35 m.p.h. Every effort to climb out seemed only to sink the car farther. In Sara's version for the Portland *Oregonian*, they tore "the starry silence into bits with cries for aid."[38]

She remembered seeing a farmhouse two or three miles back. Her companions refused to leave the car, and she set out alone. Mud sucked at her shoes and tugged at her skirt. She arrived coated in brown goo and woke a farmer and his son, who obligingly hitched two heavy workhorses to a rig and extracted the Overland.

"Well, you girls have guts," the farmer told Sara when he learned of their mission.[39] It was her one small satisfaction that dreadful night.

When the threesome reached their destination hotel in Emporia, Kansas, at 2 A.M., the staff regarded the soggy Sara with distaste. She had no other clothing, having sent her bags ahead to Kansas City. After handing over her soiled garments for cleaning, she climbed into bed. Later that day the famous Emporia *Gazette* editor and wordsmith William Allen White, a pal of Teddy Roosevelt, came to interview her. Praying she was decently covered, Sara held court from her bed.

The incident might have dampened Sara's spirits less had she been able to laugh about it with her companions. But humor was not one of their attributes. Both over sixty, the Swedish women resembled each other. In Sara's words, "they were both stout and very Nordic and stolid." Maria Kindberg, who usually drove the car, was a gentle soul. But Ingebord Kindstedt, who had mastered the Overland's anatomy and performed the invaluable role of "mechanician," was, said Sara, "always very belligerent." Kindberg seemed to fear her friend. And Kindstedt was openly hostile toward Sara, accusing her of stealing the limelight at public appearances. At one point, she spat out fiercely, "I'm going to kill you before we get to the end of this journey."[40]

Alice Paul, of course, had not investigated the background of these convenient volunteers. Said Sara, "They just seemed like good solid Swedish women who were buying a car and were driving back to the East coast, and that was enough for her."[41]

It was not until after the trip that Sara learned that Kindstedt had once been confined to a mental hospital.

From Des Moines on October 29, 1915, Sara wrote Alice that she was quitting. She had deceived herself into thinking that she could be both an envoy and a newspaper correspondent. "Either one is more than enough for my unfortunately limited strength."[42]

In her resignation letter, Sara cited the Kansas mud hole, the bitter nights in the desert, the speeches, the interviews. Tiptoeing around specifics, she mentioned her adjustment to "the peculiar, the fine, natures of my two companions." All those together, "without putting one touch of my pen to paper has taken every ounce of strength I have."[43]

That wasn't all. "Our clothes have been almost ruined by storm and mud, my coat has been stolen and my heart has been so weak during the stay in high altitudes that I have had to consult a physician."[44]

She insisted she didn't want money. That "would at once rob my message and mission of its worth."[45] No, what she wanted was to turn the mission back over to Frances Joliffe when they reached Chicago. Frances had promised to join her for the end of the journey. Surely she could come a little sooner.

Alice knew from Mabel that Sara was at the breaking point. "Pay Field whatever necessary enable her continue trip to end," she wired. Alice sent a consoling wire to Sara that arrived as she was finishing her resignation letter. The envoy also heard mid-letter from Frances, who told her Chicago was impossible. Sara rallied. She concluded with a pledge to go on. "Heaven knows I will do my best to meet the needs."[46]

Then she added a friendly reproach to Alice. "You must not inspire people with such confidence in their powers as you did me!"[47]

As their fame preceded the trio, crowds and press coverage snowballed. Standing on the steps of the Chicago Art Museum before streets clogged with people on November 5, Mayor William "Big Bill" Thompson threw his bulk behind the federal amendment. "I hope it will not be long before women have full suffrage here and throughout the nation."[48]

In the pages of the *Indianapolis News,* Sara was "a little bundle of energy" and the street meeting in that city was said to be the state's largest.[49] In Detroit, a cavalcade of forty cars adorned with flags, yellow balloons, and lanterns greeted the visitors and presented them with four thousand signatures. The governor of Ohio and his wife signed the petition.

But the mayor of Cleveland withheld his signature because the petition contained the word "demand." "He tried to freeze us," wrote Mabel. Then a real freeze set in. The unheated car was encountering the first snows of the season. En route to Geneva, New York, its axle broke. The Overland people in Rochester said they could do nothing for at least a day. But the enterprising Sara telegraphed company headquarters in Toledo and a new axle arrived by train that same evening. Wrote Mabel, "If it had not been for Sara's spunkiness our car might have been held up 2 days & caused endless complications."[50]

In Albany Gov. Charles Whitman professed amazement that a woman, especially one so diminutive, had traversed the entire country. He told Sara, "I thought you would be six feet tall." But their reception was "marked by a rather stately quiet," reported Sara.[51] No crowds were on hand to greet them, and the only scheduled event was a luncheon attended by forty women.

Well might New York women have had difficulty rousing themselves for yet another suffrage demonstration. As Sara's five thousand-mile journey entered its final month, suffrage referendums were defeated in all four states by thick margins. While suffragists mourned this devastating setback, Alice had reason to celebrate. The multiple defeats immediately boosted interest in the shortcut offered by the federal amendment. Harriot Stanton Blatch decided to throw her considerable influence to the federal campaign.

The National, recognizing that state campaigns were iffy prospects at best, dropped the tortuous Shafroth amendment.

And Anna Shaw announced she would not be a candidate for reelection at the 1915 convention. A boom immediately developed for Carrie Chapman Catt, Shaw's predecessor from 1900 to 1904, who had resigned owing to her husband's illness. Another of Anthony's protégés, with a record as a deft and hardworking manager, the now widowed Catt agreed to accept the nomination. This was not good news for Alice. Catt was, if anything, even more hostile toward the Congressional Union than Shaw. It had been she who had led the National's attack against Alice at the 1913 convention.

No longer the shiny, unscarred machine that had left California ten weeks earlier, the Overland rolled into New York on November 26, 1915. The heroic vehicle cruised Fifth Avenue trailed by a hundred other cars wreathed in white and yellow chrysanthemums and flying golden balloons. A sign on the windshield announced "On to Congress." A weathered Great Demand banner stretched across its rear.

"I thought the suffragists were dead and buried," the driver of a sightseeing conveyance was overheard to remark. "And here they are again."[52]

While the Overland hopped a ferry south from New York for the final leg of its journey, Alice planned an elaborate escort to the portals of the Capitol. On December 6, two thousand women in regalia, a band, a dozen young female flag bearers, and a cavalry brigade would precede the envoys from the outskirts of Washington. Then more marchers, more cavalry, and another band bringing up the rear. A double line would ascend the Capitol steps, holding the monster petition rolled on huge spools. Announced the *Suffragist*, "As they go up the steps this will be unrolled, and displayed in its full length and glory."[53]

The petition?

The closer they got to Washington, the more Mabel worried. She had never laid eyes on the alleged three-mile document with its half million signatures. The only place it ever turned up was in newspaper stories. "Where is it?" Mabel wrote Alice on November 1. "I have about 5,000 names in my suitcase." The whole mission was in jeopardy. "What are we to present to Congress?"[54] Either Alice didn't know or she was keeping quiet.

On November 29 Sara wrote Alice from New York that the petition, such as it was, had been sent on to Washington. Certainly it was not *her* fault that it lacked heft. The envoy pointed an accusatory finger at Mabel, who "seemed to think that the petition was an unessential matter. When the press began making a great deal of it, and the necessity for presenting something voluminous to Congress appeared, we all became anxious about the petition and have tried to secure as many names as possible."[55]

Unfortunately, they had fallen far short of their goal. But it was too late now to admit it. The antis would crow, and the National would never let the Union live it down. They would have to present what signatures they had and come up with an explanation for reporters.

The petition had been lost.

Yes, sad to say, it had traveled five thousand miles from coast-to-coast only to be mislaid, reported the *Washington Post*, by "the express company which had been entrusted with the last few miles of its long journey."[56]

But *mirabile dictu!* The "women had another petition with them." "Although less pretentious," on December 6 as scheduled, the substitute was duly proffered to Rep. Mondell, sponsor of the federal amendment, on the steps of the Capitol.[57]

The *Suffragist* mentioned neither the loss nor the explanation for the loss. Indeed, in its account the petition had grown to four miles in length. But it was unrolled to display just one hundred feet of its length.

The week before the December 6 ceremony at the Capitol, the Congressional Union had moved into Cameron House, a petite yellow-brick century-old mansion on the east side of Lafayette Square. Named for the Maryland family that owned it, the Union's new home was sandwiched between the five-story all-male Cosmos Club on the north and the six-story, 1,800-seat Belasco Theater on the south. Alva Belmont had long had her eye on the property, which had once been occupied by Dolley Madison.

The move from F Street to Madison Place signaled a new status for the Union as Congress convened its winter session. "Can't you just *see* those Congressmen opening their eyes?" Dora Lewis gloated in a letter to Alice. "And I hope shaking in their shoes at such an evidence of prosperity."[58]

From Cameron's bayed entrance the White House was visible. And vice versa.

To the delight of Union members, Alva Belmont enticed the president's daughter, Margaret Wilson, to officiate at a reception following the Capitol demonstration. Surely she would not have agreed to do so without her father's approval. The guests of honor were the envoys, now including Frances Joliffe, who had surfaced at last.

But preceding the reception, and immediately after the demonstration, was a meeting with the president himself. As a raw winter wind tugged at purple and gold banners, the bands set the pace for a parade up the Avenue, with Alva and Alice in the lead.

Alas, Wilson told them when they reached the White House, it was too late to include a suffrage appeal in his annual address to Congress. His speech had already gone out to newspapers. But he pledged to maintain an "open mind" and said he would "take the greatest pleasure in conferring in a most serious way with my colleagues at the other end of the city with regard to what is the right thing to do at this time concerning this great matter."[59]

Wilson had never gone so far before. His guests took heart.

Tacie Paul with daughter Alice Paul, age six months. Courtesy of the Alice Paul Institute, Inc. (www.alicepaul.org)

Suffrage pilgrims and reporters hiking from New York to Washington, D.C., to join the 1913 parade on the day before Wilson's inauguration. Courtesy of the Historic National Woman's Party, Sewall-Belmont House and Museum, Washington, D.C.

Lead herald Inez Milholland on "Grey Dawn" in 1913 suffrage parade, followed by the "Great Demand Banner": "WE DEMAND AN AMENDMENT TO THE CONSTITUTION OF THE UNITED STATES ENFRANCHISING THE WOMEN OF THE COUNTRY." Courtesy of the Historic National Woman's Party, Sewall-Belmont House and Museum, Washington, D.C.

(left) Anna Howard Shaw, president of the National American Woman's Suffrage Association, in undated photograph. Library of Congress, Prints & Photographs Division.

(below) Crowd spills across Pennsylvania Avenue, converging on 1913 parade and blocking its way. Army cavalry finally cleared a path. Library of Congress, Prints & Photographs Division.

Crying "Arrested at the gates of Parliament—tell the king!" Emmeline Pankhurst is arrested on May 21, 1914, while attempting to deliver a petition. Copyright Museum of London.

Headquarters of Alice Paul's Congressional Committee at 1420 F Street, Washington, D.C., just up the street from Woodward & Lothrop, the popular department store. Courtesy of the Historic National Woman's Party, Sewall-Belmont House and Museum, Washington, D.C.

(left) British suffragette being force-fed through the nose in widely circulated Women's Social and Political Union poster. Library of Congress, Prints & Photographs Division.

Mabel Vernon, Alice Paul's Swarthmore schoolmate, speaking to mostly male crowd at 1916 suffrage rally in Chicago. Library of Congress, Prints & Photographs Division.

Inez Milholland Boissevain is celebrated as the National Woman's Party's first martyr. Courtesy of the Historic National Woman's Party, Sewall-Belmont House and Museum, Washington, D.C.

Ingeborg Kindstedt, at the wheel, and Marie Kindberg (standing), on 1915 cross-country drive, with envoy Sara Bard Field (left front) and Bertha Fowler, chairman of the Colorado chapter of the Congressional Union. Courtesy of the Historic National Woman's Party, Sewall-Belmont House and Museum, Washington, D.C.

Woodrow Wilson exiting White House past Congressional Union's "Silent Sentinels." Signs read, "MR. PRESIDENT, WHAT WILL YOU DO FOR WOMAN SUFFRAGE?" and "MR. PRESIDENT, HOW LONG MUST WOMEN WAIT FOR LIBERTY?" Philadelphia Jewish Archives in Urban Archives at Temple University Libraries.

Mabel Vernon surrounded by hostile mob en route to White House. Courtesy of the Historic National Woman's Party, Sewall-Belmont House and Museum, Washington, D.C.

Woman's Party members demanding that Alice Paul be treated as political prisoner during her 1917 incarceration. Lucy Burns is third from left. Courtesy of the Historic National Woman's Party, Sewall-Belmont House and Museum, Washington, D.C.

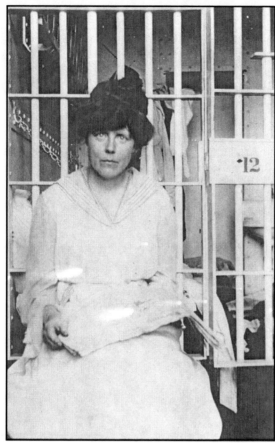

(left) Woman's Party firebrand Lucy Burns in Occoquan Workhouse, site of the "Night of Terror." Women of Protest: Photographs from the Records of the National Woman's Party, *Manuscript Division, Library of Congress, Washington, D.C.*

(below) Lucy Branham prepares to set Wilson's words afire in 1918 Lafayette Park demonstration. Women of Protest: Photographs from the Records of the National Woman's Party, *Manuscript Division, Library of Congress, Washington, D.C.*

Dora Lewis, barely able to walk after five-day hunger strike, on her release from jail in 1918. Supporting her are Clara Louise Rowe (left) and Abby Scott Baker (right). Women of Protest: Photographs from the Records of the National Woman's Party, *Manuscript Division, Library of Congress, Washington, D.C.*

Alice Paul offers toast after Tennessee becomes the thirty-sixth state to ratify the Nineteenth Amendment. Each star on banner represents a state that ratified. Courtesy of the Historic National Woman's Party, Sewall-Belmont House and Museum, Washington, D.C.

Alice Paul displays ratification banner from balcony of the National Woman's Party's Jackson Place headquarters for news photographers as fellow suffragists applaud. Library of Congress, Prints & Photographs Division.

CHAPTER TEN

MISS PAUL,
AND MR. WILSON

The suffragists' target, President Wilson, was a complex man. Scholar Arthur S. Link, who devoted a lifetime to arranging Wilson's papers and writing a five-volume biography, grew to know him as well if not better than most of his contemporaries. Surprising for an academic, Link wrote, the nation's twenty-eighth president was poorly read and had little intellectual curiosity. But he was intensely pragmatic and possessed the "ability to absorb ideas and to assimilate and synthesize them rapidly."[1]

The son of a Presbyterian minister, Wilson was endowed with spiritual resources—manifested in a strong sense of integrity, justice, and devotion to duty. His two-term administration was untouched by serious scandal.

Because he believed in predestination, Wilson could justifiably conclude that he was on earth at God's behest. He was, Link wrote, "less susceptible than other men to the force of argument. . . . Wilson's supreme judgment came out in blunt assertions of his superior wisdom and virtue."[2] The president was famously stubborn. Those who dared to disagree were not mere opponents, but enemies. He confessed to volcanic emotions that required effort to conceal. Sen. Robert Byrd, a chronicler of Senate history, reduced Wilson to seven telling adjectives: "long-faced, idealistic, self-confident, and eloquent; preachy, overbearing, and self-righteous."[3]

Raised in the South during and after the Civil War, the president was no friend of the Negro. During his Princeton tenure, the halls of ivy were closed to blacks. Too refined to stoop to the racist rhetoric of his countrymen, he nonetheless backtracked on a campaign pledge of racial "fair dealing," and allowed several cabinet appointees to introduce segregation in their departments. Screens went up to isolate black workers from white; lavatories and lunchrooms were divided by race; Negroes were forced into menial jobs. Civil service applications began to require photographs that could be used to discriminate.

Objections from individuals white and black, the nascent NAACP, and the Negro press poured into the White House. Petitions, mass meetings, and delegations protested Wilson's approval for discriminatory measures that he claimed would eliminate friction between the races and protect and advance Negroes. By 1914, these instances of overt government segregation had been rolled back.[4]

Suffragists were not so fortunate in their quest for the president's support. After three years of manufacturing excuses, Wilson had not budged from his natural bias. On the eve of the Sara Bard Field delegation, he maintained to a female friend that suffrage "will make absolutely no change in politics—it is the home that will be disastrously affected. Somebody has to make the home and who is going to do it if the women don't?"[5]

Wilson was not an unqualified misogynist. In general, he preferred the company of women to that of men, who were more likely to raise challenges. He was at his most playful in the company of his three daughters. And he craved love as much if not more than the next man. "I have never seen a man more dependent upon a woman's companionship," reflected Edward M. "Colonel" House, Wilson's close friend and unofficial adviser, in a September 1915 diary entry.[6] The president had swooned over Edith B. Galt, a wealthy jeweler's widow, whom he had met in March. She would become his second wife.

Wilson's first wife, Ellen Axson, painted dreamy Impressionist landscapes that displayed considerable talent. During their courtship she left her home in Georgia to study in New York. Wilson wrote her brooding, anxious letters. When he insisted on a June marriage, she abandoned plans for a summer of painting at the seashore. And when she mentioned the current notion "of a woman's right to live her own life," Wilson's attack on such "false talk" scorched the page. If it meant a woman living on her own, such independence was contrary to "the teachings of history, to the manifestations of Providence and to the deepest instincts of the heart."[7]

At his first teaching post, all-female Bryn Mawr College, Wilson at first perceived his students as "demure friendly damsels," who were "interesting and intelligent." By his third and final year on campus he was sick of them. He wrote a friend that they merely parroted his lectures on their exams. Their minds reflected a "painful *absenteeism.*" Teaching them history and politics was as pointless as "lecturing to stone-masons on the evolution of fashion and dress." Wilson was "hungry for a class of *men.*"[8] He jumped at the opportunity to teach at all-male Wesleyan University; it proved his stepping-stone to Princeton, another male universe.

On May 7, 1915, as his romance with Edith Galt was just budding, a German submarine torpedoed the British liner *Lusitania* fifteen miles off the coast of Ireland. Among the 1,198 victims were 128 Americans. While an angry nation waited a week for the president's official response, Wilson was distracted by his romance. He snatched time to importune Galt. Tender words fell like petals upon the page. "You may take as long as you need to accept in your heart the fact of my love, 'holding it in tender hands,' as you so sweetly phrase it, but you must accept it *as a fact.*"[9]

Writing as often as three or four times a day, he pressed his "lovely sweetheart" to marry immediately, and when she asked to wait until after the 1916 election, he pressed harder, until she agreed.

House worried that a betrothal soon after the death of Ellen Wilson would sour the president's reelection prospects. But until Wilson met Galt, he had been drowning in an ocean of loss. In the absence of a wife, said House, "his loneliness is pathetic." White House physician Cary Grayson agreed that if the never robust Wilson "does not marry and marry quickly, I believe he will go into a decline."[10] Wilson and Galt wed on December 18, 1915.

Wilson's two wives were intelligent, well-bred, adept at conversation, devoted to their marriage, and, like himself, from the South. They would no more sash up and parade for votes than smoke after-dinner cigars with the men. Summering in New Hampshire in 1914, Ellen Wilson wrote her husband that she had "just escaped" a group of suffragists, who had arrived without an appointment. "They simply *came.*" The women sent word saying it would help them greatly were she to receive them. "Doubtless it *would,*" wrote Ellen indignantly, "for it would be considered putting myself on record!"[11]

During the first two years of his presidency, from 1913 to 1915, Wilson entertained eight deputations, as they were called, of women asking for his support for the vote. To the three that visited during his first month, he had offered the same excuse. His campaign pledges came first. On November 15, 1913, with reduced tariffs to his credit and a reform of the banking system headed for passage, Wilson received the fourth deputation, seventy-three influential women from his adopted state of New Jersey. He gave them some welcome news. Just the day before he had been discussing the creation of a suffrage committee with House leaders. The Senate already had one.

Now this was more like it.

The following month, a deputation of fifty-five women fresh from the National's convention protested the president's failure to endorse suffrage in his annual message to Congress. To them, the president did not mention a suffrage committee. He had a new explanation for why his hands were tied. The Democratic Party didn't favor votes for women. As its leader, he was obliged to follow. He was not at liberty to act for himself.

Anna Shaw spoke up. "Since we are not members of any political party, who is going to speak for us—there is no one to speak for us. . . ."

"I realize that," interjected Wilson.

" . . . unless we speak for ourselves."

The president laughed. "And you do that very admirably."[12]

Deputation number six: carpet weavers and burlers, laundry workers, hosiery and lace menders, and assorted other female toilers, a total of four hundred working women whose unseen hands applied finishing touches to the fabric of America, turned up at the White House on February 2, 1914. To come, they had sacrificed wages; donations paid their way. Just twenty-five were allowed to enter.

Among those who spoke was Rose Winslow. Her health had been permanently damaged when she developed tuberculosis after working in textile mills from age eleven to nineteen. She introduced herself as "one of the thousands of women who work in the sweated trades . . . who give their lives to build up these tremendous industries in this country, and at the end of the years of work, our reward is the tuberculosis sanatorium or the street."

Her voice quavered. "I do not speak to presidents every day. It hasn't been my job, so I don't do it very gracefully." Wilson told her gently that presidents were perfectly human. Then he fell back on his now standard response. "Until the Party, as such, has considered the matter of this very supreme importance and taken its position, I am not at liberty to speak of it." The women waiting outside were invited in to shake hands with the president. Many brushed by.[13]

A few days later, in open defiance of the Democratic Party platform he had touted, Wilson called for a repeal of the free-tolls provision in the Panama Canal Act.

By the time a seventh deputation arrived in June 1914—five hundred respectable club women—these visits had become a source of amusement in Washington. Sen. John Thornton, a Louisiana Democrat, dropped a note to Wilson, wishing him a good night's sleep "in order to have steady nerves tomorrow to meet the feminine onslaught."[14]

As the club women posed ever sharper questions, the president's responses grew stiff and his jaw rigid. "I do not think it quite proper that I submit myself to cross examination," he said during one pointed exchange.

The eighth deputation, on January 6, 1915, was composed of Democratic women. The atmosphere was "far more friendly" than on more recent visits, noted the *Suffragist*, but the group fared no better.[15]

After that, women pretty much stopped counting the deputations. But they didn't stop coming. And the encounters became increasingly confrontational.

In the wake of the *Lusitania* incident, Wilson launched a preparedness campaign to ready the nation for war. On the eve of a western publicity tour, 250 suffragists showed up at his New York hotel. The president sent word he would give no interviews now or on his trip. Some women argued it was undignified to wait. "Our political position is undignified," countered one, "and that is what we should remedy."[16]

Two hours and fifteen minutes later Wilson appeared, his mood testy. After some discussion of whether they did or did not have an appointment, the president confessed that he had not honored his pledge to confer with members of Congress about the suffrage issue. He was sorry, but he had been too busy. "That has been my reason, and I think it is a sufficient reason."[17]

On the tour, the president crossed paths in Kansas with Mabel Vernon. Her request for a meeting had been turned down, but she nevertheless led seventy-five women through driving snow to the governor's mansion, where Wilson was a guest. The snow-frosted petitioners waited for an hour in near-zero weather until he stepped out onto the porch. "Where are they?" he asked softly.

They were standing on the sidewalk. Through chilled lips one member managed to stammer out a statement, then hand him a petition. "I appreciate this call very much," Wilson murmured. "I am much obliged, much obliged." As the delegation filed past, the president lifted his hat.[18]

In Washington, Alice was trying to pry the suffrage bill out of the House Judiciary Committee, a nest of hostile Democrats who hadn't forgiven her campaign against the party. Joseph Taggart of Kansas had been the target of two scrappy Congressional Union organizers from Baltimore. More than a year had passed, but now, on December 16, 1915, he would have his revenge.

Taggart lay in wait as Mabel Vernon, Sara Bard Field, and several others delivered the usual pleas for suffrage. When at last Alice rose to introduce a speaker, he lashed out. "Are you here to report progress in your effort to defeat Democratic candidates?"

Alice replied calmly, "We are here to ask this Judiciary Committee to report this bill to the House."

Had a partisan organization of men "attempted to defeat members of this committee," Taggart countered, "I do not think we would have given them a hearing. And if they had been men, they wouldn't have asked it."

"But you hear members of the Republican Party and of the Prohibition Party," Alice pointed out.

"But they aren't partisan," interjected Edwin Webb of North Carolina, prompting embarrassed laughter from partisan colleagues.

Taggart jumped back in. "You didn't defeat a single Democratic member of Congress in a suffrage state."

Paul held him in her sights. "Why, then, are you so stirred up over our campaign?"

Taggart had a final question that day: "You are organized, are you not, for the chastisement of political parties that do not do your bidding at once?"

Alice had a final answer: "We are organized to win votes for women and our method of doing this is to organize the women who have the vote to help other women to get it."[19]

But the Judiciary Committee had the last word. A majority voted to refuse consideration of any constitutional amendments until the end of 1916. Thanks to Democrats, the amendment was dead for a year, until after the next election.

Alice always knew that the Union's 1914 campaign was a trial run for 1916, when the president would face the electorate. Come fall, she would be ready with a new campaign. Until then she just needed a way to keep the issue before the public and the politicians.

On April 9, 1916, Sunday travelers encountered a bewildering crowd of women massed outside the arched entrances of Union Station. Despite an overcast sky and wintry temperatures, the women were in high spirits. Several flower-strewn cars pulled up, trailing banners of purple, white, and gold. Two dozen suffragists in traveling clothes stepped out to enthusiastic cheers.

The station manager had almost ruined the send-off, turning down Alice's request for a band and chorus. Helena Hill Weed watched the leader's face crumple like a disappointed child's. The manager relented. Now the Naval Gun Factory Band, a popular ensemble of government workers, greeted the arrivals with a brassy rendition of the Marseillaise. A chorus led a crowd of five thousand loyalists in "Onward, Christian Soldiers" and "America," anthems particularly suited to this farewell.

At 6 P.M. two bugles sounded. The sun burst through the clouds—a nice touch—and the two dozen women marched four abreast through the elegant marble cavern to their waiting train. Calls of "Godspeed" followed them.[20]

The Suffrage Special was on its way.

For six weeks twenty-three Congressional Union suffragists would tour the West on behalf of the Anthony amendment, overnighting in big cities and whistle-stopping in the little towns that chained them together. Lucy Burns was the leader of the entourage, which included some prominent names but not, alas, suffrage superstar Alva Belmont. Alva protested that she was "not strong enough or young enough to make these trips."[21]

Alva's defection was devastating news. Mabel Vernon wired Lucy, "Union's reputation irreparably injured if we fail to produce her after featuring her everywhere." Margery Ross wrote that Cheyenne women "are *pleading* for Mrs. Belmont." Unmoved, Belmont insisted she had never agreed to go. If "idle curiosity" was all that drew women to meetings, she sniffed, it wasn't "worth anything."[22]

Mabel's report was not an exaggeration. Reporter Winifred Mallon, riding along with the group and doing double duty as a publicist, told Alice that Kansas women "cursed us along the route for not bringing Mrs. Belmont. They *raged.*"[23]

In her stead, Alva proposed to pay the way of Inez Milholland, now married to a Dutch importer, the handsome and supportive Eugen Jan Boissevain. Next to Alva, Inez was the movement's biggest draw.

When Mary Beard endorsed Inez for the Suffrage Special in March, Alice had doubts. To Alice, it did not speak well that Inez had been an emissary aboard Henry Ford's 1915 "Peace Ship" to Europe, a quixotic, controversial, and ultimately unsuccessful mission that the auto magnate dreamed up to enlist neutral nations in his effort to broker an end to the war. Almost certainly, reports that Inez advocated free love and had indulged in numerous dalliances reached Alice's ears. "It seems to me," wrote Alice, "that Mrs. Boissevain (as far as her reputation goes—which might be quite unearned, for all I know) would not add to the weight of the expedition as a serious undertaking."[24]

Beard disagreed. She had seen Inez in action on a recent trip to Syracuse. "The women loved her and every man seems eager to do what she wants."[25] Persuaded, Alice made the overture. After first accepting, Inez ultimately withdrew—even with Belmont's support, she could not afford to make the trip.

By default, the daughter of Elizabeth Cady Stanton became the headliner. Harriot Stanton Blatch, "coming West in her mother's footsteps asking for help in the East, never fails to stir the people here," Lucy wrote from the Brown Palace Hotel in Denver.[26]

As the train paused in small towns, women spoke from the rear platform. A whistle-stop in an Arizona town with a water tank, a restaurant, and a picture postcard shop drew hundreds of spectators. Down a lonely stretch of track, in another Arizona town, the train pulled in at dawn. Waiting in the half-light were four women, one man, and a dog.

Eager to host these adventurous women from the East, the Sacramento Chamber of Commerce took them "autoing." Wrote Lucy, "We admired their cherries and their fig trees, and the town, and the Capitol and them, energetically all day long. . . . The people here are ruthless in their hospitality. We shall be dead before we get back."[27]

In a stunt arranged by a Seattle newspaper, Pathé Weekly filmed Lucy in cap and goggles scattering pamphlets from a hydroplane at a thousand feet. At the University of Washington 3,500 students turned out.

Caroline Katzenstein, Alice's accomplice during the 1911 Philadelphia street corner campaign, was intoxicated by the attention. "Automobiles meet us at stations, whirl us out on beautiful drives, etc., etc. It will seem queer to be a simple, ordinary individual again."[28]

Western reporters were drawn to the rolling emissaries like thirsty cattle to a watering hole. But back in the East the papers clamored in vain for news. Alice, it seemed, had made the mistake of trusting a single task—publicity—to three people. No single person was in charge. And not one of them was sending her stories.

In "deep distress," her words iced with sarcasm, she implored Lucy to intervene. Despite repeated wires, nothing had arrived from Mallon; or Abby Scott Baker, the Union's current press officer; or Katzenstein, Baker's assistant. "If Miss Mallon, Mrs. Baker, and Miss Katzenstein are all three ill, which I suppose must be the case, will you not appoint someone else to send us a daily bulletin?"[29]

Mallon, with newspaper stories to write, held Baker responsible, but promised to pitch in. Baker said it was the reporter who had fallen down on the job and called her "treacherous." The majority of the travelers sided with Baker, one of their own. Embittered, Mallon left the train earlier than planned. "After this trip is over, Mrs. Baker and I will never meet again—if I can help it."[30]

In May, the venerable wisteria that crawled across Cameron House dangled clumps of glorious blossoms in suffrage purple. But few were in headquarters to appreciate the spring show. The Suffrage Special was huffing across the Northwest, and Alice had decamped for Chicago to prepare the groundwork for a major overhaul of her movement.

As the 1916 election approached, Alice believed the time had come to launch a woman's political party. She chose Chicago, where the Republicans and Progressives would be holding their conventions. Mere suffrage organizations "have come to stand for feebleness of action and supineness of spirit," she told the Union advisory council in seeking its approval.[31] The Progressives had demonstrated the power of a third party in 1912 when they split the Republican vote and unintentionally handed the election to a Democrat. Under Alice's game plan, the nearly four million women voters in states that controlled nearly one-fourth of the Electoral College had sufficient clout to elect a president. Candidates would have to cater to their demands that *all* women be enfranchised.

The council rubber-stamped her proposal. The new party would be composed of women in the eleven voting states, plus Illinois, where women could cast ballots for president (but were still denied other voting rights). It would have a single plank: passage of the Anthony amendment.

Chicago's Blackstone Theatre held fourteen hundred people, and every seat was taken on July 5, 1916, as the Union's best speakers held forth. Inez Milholland electrified the audience when she tossed her hat on the table as if in a ring and called for "a dollar shower" to fight the Democrats. Alva Belmont pledged to raise an astonishing $500,000; Harriot Blatch promised to produce 500,000 votes.[32]

Among those who witnessed the birth of the National Woman's Party that night was the famous muckraker Ida Tarbell. A suffrage skeptic, the journalist was impressed in spite of herself. In her account for the *New York World,* she wrote that she had grown weary of the well-worn feminine scripts: "The old self-pity and talk of slavery." It was refreshing to hear women who "talk in terms of politics; work with political weapons; they know the game; they like it, and they are not afraid to play it."[33]

A cartoon in the *Chicago Tribune* depicted the new party as a winsome doe with large female eyes and a bow tied round her neck, the object of bug-eyed stares from a grinning donkey, elephant, and moose. Alice loved it. The *Suffragist* used it on its June 17 cover.

Because she was a resident of New Jersey and could not vote, Alice was not a member of the party she had just founded. Nevada's Anne Martin would serve as chairman, and Mabel Vernon as secretary. In order to qualify, Mabel moved temporarily to Nevada, the *Suffragist* reported, with her dog and a geranium. Martin put the major national parties on notice: "We do not ask you here to tell us what we can do for your Parties, but what your Parties can do for us."[34]

The Republicans and Democrats weren't willing to do much, as it turned out. Both parties passed platform planks that supported suffrage, but only through state action.

The 1916 presidential election featured two candidates who were remarkably alike. Both Woodrow Wilson and his Republican opponent, New Yorker Charles Evans Hughes, were sons of clergymen, lawyers, former college professors, and both had been progressive governors of their own states. The most obvious difference between the pair was the wiry beard that enveloped the lower third of the Republican's face. Theodore Roosevelt called him "the whiskered Wilson."[35] At the time of his nomination, Hughes was a U.S. Supreme Court justice. He left the bench with great reluctance, persuaded that the nation was seriously adrift in a bellicose world.

Because Hughes's position on suffrage was not yet on record, Alice glimpsed an opportunity to put pressure on Wilson. If Hughes were to support the federal amendment, she reasoned, Wilson might do likewise. She fired off telegrams asking her most influential members to lean on the Republican candidate. Ethel Adamson, wife of the New York City fire commissioner, tried to see him and failed; she thought it inadvisable "to camp out on his doorstep."[36] Alice felt no such compunction. She scurried up to New York and met with Hughes at least twice.

Readers of the *Suffragist* must have been startled to discover the normally composed chairman gushing like a schoolgirl. "Mr. Hughes is very quick and keen," Alice was quoted as saying, "and shows his interest with a boyish spontaneity. He was quite unlike the cold and imposing judge one expected to find. He interrupted all the time! and so did I. It was delightful." Miss Paul, the *Suffragist* said, was "charmed."[37]

Hughes came through. "My view is that the proposed amendment should be submitted and ratified, and the subject removed from political discussion."[38]

"We are so thrilled," wrote New Jersey's Alison Hopkins. "It is wonderful the weight the Woman's Party has." Wrote Mary Beard, "I really believe, if we keep our heads, we have the amendment in the hollow of our hands, now." Even pro-Wilson Carrie Catt declared herself "highly gratified" by Hughes's endorsement.[39]

Greatly encouraged, Alice wrote Dora Lewis there was "no doubt but" that they would secure the amendment. Then she crossed out "no doubt but" and substituted "a strong chance."[40]

As Alice had hoped, Wilson came under pressure to match Hughes's declaration. His back went up. From the White House came a stiff response. "The President is declared to have been irritated by statements that his indorsement [sic] of the amendment might be expected during the campaign. The President is understood never to have intended going beyond the declaration of the St. Louis platform, which was virtually drawn by himself."[41] Not only had the president not budged, but it was now official that he himself had authored the Democrats' states' rights position. So much for following the dictates of his party.

On July 4, 1916, Wilson was scheduled to speak at the dedication of a new national headquarters for the American Federation of Labor. Lucy and Alice wrangled three platform seats and summoned Mabel. The Union's leader sometimes spoke in triplets, and as Wilson launched into his address, she hissed to Mabel, "Do it now! Do it now! Do it now!"[42]

Mabel waited for the right moment. When the president asserted his support for the interests of all classes, her debate-honed voice rang out. "Mr. President, if you sincerely desire to forward the interests of all the people, why do you oppose the national enfranchisement of women?"[43]

Wilson turned toward her. He must have recognized the woman who had waylaid him in Kansas. "That is one of the things which we will have to take council over later," he replied.[44] Mabel managed to raise the question a second time before the secret service hustled her away.

Interrupting the president on a patriotic holiday smacked of Pankhurst-style militancy. Criticism rained down on Vernon. Even her mother didn't think "that was very polite." Alice was unperturbed. To one protestor, she defended Mabel's question as "an excellent thing."[45]

After her moment in the headlines—"Mabel Vernon Heckles Wilson During Speech" was typical—Alice's old chum joined the western campaign. Unlike

1914, in 1916 Alice had no trouble recruiting volunteers, many of them young and enthusiastic. By the end of August there were thirty-six, and a corps of speakers waiting in the wings for an eleventh-hour push.

The veterans knew what to expect: heat and dust, hostility and indifference, fatigue and bad food, lost baggage, mail gone astray, train wrecks. And they couldn't stay away. "Of course I will organize Kansas," declared Ella St. Clair Thompson. "*Somebody* has to do it! Might it not as well be *me?* . . . Don't mind if I seem disagreeable about the heat. It is awful—114 sometimes! But I'll work just the same."[46]

She ended up in Arizona. "If there's anything worse than Arizona, show it to me."[47]

"The fight is on and it surely is a hot one," Doris Stevens wrote cheerfully from her base in San Francisco's St. Francis Hotel. "Two floors above our room women are slaving to re-elect Wilson. Alas no-one seems to be slaving to put in Hughes! It's all very thrilling."[48]

The truth was, Hughes was turning out to be a disappointment to his female boosters. As he hopscotched across the West, appearing before crowds thick with women, he repeatedly failed to tout the federal amendment. Sounding rather like Wilson, he pointed out that his party had not endorsed it. His support was "purely a personal opinion."[49]

Alice polled her organizers on Hughes's performance. Reported Doris Stevens, in California he "made an almost universally bad impression."[50]

"If Hughes makes a few more speeches we may elect Wilson," a Democratic woman remarked within Katherine Morey's earshot. Wrote Margaret Whittemore from Oregon, "Even the strongest Republicans criticize him."[51]

Meanwhile Wilson seemed to have sprouted a halo. "Mr. Wilson is more popular than any Congressional candidates of his Party," wrote Agnes Campbell, based in Washington State. "We hear that he is a second Lincoln."[52] Progressive leaders flocked to the president's side. His support for an eight-hour day for railroad workers pleased labor. A line from the Democratic platform resonated with women. Wilson was the man who "kept us out of war." His feminist critics retorted: "He kept us out of suffrage."

Among the western organizers, only Maud Younger, a recruit from the women's trade union movement, and veteran Margery Ross, who were holding down Wyoming, seemed to be having fun.

A Californian who had come aboard during the 1915 Expo, Maud was the wealthy daughter of a well-to-do dentist and an heiress. On a trip east, she had visited New York's College Settlement in 1901, intending to stay a week; she was there five years. She would always remember a settlement party attended by teenaged factory girls too exhausted from a seventy-two-hour week to eat, let alone dance or play games. To keep his workers upright, they said, their boss spiked their drinking water with brandy. On her return to California Maud waited tables and organized a union. She became known as the "millionaire waitress."

At one county fair, competing for attention with "races, a circus show, a fortune teller, & a row of booths down the center of the street," Maud and Margaret billed themselves as the newest act in town: Maud Younger, *"who lived five years in the slums of New York, will tell the dramatic story of the Shirtwaist Makers' strike."* Margery Ross *"will tell why she left her native state to become a citizen of Wyoming."* The friendly circus manager volunteered his tent and piano, and Maud pounded out tunes under the big top, building to a patriotic crescendo with "The Star-Spangled Banner."[53]

When Maud was offered the pulpit at a Methodist church, the spunky pair scoured the Bible for passages that seemed to favor suffrage. They wrote Alice that they had found two: "Rise up ye women that are at ease," from Isaiah; "And then she shall be free," from Numbers. Elated, Margery reported, "The Church was filled and the people were delighted."[54]

Elsewhere, ill will and ill health jeopardized the campaign. In Arizona, Ella Thompson was nominally in charge of two junior organizers, Vivian Pierce and Iris Calderhead. Pierce balked at Thompson's supervision and called her "horribly incompetent." Thompson listed Pierce's faults: She debunked the Woman's Party, ran down other organizers, and criticized Hughes. The friction with Pierce prompted Thompson to consider quitting. "Her fishwife way of expressing herself is quite too much."[55]

A California organizer returned home to Texas to recuperate from illness, and another organizer left Nevada for California to check into a sanitarium. Emily Perry also fled to California after falling ill in Utah. Once there she collapsed. By the third week of September, less than a month into the fall campaign, eight women were down. "I am in despair," Alice wired Dora Lewis.[56]

And then it got worse.

One organizer after another deserted Colorado, unable to handle the altitude. When Rose Winslow descended to Arizona's more hospitable level, she landed squarely in the middle of the Thompson-Pierce feud. The latest chapter started when Rose called off two speeches in mining camps because they were advertised in circulars printed by a non-union shop. Local suffragists were irate at the cancellations; Vivian Pierce blamed Ella Thompson for the muddle. But one town *had* no printer, Thompson wailed, and the only printer in the other was non-union.

Winslow complained to Paul, who finally lost her temper and fired off a curt reply. "Why do you not remind Thompson about Union label instead of wiring me?"[57]

In late September, a half-dozen Woman's Party speakers fanned out across the prairie states for a final campaign blitz. Back in Washington, Alice struggled to coordinate their complicated train schedules. Jane Pincus in Salt Lake City was deluged with conflicting telegrams. "I feel like the inmate of an insane asylum. . . . At this moment while I am writing you I haven't the faintest idea whether Mrs. Field is coming or whether Miss Younger is coming or whether either of them are going to stay more than two days."[58]

Blatch, making her way across southwestern Wyoming, wrote that she was worn out from catching trains that left as late as midnight or as early as 4 A.M., and staying at hotels that didn't serve meals. She was "compelled to pick up what I can at Chinese restaurants." Like Belmont, she had decided that at sixty she was too old for the road. "Younger women must do that work."[59]

Fortunately, Inez was standing by.

CHAPTER ELEVEN

A MARTYR IS BORN

Inez Milholland Boissevain had agreed with reluctance to campaign against Wilson. It was, she said, tantamount to working for Hughes, who "captures my enthusiasm about as well as a feather duster."[1]

But she felt guilty for having dropped out of the Suffrage Special earlier in 1916. So, when her father offered to pay her way on the fall campaign, Inez volunteered. No speaker faced a more grueling schedule—fifty meetings in thirty days. Her tour would end on November 5, 1916, two days before the election, on the stage of Chicago's Blackstone Theatre. There, "with all possible ceremony," (said Alice) employing the newest technology, Inez would deliver a final appeal via telephone simultaneously to all twelve suffrage states.[2]

Even before leaving New York, Inez was not feeling well. Determined not to bow out, she nevertheless boarded the train to Chicago on October 4, accompanied by her sister Vida. When she arrived, her body ached, her heart was skipping beats, and she felt dizzy. A doctor recommended an immediate operation for infected tonsils. Instead, Inez asked for medication. As her itinerary took her deeper into the backcountry, she grew steadily weaker.[3]

"After each meeting she wilted and looked like a ghost," reported Vida, chronicling her sister's decline. "In Butte she looked as if she might give up. Her head was one great throb and her body was like lead." Inez could barely walk. When she tried to cancel a speech in Ogden, Paul wired that it would be a "disaster." Inez kept the date.[4]

Before audiences, she rallied heroically. In Sacramento, Vida wrote that her sister "could scarcely raise her head. . . . But when it came time for her to speak I have seldom heard her make a better one. The women were delighted & a great many promised to stand together against the Democrats." Organizer Julia Hurlburt wired from Seattle, where three thousand people turned out, "Milholland made wonderful impression everywhere and dozens of converts."[5]

Thinking it would ease the strain, Paul scheduled other speakers to appear with her. But Inez felt intimidated in their presence. She insisted on solo performances, which gave her a reputation as a prima donna. "The Lady Milholland refused to share either platform or audience with any other," griped another speaker after she was shunted aside.[6]

While Inez's tour was underway, the campaign took an ugly turn. In Chicago, a hundred members of the Woman's Party lined up on Michigan Avenue on October 20, 1916, as Wilson arrived at the Congress Hotel. The women were silent, but their banners shrieked.

PRESIDENT WILSON! WHY DO YOU SEEK VOTES FROM WOMEN WHEN YOU OPPOSE VOTES FOR WOMEN!

PRESIDENT WILSON! HOW LONG MUST WOMEN WAIT?

WHY DID PRESIDENT WILSON OPPOSE WOMAN SUFFRAGE IN CONGRESS, WHERE HE HAD GREAT POWER, AND VOTE FOR IT IN NEW JERSEY, WHERE HE KNEW IT WOULD FAIL!

A mob gathered and surged toward the women. A *Chicago Tribune* reporter watched as "the line of women sashed in the colors of the party crumpled up like a rank of paper dolls."

His story, published the next day, continued: "Michigan avenue in front of the Congress Hotel rang with screams and oaths. The 'insulting' banners bobbed for a sudden, agitated moment above the crowd like a fishing fleet hit by a squall, and then sank."

Wielding umbrellas and canes, the attackers ripped the banners and snapped the staffs, knocking down and trampling many of the women. "Those who attempted to defend their banners were beaten on the knuckles until their grip relaxed. Hats were torn off. Hair fell in cascades. Hairpins jumped like Mexican beans on the pavement. Wails rose, tears fell, waists parted, stays creaked, and women were wild in Michigan avenue."[7]

Seated in his car just a few feet away, Wilson did not react.

Though clearly ill, Inez soldiered through three packed days in San Francisco before leaving for Los Angeles at 3 A.M. on October 23. She and Vida almost missed their train because of car trouble. "Dragged *at a run*"to the train, "she lay half dead and panting," Vida reported, as she and the porter tried to revive her. Then a wreck delayed the train's departure by six hours. When at last the sisters arrived in late afternoon, they had been nineteen days on the road. A doctor was summoned to Inez's hotel room; she instructed him to "fix her up."[8] Fortified by painkillers, the pale young woman took her place for a heavily advertised appearance at 8 P.M. on the stage of Blanchard Hall, a four-story art and music emporium on Broadway across from the Los Angeles City Hall.

In the middle of an impassioned plea to Wilson, Inez suddenly crumpled, falling to the floor, as Vida put it, "like a log." She was helped off stage. Fifteen minutes later she reappeared, finished her address, answered questions, and returned to her hotel.[9]

Not even Beulah Amidon, who was with her all night, realized the severity of her collapse. "Miss Milholland was thrilling and they were thrilled," she wrote Doris Stevens. "She fainted in the midst of things, but I managed to hold the crowd, and she insisted on coming back. You can imagine how that 'got' people. We got over fifty dollars in cold cash and some very valuable enthusiasm."[10]

The gravity was also lost on Alice, who knew few of the details of Inez's condition. Although Inez's doctor wired that it was "quite impossible" for her patient to continue the tour, the Union's leader wanted her to come to Chicago for the phone call to the suffrage states, "even if she says only a word or two."[11]

Inez asked Amidon to relay to Alice "how deeply she regrets her inability to continue the work." Sympathy was not in Alice's repertoire; perhaps Inez could merely sit on the stage without speaking. Alice wired back to a Milholland caretaker, "Calamity not to have her appear only week of campaign left surely she can pull through this."[12] Though she, too, was not well, Harriot Blatch pitched in and agreed to finish Inez's schedule.

Inez was hospitalized on October 26. Tests showed she was anemic and too ill to survive an operation on her tonsils, or the removal of several infected teeth that were also poisoning her system. As her condition steadily worsened, she clung to life in a Los Angeles hospital room.

On November 7, Wilson defeated Hughes, but not by much. The electoral vote was 277 to 254; the popular vote favored Wilson, 9,126,300 to 8,546,789.[13] "Two classes of voters, and two only accomplished the result," the *New York Times* concluded: Progressives and women.[14]

Among the dozen states where the Woman's Party deployed organizers, Wilson captured ten. Only Oregon and Illinois stood for Hughes. Declared the *Times*, with evident satisfaction, "The reports from the States where women vote show that the dream of solidifying woman as a sex and swinging her vote this way and that at the order of female political leaders is shattered forever." The Woman's Party had "failed utterly."[15]

There was some consolation in the congressional election. The House Democrats, who tilted anti-suffrage, had lost their majority. Among those unseated was Joseph Taggart, Alice's nemesis on the House Judiciary Committee.

Belmont had not come close to raising the promised $500,000 for the western campaign. To keep it going, Alice had plowed in $1,500 of borrowed money.[16] Following the Chicago rally, she returned to Washington to begin erasing the party's $10,000 debt.

On November 25, 1916, in Los Angeles, California, Inez Milholland Boissevain took her final breath.

What were her last words? Anne Martin asked.[17]

Beulah Amidon wired back: "president wilson how long must this go on no liberty." Soon it became, "President Wilson, how long must women wait for liberty?"[18]

Even before her sister's death, Vida Milholland had glimpsed possibilities for the future. Writing from the hospital when there was still hope of recovery, she asked Alice, "Can't we in some way capitalize her illness and get some votes in that way? It sounds cold blooded but you understand the situation too well to think that."[19]

In life Inez had been the suffrage movement's glamour girl. In death she was its martyr.

In late November, supporters of the Congressional Union had received a request to snag invitations from friendly congressmen to the president's first speech to

Congress since his reelection. No reason was given. By December 5, ten tickets were in hand.

Although the speech would not begin until 1 P.M., the ten ticket holders, all women, arrived at the Capitol at 7 A.M. They wanted to be—*had* to be—first in line. One of them wore an oversized large brown coat and appeared to be pregnant. A solicitous guard found her a chair.

When the doors opened, the guard escorted the pregnant woman to the front row of the gallery, a balcony that overlooked the House floor. Her companions claimed seats on either side and in the row behind.

Reporters no doubt recognized at least two of the front-row spectators— Lucy Burns and Mabel Vernon. Why would they want to see the man they had failed so utterly to defeat on this particular day, when he would be at his most presidential? Alice Paul usually kept the press informed when something was up, and there had been no advance notice.

The president, dressed formally in a black coat and gray trousers, entered with his entourage. Men rose to their feet and applauded. A fervent Democrat was heard to cheer "Amen." Wilson waited for the clapping to die down, then began to speak. His usual eloquence was tempered by a lingering cold; his voice was husky and he spoke slowly.

Mabel Vernon discreetly opened her brown coat and unpinned the bulky object it concealed. She unfolded it and positioned it within reach of her companions on each side.

The president had enacted many of his first-term goals. Now he announced plans to follow through with more tariff reforms and a bill mandating an eight-hour day for railway workers. He was also proposing to extend voting rights to the territory of Puerto Rico. If Congress approved, Puerto Rican men would be voting, while most women—black, white, Puerto Rican, and every other kind— would still be disenfranchised.

"Puerto Rico" was the cue. When they heard the words, the five front-row women grabbed the object by five cords and lowered it over the gallery rail. It snapped open. Wilson looked up. He was staring at a golden banner crying out in bold black letters: "MR. PRESIDENT, WHAT WILL YOU DO FOR WOMAN SUFFRAGE?"[20]

They had struck again! With a strained smile, Wilson went back to reading his text. A page succeeded in pulling down the banner. Capitol police scrambled up into the gallery and squeezed through clogged aisles to the front row. They took up positions at each end, but did not attempt to remove the women, who sat quietly through the rest of the speech.

After the incident, a photographer captured Mabel Vernon in her roomy coat and a broad-brimmed hat, standing with her co-conspirators on the Capitol steps, a wide grin on her face. She had one regret, she told the press. The cords should have been shorter. "If it hadn't been for those long tapes, they never could have got it until the president finished his speech."[21]

Front-page stories carried headlines such as "HANG SUFFRAGE BANNER AS PRESIDENT SPEAKS" and "SUFFRAGISTS BOTHER WILSON." The Associated Press cast the incident as a turning point: a "woman suffrage coup" and "the first real show of organized militancy in the capital."[22]

On Christmas Day, the Capitol's Statuary Hall was transformed into a small cathedral, fragrant with massed laurel and pine boughs, for a memorial to Inez Milholland Boissevain. Chairs decorated with purple, white, and gold pennants were arranged in rows on the checkerboard floor of white and black marble. Statues of distinguished Americans, all males save for temperance crusader Frances Willard, ringed the circular space. Alice boasted to Elizabeth Rogers about acquiring the site. "It is the first time, as far as I know, that the Capitol has ever been given for a memorial meeting for anyone who is not a member of Congress." That alone, she thought, "ought to lift the event to national prominence."[23]

Maud Younger, she decided, would speak for the Woman's Party. Maud at first refused. "I can't," she told Alice. "I don't know how." Alice's airy reply became part of Woman's Party lore: "Just write something like Lincoln's Gettysburg address."[24]

Some had predicted that people would not come on Christmas Day. But the hall was full. Mourners heard first the pure, high voices of an approaching boys' choir, chanting the stirring words from a hymn quoted on the banner that Inez had carried in the 1911 New York suffrage parade. "Forward out of error / Leave behind the night / Forward through the darkness / Forward into light."[25]

People wept as the banner itself appeared, held aloft by a girl in white. More young girls followed, clad in purple, white and gold surplices, carrying high the tri-colored banners of the Congressional Union. They formed a circle of color around the hall as the choir stood at the front against a velvet backdrop. An organ and orchestra accompanied the singers in a musical program. Because of an acoustical quirk, voices appeared to come from above in an effect that the *Suffragist* labeled "peculiarly beautiful."[26]

Rising to the occasion, Maud spoke eloquently of her fallen sister. "She was brave and blithe beyond most leaders—blithe and valiant and unafraid to be herself, even though she knew that self, marching in advance, with eyes on tomorrow, would not be understood by the many with eyes on today."[27]

The procession re-formed and marched out, led by the choristers singing a recessional. The high boyish voices faded to a whisper, and the audience sat, lost in the splendor and in their grief. Suddenly a throaty burst of the organ rent the silence. It was a call to arms: the opening strains of the Marseillaise.[28]

CHAPTER TWELVE

SILENT SENTINELS

Wilson must have thought it quite amazing that the same women who opposed his election would ask to see him. But how could he say no to their request? They merely wanted to deliver resolutions from several memorials held in honor of Inez Milholland Boissevain, their fallen heroine.

Three days before the agreed-on date of January 9, 1917, the president received a warning from his chief clerk. It was going to be bad. The president should expect three hundred from "the militant branch of the Suffrage women."[1]

The speaker that day was Sara Bard Field, whom Wilson likely recognized as the small dynamo who had addressed him a year ago. Sara turned the full force of her conviction upon him. "We have come in the name of justice, in the name of democracy, in the name of all women who have fought and died for this cause, and in a peculiar way, with our hearts bowed in sorrow in the name of this gallant girl who died with the word 'Liberty' on her lips." Sara begged Wilson to "speak some favorable word to us."[2]

At some point in her speech, however, she made the mistake of quoting Charles Evans Hughes, Wilson's erstwhile opponent. Wilson had greeted the women sympathetically. Suddenly his mood changed. In a recap for *McCall's Magazine,* Maud Younger wrote, "The look in his eyes became so cold that, as Sara says, the words almost froze on her lips."[3]

When the president answered, the women "heard words to the effect that he could not dictate to his party." It was the same old story. Seeing their disappointment, "he grew still colder" and "abruptly left the room. . . . Where the president of the United States had been was now a closed door."[4]

Filled with indignation, the suffragists walked back to Cameron House. Over tea they discussed their options. "We had had speeches, meetings, parades, campaigns, organization," Younger wrote. Not even Inez's death had moved him. "What new method could we devise?"[5] No one felt the frustration more than Harriot Stanton Blatch. After a childhood steeped in the women's struggle, she had spent her adult years writing, organizing, and speaking for suffrage. She had known personal privations because of her sex. As a woman, she lost her American citizenship when she married an Englishman. Not until he died did she regain it.

In a private meeting with Wilson on July 24, 1916, she had tried to make the president understand. "I have worked all my life for suffrage," she told him, "and I am determined that I will never again stand up on the street corners of a great city appealing to every Tom, Dick and Harry for the right of self-government." Nothing was more humiliating than begging foreign-born male citizens, who had the vote, to give women the same right. At least, she told him, when suffragists lobbied the U.S. Congress for the federal amendment, they were dealing with men who "understand what we are talking about and can speak to us in our tongue."[6]

His own tongue loosened perhaps by her dig at immigrants, Wilson swept away months of obfuscation to tell her, in a lowered voice, that if women cast ballots, in two states "the blacks would still preponderate."[7] She realized then that this southern president would never change his convictions. But that didn't mean he couldn't be moved.

She spoke now to her suffrage sisters in Cameron House. "We can't organize bigger and more influential deputations. We can't organize bigger processions. We can't, women, do anything more in that line. We have got to take a new departure."[8]

That departure would be something never before done in America. Alice, Harriot, and others had been mapping out a bold plan. Harriot made it official:

> Won't you come and join us in standing day after day at the gates of the White House with banners asking, "What will you do, Mr. President, for one-half the people of this nation?" Stand there as sentinels—sentinels of liberty, sentinels of self-government—silent sentinels.[9]

The following morning, January 10, 1917, the *Washington Post* warned that on that very day the Congressional Union planned to post "silent sentinels" at the twin gates of the White House in a new phase they were calling "mild militancy."[10] There they would remain until Woodrow Wilson's second-term inauguration on March 4, 1917.

Shortly before 9 a.m., a dozen women spilled out of Cameron House. They wore wide-brimmed hats and heavy winter garments that stopped short of their ankles, and their torsos were bisected by purple, white and gold sashes. They carried banners that were high and unwieldy, almost as long as the women were tall, and the message was to remain visible at all times.

Mimicking a military maneuver, Alice Paul issued "General Orders No. 1," according to which she was the "Commandant" and Mabel Vernon the "Officer of the Day." Each of the two White House gates had a "Morning detail" composed of "Privates."[11] "Sergeant of the Guard" Mary Gertrude Fendall, a recent Bryn Mawr graduate, was the only picket authorized to speak to the press.

Alice snapped out orders: "Stand on either side of the two gates with your backs to the wall. If the police interfere with you, move out from the wall and step from place to place on the sidewalk in front of the gates. If the police press you further, go out to the curb and stand there. If they press you still further, move your lines into the gutter. If they won't allow you to remain there, get in parade formation and march through the grounds going from gate to gate."[12]

She took a breath and gave them their final instruction before leading them down the block past the statues of dead military heroes in Lafayette Park and across Pennsylvania Avenue.

"Don't come back here until your time is up."[13]

January 10, a Thursday, was a good day for golf in the nation's capital, with unusually balmy temperatures in the mid-fifties, and Wilson had left for his daily round by the time the women arrived. Three pickets took up positions to the left and three to the right of each of the twin iron gates. A yellow banner shouted in black letters: "MR. PRESIDENT, WHAT WILL YOU DO FOR WOMAN SUFFRAGE?" Another, Inez Milholland's final plea: "HOW LONG MUST WOMEN WAIT FOR LIBERTY?"[14] The others displayed the Congressional Union's tri-color. Visible from a block away, the bright colors flamed against a wintry backdrop of leafless dark-skinned White House trees and drew onlookers throughout the day. Six Comanche Indians from Oklahoma took in the scene, clearly mystified.

When Wilson returned at 10:40 A.M., he could not miss the audacious legends whipping in the wind. "He looked neither to the right nor the left and he didn't change expression once," Fendall announced. Edith Wilson likewise ignored the women. But the president's suffrage-friendly daughter, Margaret, waved. Passersby cheered them on, Fendall said, telling them "good work and keep it up" and "That's the way to get it." There was, she said, "no rudeness at all. Not one unkind or insulting word from anyone."[15]

Contrary to Alice's fears of official harassment, White House officials said that the women would be left alone as long as they caused no trouble. Indeed, the White House police smiled as the pickets took up their positions and joked that the next day, when the weather was expected to turn sharply colder, they would bring them hot bricks to stand on. At 1 P.M. a dozen reinforcements arrived for the next four-hour shift. Occasionally a picket left, citing tired feet, but a replacement always turned up quickly.

Thanks to Roosevelt, the first president to set aside a room for reporters, the White House now had a permanent press corps, which guaranteed that stories on the pickets would appear in every city and town across America. The day after the picketing began, Alice entered the Cameron House dining room for breakfast with a large bundle of papers tucked under her arm. The chairman could scarcely contain her delight at how well things had gone. Her face "flushed with pleasure and her eyes sparkling," Alice told Hazel Hunkins, a new recruit from Montana, that the picketing had been "peaceful, harmless and compelling." Meanwhile, "the coverage of the event in the press had been colossal."[16]

Although picketing was common in labor disputes and had been legalized by the 1914 Clayton Antitrust Act, the line of shivering, defiant women in front of the White House was unprecedented. The *Suffragist* boasted that it was "the first time in history the President of these United States is being picketed."[17] Newspapers were largely unimpressed by this historic feat, and many editorial writers were apoplectic. The *New York Times* labeled the picketing "silent, silly, and offensive." Had Socialists followed the same course, "the police would unceremoniously assemble the offenders in a patrol wagon and deposit them in a body in the District jail." But even Socialists, the *Times* was certain, would not picket in such a fashion, nor would any other organization run by men. "There is something in the masculine mind that would shrink from a thing so compounded of pettiness and monstrosity."[18]

"They savor too much of the Pankhurst hysteria and rowdyism," fumed the editorial writer for the *Lowell Sun*. "It is a pity that the suffragettes do not realize how they hurt their cause and their entire sex, but they never did and probable [*sic*] never will," said the *Fitchburg Daily Sentinel.* The "spectacle" was "a cheap and uninspiring one," declared the *Oakland Tribune*. "The real friends of suffrage must be ashamed of it."[19]

Objections poured into Cameron House, along with a flurry of resignations from members and cancellations to the *Suffragist*. When the picketing was first announced, Michigan's Marjorie Whittemore wired that she had been besieged all day by unhappy Detroit suffragists. She herself thought the picketing might well "arouse the 'mule'" in Wilson. Back in New York, advisory council member Ethel Adamson had the same worry. The president, she warned Alice, was "so adamant I believe that he can stand any amount of 'picketing.'"[20]

A New York anti-suffragist, Ruth Kimball Gardiner, suggested that any crank could stand at the White House gate "protected by suffrage colors, with a weapon concealed under suffrage banners. This is not at all a far-fetched accusation. Ten percent of our Presidents have been assassinated."[21]

When Alva Belmont sent a check for $5,000 that first week, Alice was overwhelmed. "It was indeed a joy to open your letter after all the other hostile ones that have come and find this wonderful gift."[22]

Shortly after the daily demonstrations began, Alice opened a letter from Moorestown addressed to her in familiar handwriting.

"Dear Alice," Tacie Paul wrote.

"I wish to make a protest against the methods you are adopting in annoying the President. Surely the Cong. Union will not gain converts by such undignified actions. I hope thee will call it off."[23]

The second day, January 11, the thermometer never topped 35 degrees. Stiff as icicles and just as cold, the pickets stood on wooden planks and hot bricks wrapped in newspaper, occasionally taking refuge from piercing winds behind the stone pillars that supported the gates. Tolerant policemen looked the other way at this trespass onto White House property. The sentinels took turns wearing a capacious muskrat coat that Florence Hilles, the head of the Delaware branch, had sent, along with a plum pudding "for the household." Alice thanked her with uncharacteristic fervor for the fur coat. "I don't know how we could have done without it. It is so cold today that we have all been most grateful for it." An anonymous Pennsylvania donor supplied six pairs of tights, four pairs of galoshes, and eight capes.[24]

Shifts were shortened to half an hour. On his return from golf, the president smiled broadly at the women in anticipation of the magnanimous gesture he was about to make. From within the White House emerged a messenger with an in-

vitation to warm up inside. The pickets declined. Reported the *Syracuse Herald,*
"Some of the guiding spirits in the organization felt that it was not the part of a
besieging force to be resuscitated by the besieged."[25]

A letter writer complained that their refusal was rude. Alice replied that the
point of the picketing was "to advertise the attitude of the President toward suffrage" and they would not accomplish that "by sitting within the rooms at the
White House which are open to the public."[26]

In short order, Alice's initial ebullience dimmed. She was almost alone in dealing with the backlash. Doris Stevens was recuperating in Bermuda from illness.
And Lucy Burns had announced her intention the preceding November to work
for the Union only as a volunteer. She had left for Brooklyn the day after the
Milholland memorial. Lucy was devoted to her family and returned frequently
to Brooklyn, but this time she gave no indication of when, if ever, she would return. In Lucy's absence, Alice was compelled to take on her duties as editor of
the *Suffragist.*

From New York Harriot Blatch questioned the wisdom of allowing women
from non-voting states to picket. She believed that a picket line composed only
of voters offered a more forceful statement. Mabel Vernon was on hand, loyal
Mabel, but she was consumed with recruiting and scheduling pickets. The Pennsylvania chapter was slated to send reinforcements on January 24, but didn't quite
understand the commitment. "What were the hours?" they wrote. One of their
members had a breakfast meeting in New York the following morning; "Can we
go and come in one day?"[27]

The line had an insatiable hunger for fresh bodies. Just three days after the
start, Alice wrote a Massachusetts member, "We are already worn out by the
picketing and how we shall keep it up until March 4 is a problem which we cannot face with equanimity."[28]

To lure volunteers, Alice created Pennsylvania Day, Virginia Day, Maryland
Day, and other state days, and also set aside days for doctors, nurses, lawyers,
teachers, college students, artists and musicians, and other professional women.
Cameron House staffers were expected to do a turn each day.

"Please don't think I am forgetting the pickets on Jan. 30," New Jersey chairman Alison Hopkins wrote Mabel. "Far from it! They hang over me like a black
cloud, which I am vainly trying to lift." She summed up her dilemma. "To begin
with, all our active members who have money are much opposed to the pickets; two
or three nearly resigned! The others are so poor, that the ten or twelve dollars

necessary to take the trip make it out of the question." Compounding the difficulty, the Union's convention was coming up on March 1. "Those who can afford to make the trip once want to save up to attend the convention."[29]

In the end, not only did Hopkins pull together a delegation for New Jersey Day, but she was its headliner. Just a month earlier she and her husband, J. A. H. Hopkins, a prominent Progressive and Wilson ally, had dined at the White House. The *Trenton Evening Times* took note of the irony: One month she was dining with the president, and the next "she was holding a banner, 'Mr. President, What will you do for woman suffrage?'"[30] Passing in his limousine, the president gave no sign that he recognized her.

On their assigned day, pickets from New York displayed words that Wilson couldn't fail to recognize. They were his very own, lifted from his 1913 book *The New Freedom:* "LIBERTY IS A FUNDAMENTAL DEMAND OF THE HUMAN SPIRIT; and, WE ARE INTERESTED IN THE UNITED STATES, POLITICALLY SPEAKING, IN NOTHING BUT LIBERTY."[31]

On Lincoln's birthday, the sentinels held up a banner that said, "LINCOLN STOOD FOR WOMAN SUFFRAGE SIXTY YEARS AGO—MR. PRESIDENT, YOU BLOCK THE NATIONAL SUFFRAGE AMENDMENT TODAY. WHY ARE YOU BEHIND LINCOLN?"[32]

On February 15, Susan B. Anthony's birthday, a holy day for suffragists, the women hoisted aloft her words. "WE PRESS OUR DEMAND FOR THE BALLOT AT THIS TIME IN NO NARROW, CAPTIOUS, OR SELF-SEEKING SPIRIT, BUT FROM PUREST PATRIOTISM FOR THE HIGHEST GOOD OF EVERY CITIZEN, FOR THE SAFETY OF THE REPUBLIC, AND AS A GLORIOUS EXAMPLE TO THE NATIONS OF THE EARTH."[33]

The *Washington Post*, especially, kept a cynical watch over the pickets, counting the ranks daily and rejoicing when the numbers dwindled. The newspaper was there, too, when the financially hard-pressed Union ran short of money for bills. "Militant suffragists, preoccupied with their heckling campaign, have overlooked the demands of the rent man," the *Post* crowed.[34]

Alice settled in for the long haul. She offered up an everyday analogy to explain their rationale for picketing: "If a creditor stands before a man's house all day long demanding payment of his bill, the man must either remove the creditor or pay the bill."[35] By that measure, Wilson had two options. He could remove the pickets. Or he could give them the ballot.

As the suffragists sallied forth, they often spied the distinguished men of the Cosmos Club, many of them scientists, most of them well-traveled, peering at them through the club's large windows as if they were females of an aberrant and previously unknown species of Homo sapiens. Women were so irrelevant when Cosmos was founded three decades earlier that no one thought to propose a formal ban on their presence. A tacit anti-female policy was made explicit in 1906.

The rebellious young pickets delighted in the shocked conversations they imagined to be taking place among the "wise elderly gentlemen" in their cushioned chairs, snug in the smoke-filled environs beneath the hanging heads of slain prey.[36]

"'Silly women' . . . 'unsexed' . . . 'pathological' . . . 'They must be crazy'"— and so on, Doris Stevens would write in her account of those months. "The strain on them day by day, as our beautiful banners floated gaily out from our headquarters, was, I am told, a heavy one.

"Yes, of course we enjoyed irritating them. Standing on the icy pavement on a damp, wintry day in the penetrating cold of a Washington winter, knowing that within a stone's throw of our agony there was a greater agony than ours— there was a joy in that!"[37]

The pickets were grateful to the men who tipped their hats, and the women who brought them hot bricks to stand on, thermoses of coffee, and sometimes mittens or fur pieces. One day a limousine pulled up and the woman within invited one of the freezing suffragists to warm up while she took her place on the line. An ancient Civil War veteran pressed a crumpled $2 bill into the hand of another. "I am living at the Old Soldier's Home," he said, "and I ain't got much money, but here's something for your campaign."[38]

But the initial excitement soon faded into a sense of obligation toward "an unpleasant job." The most frequent comment, Doris wrote, was "When *will* that woman come to relieve me?"[39]

Naturally people wanted to know what Carrie Chapman Catt, elected in 1915 to succeed Anna Shaw at the helm of the National, thought about the women on the picket line. Although Catt endorsed the federal amendment, she believed the surest route to passage lay in first gaining the vote in individual states, whereupon voting women would elect sufficient legislators to Congress to constitute a pro-suffrage majority—a strategy she formulated in 1916 known as her "Winning Plan." The crucial test for the plan was the New York referendum coming up in November 1917. National members were fearful that picketing would provoke a backlash among male voters. Of course Catt didn't approve. "A childish method of appeal," she said, "and will never bring a result."[40]

On January 31, 1917, the German ambassador announced that his country would resume submarine warfare in retaliation for a British blockade against Germany. Any vessel that ventured into a watery arc of several hundred miles surrounding Great Britain would henceforth be a target.

This was a direct threat to the U.S. supply ships and passenger liners that plied the Atlantic. "The United States Government tonight faces its greatest international crisis since the Lusitania was sunk," warned the *New York Times*. "The gravity of the situation cannot be exaggerated."[41]

As a consequence, Wilson announced to a somber Congress on February 4 that the United States would sever relations with Germany. War now was a foregone conclusion. On the Mexican border, the American expedition that had sought to tame Pancho Villa and his raiders packed up and began the trek home—405 officers, 12,513 men, 9,532 animals, and 405 wagons. Their commander, General John Pershing, who had begun his military career in the Indian wars, would soon be en route to France.

Carmaker Henry Ford set aside his pacifist leanings and put his automobile works at the disposal of the government. Thomas Edison celebrated his seventieth birthday with a cake glowing with seventy electric candles. Asked for a birthday message, he wrote, "I feel fine and am working hard just now for my uncle Sammy."[42]

Support for Wilson rang out from pulpits across the land. University students proclaimed themselves ready to serve. Wool manufacturers pledged their output for the military's use. The National League for Woman's Service opened headquarters in New York and announced it would emulate British women, who were driving ambulances, working in factories, and tilling farms.

Three years earlier, when Britain declared war on Germany, Emmeline Pankhurst had called an abrupt halt to the WSPU's campaign of militancy. In its place she took up a new cause, urging women to do war work. What good, she asked, was the vote if there was no country in which to exercise it? In America, the deteriorating international situation placed similar pressure on suffragists.

When Mary B. Anthony of Providence, Rhode Island, addressed a contribution to the Congressional Union on February 1, she felt impelled to add a postscript. It might be well to call off the picketing lest the president be "so irritated that he might not keep complete control of his judgment. At this terrific crisis the nation needs to have the president at his best."[43]

But Alice recalled what had happened a half century ago. "When the civil war began, Susan B. Anthony was told the same things we are being told today," Alice lectured reporters in February 1917 when they sought her reaction to the international crisis. "If she'd only drop her suffrage work and become an abolitionist, women would be given the vote as a reward as soon as the war was over. She did drop her work and as a result all legislation in which women were interested was promptly dropped."[44] After the war, supporters of the Fifteenth Amendment enfranchising black males counseled suffragists to wait their turn. This was, they said, the "Negroes' Hour." A half century later the suffragists were still waiting.

Alice would not make that mistake. The picketing would continue. To conflicted members of the Congressional Union, she wrote in the *Suffragist* of February 7 that each person was free to work for peace or join in war preparations; the Union would neither sanction nor endorse either action.

The once hotheaded suffragette who had written letters home from England brimming with emotion had matured into a pragmatic leader. Even women who angrily canceled their membership received polite notes of regret from Alice, designed to soothe their passions and leave a door open to return.

Carrie Catt, until now an ardent pacifist, reversed her stand and announced that she would ask the National's executive board to consider how their two million members might aid the country. The National's position spurred an exodus of disillusioned socialists and peace activists to the Congressional Union. Alarmed, press chairman Abby Scott Baker issued a statement that the Union was not a refuge for pacifists or any other shade of political belief.[45]

On hearing that the Rochester, New York, headquarters had become "a sort of gathering place for a following of Socialists and Pacifists," Alice issued orders to recruit new members who were uncommitted and in that way "neutralize those who are."[46]

That summer Alice decided she needed a full-time professional to manage publicity. In the past the Woman's Party had mailed its stories to individual newspapers, but these days it would be far more effective to tap into the burgeoning network of news syndicates that most papers now subscribed to.

Even with Alva Belmont's help, Alice did not have the funds to match the National, which had just come into a $1 million bequest from a wealthy suffrage sympathizer and canny businesswoman, Mrs. Frank Leslie, in January 1917. No sooner had the National harvested its financial windfall than it mounted a mighty press operation, the Leslie Bureau of Suffrage Education. Eventually the bureau would employ twenty-five people, occupy the entire fifteenth floor of a large Madison Avenue office building, and crank out news and features totaling 250,000 words a year.

Alice hired Charles Heaslip.

Either because he had until recently been a press agent for the National, or because he had recently decided to leave it, Alice thought Heaslip was just the man to sharpen the suffragists' public profile. He had contacts at the news syndicates and the knowhow to peddle stories and photos. Perhaps it was his enthusiasm for what he called the "picket stunt" that really sold her. He *was* enthusiastic about the pickets, highly so, and immediately foresaw "excellent photographic possibilities." "If it has not already been done, get six of your prettiest pickets at once together with the sign which they are holding at the White House gates."[47]

Prettiest pickets?

To his newspaper contacts Heaslip announced that he was now "taking care of the publicity for a more progressive suffrage organization—the Congressional Union."[48]

Heaslip's first assignment was to drum up coverage of the procession that would climax the picketing campaign. As in 1913, it would be timed to Wilson's inauguration. But as he unsuccessfully tried to promote stories about suffrage warriors to editors buried under war news, Heaslip's enthusiasm turned to the desperation of a car salesman stuck with last year's model.

Now based in New York, where she had many contacts, Doris Stevens was the recipient of Heaslip's "cry for help of one nerve-wracked soul to another. . . . Our demonstration on March 4th is going 'blooey' so far as the New York City publicity is concerned." The papers were jammed, he moaned, and "it is almost impossible to jimmy a suffrage story into the New York papers from this end of the line." In addition, "the stand we have taken is very unpopular with the individual newspaper men, and they are anything but eager to help us."[49]

He thought their best shot was a story on Vida Milholland, who would lead the march. She would be stepping "into the vacancy left in the front ranks by the death of her sister. That is what is technically known as 'good sob stuff,'" Heaslip said, oozing confidence, "and all the newspapers will eat it."[50]

In a pitch to the syndicates, he offered a "pretty girl" story on the attractive and competent Edith Goode, who was working non-stop to find housing for the hundreds of women coming to town for the procession. If you "wanted to boil the copy down to a caption," Heaslip told one editor to whom he sent a photo, "you might just mention that Miss Goode is Hospitality Chairman for the Congressional Union and the little lady who evolved the bright idea of converting garages into suffrage dormitories."[51]

"And for the love of mike," he begged the head of the Newspaper Enterprise Association, "please send me a proof of whatever you use. Otherwise, how do you expect me to convince my people that I am actually earning my living?"[52]

Two months after he had started the job, Heaslip resigned, doubtless under pressure. In a farewell letter, he announced that he would take on no more suffrage work, having concluded after stints with both the National and the Union that "it is almost impossible for a man to do suffrage publicity work without being in continual conflict with his co-workers."[53]

The feeling was mutual. "We are all anxious to have a woman take this place," wrote press chairman Abby Scott Baker. She offered a job as her assistant to a young New York woman.[54]

Lucy Burns was still in Brooklyn, her absence deeply felt. "When are you coming back?" Anne Martin, president of the western Woman's Party, who was handling legislative matters in Washington, wrote to the redheaded firebrand in February. "We all miss you very much and wish you would return." Alice, too, penned an awkward entreaty that month to her onetime comrade-in-arms. "Can you not come to the Washington convention? It would help so much to allay the suspicions of those who insist that we are hopelessly rent in twain because of the dissension over our 'near militant' policies."[55]

Meanwhile, Harriot Blatch, the very person who had coined the term "Silent Sentinels," was undermining the picketing campaign. She was adamant that the current international crisis required its termination. When Alice refused, she resigned. Newspapers reported that she had "taken up the work of making bandages for use in case of war."[56]

Bandages, indeed! Appearing at the Union's March convention to make a last stand, Harriot indignantly denied the bandage report. "The instant that there is a rumor of war, hosts of people who will not be called upon to shed any blood come forward and say they are going to make bandages." Her colleagues must have tittered, for she added, "To me there is something awful—I mean it seriously—in bandages. It is terrible for the women to say they are waiting for the men of their nation to bleed."[57]

The major item on the convention's agenda was an overdue merger between the National Woman's Party, composed of western voters and headed by Anne Martin, and the Congressional Union. It was a good decision: Alice Paul was in charge of both organizations, nobody could keep them straight, and they were working for the same cause. Run by Alice, the new organization would keep the name of the National Woman's Party.

Perhaps it was just as well that Inauguration Day brought a steady soaking rain and a biting wind. Had it been one of those bright, dry days in late winter, in Washington's bellicose atmosphere, the March 4 inaugural procession of the reconstituted National Woman's Party might have received less sympathetic coverage.

Unlike the 1913 suffrage parade, there were neither floats nor pageants, just long lines of bedraggled women circling the White House in wool garments that grew wetter and heavier, marching steadfastly to ever fainter music as rain clogged the bands' instruments. The *New York Times* was moved to something resembling sympathy:

> Every woman carried a banner—the insignia of a State, some printed slogan of the campaign, or the party's tricolor, purple, white, and yellow. In order to hold their banners the women had to leave their umbrellas behind and expose themselves to the rain. Less than half of them had provided themselves with waterproof coats, and many did not even have gloves. Before they had been marching half an hour most of them were soaking wet and cold. As the afternoon advanced the sting in the wind increased.[58]

(After Baker wrote a thank-you note to the *Times's* Washington bureau, she learned that the reporter's mother-in-law was a dues-paying Alice Paul supporter.[59])

Colors drained from banners and rain traveled down uplifted arms as the procession circled the White House four times, a distance of nearly four miles. Thousands of spectators huddled in doorways and under porticos and umbrellas. No drunken men or wild boys caused trouble. The *Times* reported that the police department had fielded more police than there were marchers.[60]

On February 8, Wilson's secretary Joseph Tumulty had turned down a request for a meeting, saying, "it would be literally impossible for him at such a crowded time."[61] So it was perhaps for show that a delegation approached the White House gates with the stated aim of handing Wilson a newly coined resolution. They were astonished to find every gate locked. No guard would accept their resolution, and the one who agreed to deliver their calling cards was sent back to his post and reprimanded before he could do so.

In late afternoon, the front gates swung open and the presidential limousine nosed through the procession. President and Mrs. Wilson stared fixedly ahead, Doris Stevens wrote, "as if the long line of purple, white and gold were invisible." The soggy marchers were incensed. The misery and frustration of that day ignited a "passionate resentment [that] went deeper than any reason could possibly have gone. This one single incident probably did more than any other to make women sacrifice themselves."[62]

For the first time since the picketing began on January 10, on March 5 the men of the Cosmos Club had only their morning newspapers for entertainment. No women gathered outside Cameron House for the walk to the White House. The National Woman's Party announced without explanation that picketing the president had been "temporarily abandoned."[63]

By the end of winter 1917, Americans were waiting anxiously for the "overt act" that would prompt Wilson to request a declaration of war. Noting that the Germans had sunk seventy-five vessels without notice since February 1, possibly including at least one American ship, North Dakota Sen. Porter James McCumber wondered: "Just how the German Government can do more than it has done to constitute an overt act is difficult for me to understand."[64]

As the nation waited for Wilson to act, Czar Nicholas and his wife Alexandra were forced from the Russian throne. Suffragists the world over celebrated as the new socialist government trumpeted plans for universal suffrage and British premier Lloyd George announced on March 28 that he now supported woman suffrage. Former premier Herbert Asquith, onetime enemy of Emmeline Pankhurst's WSPU, made the motion for electoral reform. He hastened to say that he was not responding to feminist pressure. Rather, the vote rewarded women for their war work and sacrifices. Because so many soldiers had lost their lives, however, only women over thirty would be allowed to cast ballots. Men who had seen active service could vote at nineteen; all others at twenty-one. Were all women to vote, they would outnumber men.

In the end, it was an almost comical misstep on Germany's part, a secret offer to Mexico, which tipped the balance of war. If Mexico would join the Central Powers when America entered the war on the Allies' side, Germany would aid her in recovering the territories of Texas, New Mexico, and Arizona lost to the United

States in 1848. Part of the deal was that Mexico would try to recruit Japan. This wasn't quite as crazy as it sounds. For years there had been reports of Mexican-Japanese conspiracies, not to mention Germans lurking around Mexican ports.

News of Germany's offer was leaked to the Associated Press. Beginning with the evening editions of February 28, every paper in America had the story. "German Plot against U.S. Revealed" screamed the *Cedar Rapid Republican.* "Germany Plotted with Mexico Against America" bannered the *Newark Advocate* (Ohio). "Plot awakens Congress" declared the *New York Times.*

It was less the belief that Mexico, a peasant nation of 15 million, constituted a dangerous threat than the duplicity of the Germans that angered Americans. Just as the British had hoped, the revelation put pressure on Wilson to break his silence.

With spring and the return of Congress, the pickets reappeared. On April 2, 1917, they marched past blooming crocuses and budding daffodils in Lafayette Park, and took up their customary positions on the White House sidewalk. Within, Wilson was putting the finishing touches on his long-awaited message to Congress, which he would deliver at 8:30 that evening.

A second contingent of women appeared at the Capitol to greet returning senators and representatives. Their banners carried a fresh message: "RUSSIA AND ENGLAND ARE ENFRANCHISING WOMEN IN WARTIME. HOW LONG MUST AMERICAN WOMEN WAIT FOR LIBERTY?"[65] The pickets had other protestors as company. In anticipation of Wilson's call for a declaration of war, peace advocates thronged the halls of the Capitol and camped out on the lawn.

By nightfall, the suffragists had left, the pacifists had been cleared away, and cavalry troops guarded the Capitol entrances. Other troops escorted Wilson to the House chamber. Addressing "an audience that cheered him as he had never been cheered in his life," Wilson was at his most eloquent. His voice was filled with sorrow that war had come to pass. He professed "sympathy and fellowship" for the German people. He spoke the never-to-be-forgotten line, "The world must be made safe for democracy."[66]

And he concluded with words that would come back to haunt him:

> It is a fearful thing to lead this great, peaceful people into war, into the most terrible and disastrous of all wars, civilization itself seeming to be in the balance.

But the right is more precious than peace, and we shall fight for the things which we have always carried nearest our hearts—for the right of those who submit to authority to have a voice in their own Governments, for the rights and liberties of small nations, for a universal dominion of right by such a concert of free peoples as shall bring peace and safety to all nations and make the world itself at last free.[67]

When British foreign secretary Arthur Balfour called at the White House later that month, the suffrage pickets held up a thicket of words:

WE SHALL FIGHT FOR THE THINGS WHICH WE HAVE AL-WAYS HELD NEAREST OUR HEARTS—FOR DEMOCRACY, FOR THE RIGHT OF THOSE WHO SUBMIT TO AUTHORITY TO HAVE A VOICE IN THEIR OWN GOVERNMENTS.

—President Wilson's War Message, 2 April 1917

CHAPTER THIRTEEN

"WOMEN ARE ALWAYS HIPPODRONING AROUND HERE"

Separated by the woman they had come to welcome, the two feuding bands of suffragists attended a breakfast in Washington on April 2. Alice sat to the left of Jeannette Rankin, the nation's first female member of Congress, and Carrie Chapman Catt to the right. Alice and Jeannette had much they could talk about. Like Alice, the congresswoman, five years her senior, had trained at the New York School of Philanthropy as a social worker, a profession she had abandoned shortly thereafter to work for suffrage. In 1914, she had captained Montana's successful campaign for the vote. Her historic post was the electorate's reward.

Rankin declared that the joint breakfast showed "that the women are standing together."[1] But the women weren't standing together. The Montana congresswoman, a committed pacifist, was under enormous pressure from members of the National to cast a vote for war; to do otherwise, they felt, would reflect badly on women and damage the suffrage cause.

As Congress debated the war resolution on April 5, Alice slipped into the Capitol to offer Rankin a contrary view. She brought along Hazel Hunkins, who had worked with Rankin in the Montana campaign. The congresswoman met them in the gallery.

Rarely did Alice allow her personal opinions to surface on any subject other than suffrage, and in her public pronouncements she had studiously avoided taking a position on the war. Alice did not dwell that evening on the Quaker belief that warfare was unjustifiable. She and Hazel merely told Rankin, as she recalled decades later, that "we thought it would be a tragedy for the first woman ever in Congress to vote for war." It was Rankin's decision to make, of course, but Alice and Hazel stressed their conviction that "women were the peace-loving half of the world and that by giving power to women we would diminish the possibilities of war."[2]

Shortly before 3 A.M. the clerk began the roll call. The "ayes" and the "noes" rang out clearly in the hushed chamber. When the clerk came to Rankin's name, there was no answer. He moved on to the next member. When he called on Rankin a second time, all eyes turned in her direction. In a strained voice, she said, "I want to stand by my country, but I cannot vote for war." Her voice dropped. "I vote no." Not everyone heard her. "Vote, vote," came their cries. Rankin repeated her "no," with what many thought was a sob.[3]

Although 50 legislators opposed the resolution, against 373 in favor, headline writers singled out the congresswoman from Montana. She was the one who had cried, who had covered her face with her hands, who had left the chamber immediately afterward to applause from pacifists in the galleries. The war was now a reality. But so, too, was the impression that women could not be relied upon when the nation was under siege.

War preparations swept the White House pickets off the news pages and out of the public eye. Still they stood. When the May skies unloosed an unseasonable fusillade of hail, and rain sheeted down, the Cameron House staff did its daily duty. Executive Secretary Virginia Arnold knew the chairman always fretted about too few bodies on the line, especially when she was away. "The Picket never faltered," Virginia wrote her boss on one such occasion. "Everybody got soaked, even thru the slicker coats. . . . You should have seen us 'ford' the regular streams that rushed down the streets. We simply waded. It really was quite funny, except for the lightening."[4]

At the opposite end of Pennsylvania Avenue, where the Sixty-Fifth Congress was in session, Maud Younger commanded a tribe of lobbyists, their feet sounding a tattoo along marble pathways as they hunted down supporters to stroke and opponents to convert.

Maud had become one of Alice's most valuable lieutenants. True, she favored capacious chiffon dresses that swallowed her five-foot-three frame and dismayed her colleagues. "I tremble at the thought of Maud," moaned Ella St. Clair Thompson, a refined Carolinian. "She wears such terrible clothes."[5] But she had speaking ability, trade union connections, and, at forty-seven, a maturity lacking in some younger members. Her gritty determination, formidable wit, and boundless energy endeared her to Alice.

In 1917, Senate Democrats outnumbered Republicans, 54 to 42, while the newly elected House was almost evenly divided, with 215 Republicans, 214 Democrats, and 6 members of minor parties. But the critical division was between the South and everybody else. When the old Congress ended, House suffrage supporters were one hundred votes short of the two-thirds majority needed to win the Anthony amendment, and the bulk of those holdouts were Democrats who railed against suffrage in Dixie drawls.

Congressmen could—and did—take cover from controversial issues by focusing on the coming cataclysm. House Democrats voted to consider only emergency war measures, as designated by the president. In such a climate, Maud wrote, suffrage had become "a bit of driftwood on a stormy sea."[6]

Maud took charge of a card file that Alice had set up to monitor each legislator. "Every fact that has any bearing on his personality, opinions and mental make up is minutely detailed," boasted the *Suffragist*, "where he was born, where he went to school, what his special studies were if he went to college, his family, his home, his church, his clubs and his lodges—no detail is overlooked that might give a lobbyist insight into how best to approach him."[7]

The file bristled with verbatim quotes from hostile southerners. "Women are always hippodroning [*sic*] around here with some kind of propaganda," George Huddleston of Alabama complained to Maud. "We are very busy. We've got important things to do. I'll talk with my constituents and not with outsiders." She added a comment: "A little man with a district mind struggling to settle international problems."[8]

John Tillman of Arkansas, Ella St. Clair Thompson reported, was "exceedingly rude; almost insulting. Said that women are a thousand years behind man." She concluded, "He is hopeless."[9]

Though friendly, Samuel Taylor, also from Arkansas, was willing to talk to a pair of female visitors about anything *but* suffrage. As the lobbyists fidgeted, "He read us a loving letter from his wife in which she said she was busy planting garden seeds, 'on account of the war.' He advised us in the most ingenuous way to do likewise and even offered us some garden seeds, so anxious was he to be thought well of in spite of his dodging suffrage."[10]

$\mathcal{A}$t the moment southern lawmakers appeared to constitute a united front against suffrage. And women couldn't win the ballot without at least some of their votes. That spring, organizers dispatched by Alice to form Woman's Party chapters burrowed into congressional districts in the South. In North Carolina, Beulah Amidon, a 1915 Barnard graduate teamed with Doris Stevens, was swept away by nature's lush display, so different from her native North Dakota. "It's peach blossom time here, and balmy summer, and it makes you feel like lying under a tree and sighing for your lover," the young woman wrote a friend.[11]

Behind the glorious flush of spring foliage, however, she discovered a human universe much less benign. "They hate us for being young, for being energetic & for being Northern & for getting publicity & for putting on street meetings & for getting headquarters. The upper crust scorns us & the rest can't do much for us. . . . The women all say 'Thank you, ma'am' every time you ask them to do anything & do nothing."[12]

When Beulah and Doris announced a conference at the end of March for prospective members, women from the National spread the word to stay away. Curiosity won out. "Three quarters of the conference came in an inquiring and often hostile frame of mind but they caught fire easily," Doris wrote Alice.[13] Among the recruits was the granddaughter of Confederate Gen. Thomas "Stonewall" Jackson.

In South Carolina the pair were as welcome as moles. One of their prospects recommended they abandon their mission, saying, "The women of S.C. neither desired nor ought to be organized," Doris reported. "I'm sorrier than ever that the South didn't secede successfully."[14]

Alone in Birmingham in April after Doris had to leave, Beulah begged for help. Alice herself came to the rescue, along with Ella St. Clair Thompson, whose North Carolina accent resonated with Alabamans. But her southern roots did not protect her from the hostility born of the 1914 and 1916 campaigns. She wrote a friend in mock despair, "Every time our opposition to the Democratic party is mentioned I have to put on the soft pedal and play Beethoven's 'Moonlight Sonata.'"[15]

By May, summer was rolling into the delta, unfurling a blanket of heat and humidity that nurtured swarms of mosquitoes, gnats, and flies. As Beulah and Ella hurried on to Mississippi, many inhabitants already were fleeing to cooler climes.

Their destination was Vicksburg, situated on a bluff above the Mississippi River. The oldest residents still remembered how in the Civil War southern troops had lost control of the mighty river to the Union, splitting the Confederacy and resulting in a humiliating surrender to Gen. Ulysses S. Grant. Not until 1945 would Vicksburg set aside its bitterness and observe Independence Day.[16]

Into this Confederate redoubt steamed Ella and Beulah, intent on birthing a state chapter of Woman's Party suffragists. It was a remarkable testament to Ella's persuasive powers that sixty "enthusiastic and sincere" people came to the conference.[17] She recruited as state chairman the daughter of a former senator, and for other offices, the wives of a prominent doctor, the commandant of the Gulf Coast Military Academy, and a noted surgeon.

She was surprised by her own success. "Apparently the war conditions are bringing the women of the south to a realization of their anomalous position in war preparation, when they are called on for all sorts of sacrifices, and can have so little to say about plans for national defense."[18]

But that success was short-lived, thanks to Carrie Chapman Catt, who was conducting a high-visibility campaign to discredit the White House pickets. On May 24, she sent newspapers an open letter addressed to Alice in which she claimed the picketing was "hurting our cause in Congress."[19] Mississippi Rep. Byron Harrison, a member of the House Rules Committee, said he would oppose a dedicated suffrage committee so long as pickets were in place.

Alice declined to answer. The letter had been intended not for her eyes but for public consumption, she told people, and Harrison had *never* been on the side of suffrage.

In Harrison's home state, however, Catt's letter hit its mark. After it ran in the Vicksburg paper, Ella's trophy officers resigned. The new chapter had lost its chairman, secretary, and treasurer.[20]

On the other side of the continent during late May and early June, Margery Ross and Margaret Whittemore, two veteran organizers, were junketing merrily up the West Coast in a beribboned vehicle they called "Susan, The Suffrage Ford," traversing three states where they were to arrange conferences like Thompson's in Mississippi. Alice had misgivings about the Ford, a loan from Margaret's parents. But Margaret insisted it would attract publicity—the magic word—and that she was handy enough to handle her own road repairs. Alice consented against her better judgment. The chairman thought train travel more efficient and economical.

Weeks passed. The pair motored north through California, then Oregon, and into Washington without managing to hold a single conference, let alone secure the first state chairman or come through with money.

Margery, so small and delicate that one reporter thought she looked "like a bit of wedgewood [*sic*] in her blue and white suit," admitted privately to Doris Stevens that she and her companion had accomplished little. Alice had been right in her misgivings about the Suffrage Ford. Unfortunately, Margery's partner was *extremely* fond of the car, "which is delightful but not altogether practical & expensive as you know." Knowing how hard Alice struggled to raise money, Margery felt guilty. She asked Stevens plaintively, "Do you think Miss Paul will be cross with me if I run away from Miss Whittemore & the car, go off to my own territory and try to find chairmen for Boise & Salt Lake?"[21]

By early summer 1917, the picketing, the organizing, and the lobbying, following so closely the exhausting 1916 electoral campaign, had taxed the resources and energy of all the officers. An epidemic of ill-temper and actual illness was claiming one victim after another.

Troubled by "criticisms of extravagance of the national headquarters" from her Philadelphia colleagues, Caroline Katzenstein felt compelled to question Alice about the daily teas at headquarters: "cakes, costing $1.40 a pound, are used as if they were the main part of a meal, etc."[22]

In the almost too cozy Cameron House, where Alice lived and worked with other party regulars, the atmosphere grew as heated as the tropical temperatures baking Washington. Legislative chairman Anne Martin and Maud Younger were barely speaking. Under Anne's interpretation of her duties, she was in charge of Maud, and that meant she was in charge of Maud's lobbying reports, which were filed weeks and sometimes months after interviews, Maud not being, as Alice had once acknowledged, the "clerical type."[23]

Alice quenched the fires as best she could—the money for the afternoon teas came from the District of Columbia chapter, not party funds, she told Katzenstein. And whatever she said to Anne Martin and Maud Younger managed to smooth their ruffled feathers.

As for the wandering West Coast waifs in the Suffrage Ford who were now, as far as she knew, in Seattle, Alice offered to send the guilt-ridden Margery Ross to Wisconsin, where the state branch had offered to pay an organizer for a month. And she told the peripatetic Margaret Whittemore, as politely as she could manage, to stay in one place until she accomplished something. Alice made a final effort to fire the Ford, adding, "I think however that this cannot be done by motor."[24]

Alice herself was irritated with organization secretary Grace Needham, whose job was to coordinate and communicate with people in the field. Many organizers preferred to deal with Grace rather than Alice. Beulah Amidon wrote the secretary, "You seem to be one person on whom we can depend, always, for advice and action and, also, one person who has time to keep track of our wanderings and supply us with the information, etc. that we so constantly need."[25]

But Alice was not about to yield authority over her organizers. She scolded Grace for not keeping her better informed about their activities. Deeply hurt, Grace wrote out her resignation a few weeks later.

Alice was a formidable presence. When Rebecca Hourwich, the daughter of middle-class Russian Jews with several years of suffrage work on her resume, reported to Woman's Party headquarters on August 1, 1917, in the hopes of landing a job, Alice looked her over and seemed to conclude "that I was just a little softy, and needed toughening up."

Rebecca's job interview took place in Alice's office, a dark room illuminated only by a small lamp. The chairman was seated at her desk. "I felt she deliberately created an atmosphere of the tough executive. There was no subtlety about her. Direct, blunt, she asked why I wanted to do this. She wanted to probe sufficiently, without wasting time, to discover if I had any weaknesses, and to what extent she and the movement could depend on me."[26]

Rebecca was hired and worked for the Woman's Party off and on from 1917 to 1927. As she grew to know Alice, she thought of her as having "all the attributes of a corporation president, and by that I mean praise, because she ran the organization with great precision, single minded devotion, pared-down economy, and with an uncanny gift of getting the most out of what she had in limited resources, human and financial, for her ever present goal."

Unlike Mabel Vernon, however, who was warm, good-humored, and always interested in the lives of her friends, Alice was "a dedicated leader to whom you couldn't possibly sit down and tell a funny story, who wouldn't enjoy just something that had no relation to her work."[27]

Only once did Rebecca remember making Alice laugh. Rebecca had returned from a fundraising expedition to a wealthy woman, a health fanatic, with nothing to show but a new cracker called a Triscuit that the woman wanted her to try. "Even Miss Paul, not always given to humor, laughed merrily when I handed her the fruits of my visit."[28]

Alice ruled not only the Woman's Party, but its headquarters. She banned smoking on the first floor, to the irritation of young rebels who equated cigarettes with sophistication. Rebecca summed up Alice years later to oral historian Amelia Fry. "I think we all felt that Miss Paul was too narrow-minded and strait-laced, but that she did have a good program and good goals, and if we worked with her . . . and for that program, we owed it that kind of faithful allegiance."[29]

She didn't dislike Alice, Rebecca said. She simply didn't *like* her.

As a carefree college girl, Alice had filled her diary with confidences and hijinks. How funny it was when the German professor commanded a student to instruct three tennis players to halt their game outside his window while his class was in session. "Only he told her in German and she didn't understand." Alice's girlish laughter almost floats off the page. Once she and a friend tied together three towels and lowered them from their dormitory window to make the girls below "think they were ghosts." And "Then we danced until the proctor stopped us."[30]

If most of her innocence had vanished, even during the suffrage battle Alice, it seemed, still danced. "I was thinking the other day of how you seemed born to dancing in those evenings around a Victrola," reminisced one of her organizers, Pennsylvania artist Kate Heffelfinger, in 1920 after a small fire in headquarters had knocked out the electricity and heat. Heffelfinger suggested that dancing "would be a corking way to keep warm in the drawing room."[31]

Alice rarely acted from impulse, but seemed always to have a plan. Her mind was as uncluttered as her room, which was "simple to austerity," a visitor from a woman's magazine would write in 1925. It was "lined with paneled cupboards, within which are laid out in orderly rows all her wearing apparel, hose, gloves, shoes and hats, each have their appointed pigeonholes, even ribbons are rolled and laid in neat little piles. Papers and books are kept in as immaculate order, her books ranged [*sic*] on classified shelves. Aside from the necessary bed and table, chairs and mirror, there are only two ornaments."[32]

Unlike many of the young Woman's Party members who formed close relationships and frolicked together on holidays, there is no record that Alice took vacations alone or with others during the suffrage years, except for occasional trips to the Home Farm.

Alice's failure to forge a link with Lucy Burns that would permanently tether the spirited redhead to the campaign is a mystery that is unresolved in Woman's Party archives, where most controversies eventually surfaced in the often gossipy correspondence. Perhaps it puzzled Alice herself. Although she always credited Lucy with hard work, many years later she would tell an interviewer that Lucy "was never quite as committed as we'd like."[33]

But at those times when the campaign was most in need, Lucy Burns rallied to Alice's side. In one bit of good news for the weary Washington troops during the difficult summer of 1917, New York activist Marion May persuaded her to return to the capital. "I have got Lucy Burns to go," Marion wrote. "Now it is up to you to get her to *stay*."[34]

CHAPTER FOURTEEN

BANNER DAYS

At 12:23 P.M. on June 20, 1917, seven minutes before a Russian diplomatic mission was scheduled to meet with Wilson, Lucy Burns and Dora Lewis stepped from the car that had delivered them to the west gate of the White House and unfurled a banner so large that it required both pairs of hands and so provocative that it would incense the nation.

The wording of the banner was inspired by a speech that U.S. Envoy Elihu Root had delivered a few days earlier in Petrograd. Calling for cooperation between Russia and America, Root cast his country as a liberty-loving democracy, where "we value freedom more than our wealth" and leaders were elected by "universal, equal, direct and secret suffrage."[1]

Cameron House buzzed. How dare Root claim "universal suffrage" or "equal suffrage" when American women couldn't vote? In fact it was Russia that had given women the vote, in one of the first reforms to follow the ousting of the czar. Root's high-flown phrases, and his status as an avowed anti-suffragist, were duly noted.

Fully ten feet wide, what would forever be known as "the Russian banner" declared:

TO THE RUSSIAN MISSION: PRESIDENT WILSON AND ENVOY ROOT ARE DECEIVING RUSSIA. THEY SAY, "WE ARE A DEMOCRACY. HELP US WIN A WORLD WAR, SO THAT DEMOCRACIES MAY SURVIVE."

WE, THE WOMEN OF AMERICA, TELL YOU THAT AMER-
ICA IS NOT A DEMOCRACY. TWENTY MILLION AMERICAN
WOMEN ARE DENIED THE RIGHT TO VOTE. PRESIDENT
WILSON IS THE CHIEF OPPONENT OF THEIR NATIONAL
ENFRANCHISEMENT.

HELP US MAKE THIS NATION REALLY FREE. TELL OUR
GOVERNMENT THAT IT MUST LIBERATE THE PEOPLE BE-
FORE IT CAN CLAIM FREE RUSSIA AS AN ALLY.[2]

To the Russians who drove quickly through the gate at 12:30 P.M., the
lengthy message was merely a blur of foreign words. But several hundred government workers on their lunch break read them and raged. "Traitors," they
yelled at Lucy and Dora. "Treason!"[3]

"Why don't you take that banner to Berlin?" a woman shouted. "You are
helping Germany," cried another. As a policeman furiously scribbled down the
words, an onlooker demanded that the police destroy the banner. The officer
protested. "Can't you wait till I finish copying this?"[4]

"Come on, boys, let's tear that thing down," a man in a large checked cap and
plaid suit called out, pushing forward. Pulling out a penknife, he slashed the offending cloth, then he and another man ripped it from the poles. While Lucy
and Dora stood with the shreds, solemn as martyrs, the police diligently collected the scattered pieces for evidence. Listening to Lucy and Dora's account afterward, Alice Paul felt a twinge of the exuberance she had experienced in the
streets of London years earlier. She wrote a New York ally, "We had a very exciting time today."[5]

"WHO wrote that Russian banner?" Ethel Adamson wanted to know. "Not
Miss Paul, was it? We fairly gasped when we read it! . . . I figured Lucy Burns
must have written it with one of her red hairs!"[6]

But the banner was a group effort. "We spent many hours on wording and
did best we could," Alice wired to a member troubled by the word "deceiving."
"We thought it was absolutely true in every word." Lucy had even consulted her
brother, a lawyer, over the language. He would have preferred "misrepresenting,"
he told her, but conceded that "deceiving" had "put the kick into the banner."[7]

The Russian banner was more than a minor escalation in a battle of words.
In openly accusing the president of deception, the Woman's Party had breached
a wall of decency. Reelected as a man of peace just a few months ago, Wilson now
deserved loyalty as the leader of a nation at war.

The reaction in the press was swift and harsh; mob action was judged under-standable and perhaps even warranted. "When the banners displayed by the women in front of the president's home assumed an aspect of unveiled treason, the mob that assailed them acted dangerously nearly within its rights," snapped the *Lincoln Daily Star.* "Every good citizen is justified in suppressing treason by force."[8]

The *New York Sun* asked, had the Woman's Party "been transformed into a Bureau of German propaganda?" Said the *Reno Evening Gazette.* "The entire country is disgusted."[9]

May's Declaration of War focused the nation as never before. Everyone wanted to help. Supplies of food to fill the stomachs of both the starving allies and the American boys heading overseas were just a planting season away. New York ar-chitects prepared to give up half their vacations to till the soil. Film and stage star Billie Burke signed up to tend strawberries, while other actresses committed to raising lettuce, turnips, carrots, cucumbers, and asparagus. Rich women offered space for vegetable gardens on their Long Island estates.

By mid-June, sixty-seven young women nicknamed "farmerettes" had com-pleted two months of training in plowing and planting. Boy Scouts picked up hoes. "Every time you put up an American flag you've got to have beans at its base," author and exemplar Daniel Carter Beard exhorted them.[10] The *Times* reported that by July 1, 12,000 teenaged boys were digging in the fields and 10,000 more were needed. Colonel Teddy Roosevelt enthusiastically called upon the nation to "farm and arm," and in addition offered to storm the continent with a volunteer regiment. Wilson turned him down.[11]

The wealthy made their sacrifices, as well. In Manhattan, the Waldorf Asto-ria's restaurant slashed its vegetable choices from forty to seventeen. Fifty wealthy New York women, including Alva Belmont, pledged that they too would curb waste, by cutting the midday meal to two courses and the evening meal to three. Prohibitionists seized on the war to protest alcohol as a wasteful consumption of grains. Edith Wilson set the tone for the nation when she and cabinet wives an-nounced they would forgo social activities to pare government expenditures.

So many women took up war work that sales of light novels plunged. Pub-lisher Henry Holt & Co. advised worried booksellers to target men with a sign that said "You read while she knits." (The husband of New York's champion Red Cross knitter did precisely that, reading aloud while his wife, her needles twirling at warp speed, produced ten sweaters in one week.) But books *about* the war were much in demand, and soldiers in the trenches were asking for detective stories and other light reading. Overall, publishers agreed happily that Americans were undergoing "a stiffening of moral fibre, a broadening of outlook, a deepening and enriching of intellectual interests that are of the greatest promise."[12]

Evangelist Billy Sunday railed against marriage "slackers" who sought brides to avoid the draft that everyone knew was coming. (Wising up, the war department announced that men who had married since the beginning of the war would be treated as single, dashing hopes for what the *New York Times* labeled "petticoat protection."[13]) Sunday told his flock of thousands to buy a Liberty Bond or never return to his rallies.

As conscientious objectors, Quakers were exempted from the draft. Far from rejoicing, they complained that they had been deprived, the *Times* said acidly, "of their much cherished privilege of suffering for their convictions."[14] So many young men were trying to convert that the Quakers agreed to reject applicants of military age.

As with all wars, this one had a dark side, with grave implications for the National Woman's Party: a deep and widespread suspicion of anything or anyone that smacked of disloyalty.

Germans were the first targets. Under a law not invoked since the 1812 conflict with England, aliens could be arrested without warrants when the country was at war. Federal agents quickly apprehended sixty alleged ringleaders "in German plots, conspiracies and machinations."[15] Public schools canceled German classes and introduced patriotic study plans endorsed by the government.

Wilson and his congressional operatives rammed through the Espionage Act, with a penalty of up to twenty years in prison for statements that might in some way impede the war, weaken loyalty in the military, or interfere with recruiting. The broad wording allowed the administration to move against anarchists Emma Goldman and her lover Alexander Berkman, already regarded as dangerous radicals. Federal agents also swooped down on the offices of the left-leaning Industrial Workers of the World, confiscated tons of documents, and took national secretary William "Big Bill" Haywood into custody along with 160 other members, claiming that the union intended to block supplies needed for war.

Those were the high-profile cases, but there were many, many others. On a single day in June 1917, the *New York Times* reported the arrest of six people in New York for distributing "treasonable literature."[16] On similar charges nine men were arrested that same day in Cincinnati, three in Kansas City, and two in Detroit.

Wilson gave free rein to Postmaster General Albert Burleson to silence anti-war publications by denying them second-class mailing privileges. Among the targets were *The Masses,* whose editor was Max Eastman, Crystal Eastman's brother. Crystal, an early ally of Alice Paul, was head of the Woman's Peace Party and a member of a pacifist coalition called the People's Council of America. Seeking to hold its annual convention in the heartland, an advance delegation from the People's Council, traveling by train, was turned away by angry citizens in town after town.

The great Progressive senator Robert La Follette, condemned for his vote against the declaration of war, rose on the Senate floor to denounce the government's actions. "Private residences are being invaded, loyal citizens of undoubted integrity and probity arrested, cross-examined, and the most sacred constitutional rights guaranteed to every American citizen are being violated."[17]

The morning after the Russian banner confrontation, pickets trotted to the White House with a duplicate; young boys quickly tore it down. Later, as a lunchtime crowd variously estimated at 1,000 to 10,000 by the overheated media gathered in anticipation of another suffrage sideshow, four pickets left Cameron House and made their way across Lafayette Square. Two positioned themselves at each gate. The infamous Russian banner was conspicuous in its absence.

At the east gate Hazel Hunkins clutched the words, "WE DEMAND DEMOCRACY AND SELF GOVERNMENT IN OUR OWN LAND." A chemistry major at Vassar with a master's degree from the University of Missouri, Hazel saw votes for women as a way to fight back against the discrimination she had experienced first-hand. When in 1916 she sought a post at her hometown high school, the principal informed her that the school board wanted a man to teach chemistry and physics. She applied to commercial laboratories around the country, but the answer was always the same. "We do not employ women."[18]

At her side at the east gate, holding one of the party's tri-colors, stood Catherine Heacox, the wife of an army officer. Suddenly a redheaded woman in a white dress and a black straw hat darted out of the crowd and turned to the men behind her. "I'll spit on those banners if you men will follow me," she cried, whereupon she sent saliva flying at Hazel's banner.[19] After an angry exchange with Catherine, the redheaded stranger snatched the suffragist's tri-color, threw it to the ground, and trampled it. Shrieking, according to some accounts, "You're a dirty yellow traitor," she spun toward Hazel, who climbed a pedestal and tried to toss her banner over the gate onto the White House lawn.[20]

The woman caught Hazel around the waist, grabbed the banner, and wrestled her to the sidewalk. As Alice had counseled, Hazel countered her instincts to fight back, but rather, as she wrote her mother afterward, decided to be "a non-resistant pacifist and not an offender in any way."[21]

Her hair loose, her clothing disheveled, the attacker emerged victorious with the banner. She ripped it apart to approving shouts and, according to the *Iowa City Citizen*, threw it to "the howling crowd." Identifying herself to reporters as Mrs. Dee W. Richardson from Missouri, the redhead declared, "These women are a bunch of traitors. I'll tear down every flag they put up."[22]

By now the crowd was with her. Richardson sped toward the two pickets at the west gate. She and others reduced their banners to kindling wood and tatters. Arrested, taken to the station house, and released, Richardson showed the press sandy-colored strands of suffragist hair yanked from Hazel's head and also a photo of her own son in a soldier's uniform.

Afterward, Hazel replayed the scene repeatedly. Never before had she "seen such venom," she wrote her mother. "I never felt so helpless in my life." She remembered, of all things, that the woman's shoes were run over—"her heels leaned in"—that she had red hair, of course, and a "hair lip" [*sic*]."[23]

That afternoon, a squad of uniformed police and plainclothesmen were waiting outside Cameron House when Lucy Burns and Katherine Morey left headquarters with another Russian banner, intending to pose for a photograph. Police ordered them back inside. When the pair protested, the officers stripped the banner from the pole. Trophy hunters pounced. A detective emerged from the scrum with his straw hat badly battered and his clothing somewhat the worse for wear, but under one arm he carried most of the offending banner.[24]

Why had no pickets been arrested? It was widely reported that Wilson opposed arrests because the women sought to become martyrs. But official forbearance did not last long.

Richard Sylvester, the former police superintendent, had retired two years after the parade debacle and moved to Wilmington as head of security for E.I. du Pont de Nemours & Co. Raymond Pullman, Sylvester's replacement, was the city's youngest police chief, just thirty-two, and a Washington correspondent for the *Detroit News* when he accepted the job. Early in his term he had spoken in favor of woman suffrage at a Congressional Union meeting. Now his goodwill would be tested. On the evening of June 21, after the Dee Richardson attack, Pullman appeared in person and ordered Alice Paul to withdraw the pickets. She refused.

Advancing on the White House the next day, Lucy Burns and Katherine Morey lifted heavenward these words: "WE WILL FIGHT FOR THE THINGS WE HAVE ALWAYS HELD NEAREST OUR HEARTS, FOR DEMOCRACY, FOR THE RIGHT OF THOSE WHO SUBMIT TO AUTHORITY TO HAVE A VOICE IN THEIR OWN GOVERNMENTS."[25] The women could have been displaying a harmless Mother Goose rhyme. The police had orders to bring them in under any circumstances. But on what grounds? The high-flown words were the president's. And peaceful picketing was a right guaranteed by the Clayton Act.

At the station house, wrote Doris Stevens, "The doors opened and closed mysteriously. Officials and sub officials passed hurriedly to and fro. Whispered conversations were heard. The book on rules and regulations was hopefully found. Hours passed." Finally the two prisoners were told that they had "obstructed the traffic" on Pennsylvania Avenue. They were dismissed on their own recognizance and never stood trial.[26]

In Hazel Hunkins's hometown, the local paper headlined the episode, "Billings Girl Star Performer in Suffrage Demonstration at Main Gate of the White House." Hazel learned that the Federated Women Clubs in Billings had written her mother "denouncing the part I had taken in these 'disgraceful proceedings.'"[27]

The young Montana suffragist was furious. "I can imagine you walking up town and feeling that every eye is on you as the mother of a notorious character," Hazel wrote "Dear Little Mother of Mine." Feeling guilty, she made a half-hearted offer to be "from now on and forever a school teacher in the Billings High School; or if you want me to come home and marry some dub for money or so that I won't be an old maid—if any of those things would ensure you of happiness and nothing else would, why I would do it."[28]

She didn't really mean it, of course. Hazel had been deeply unhappy in Billings. In suffrage, she had found a calling. Hazel leveled with her mother: "I am in some what [sic] the same position as a soldier in the trenches who has the choice of going back or of going on—and he chooses to go on."[29]

A letter from a suitor named "Jack," one of those "dubs" perhaps, castigated Hazel for ruining her "chances for every opportunity that will come to you . . . when your name is being heralded so unpleasantly all over the U.S." For his part, "I simply want to wilt up and die before you plunge into any more horrible notoriety."[30]

But Socialist siblings Crystal and Max Eastman cabled their "endless admiration" for the banner bearers. And a group called the "Mothers' Anti High

Price League" wanted one of the women who had held the banner to speak at a rally, or, failing that, the loan of the banner, or, failing that, one just like it.[31]

The incendiary Russian banner was quickly weeding out the faint of heart. Two members of the advisory council resigned. In New York, city chairman Alice Carpenter asked to have her name removed from the party's stationery, then quit altogether.[32] Ethel Adamson, who had never liked Carpenter, thought the loss of wavering members was a "healthy pruning."[33] The controversy made raising money even more difficult. "If you go to pieces through lack of financial support, so much the better for you," wrote Abby Roberts of Marquette, Michigan.[34] In Georgia, a new state chairman reported that she had been hanging on, "hoping little by little to win some of these women over. . . . I am afraid this little plan has been knocked in the head for some time to come, and I can only make enemies by persisting now."[35]

Anna Howard Shaw called the picketing "the greatest obstacle now existing" to the federal amendment; Catt labeled it "unwise, unpatriotic and unprofitable to the cause of suffrage."[36] If it kept up, Catt argued, the House would never create a woman suffrage committee; the Senate would never receive a favorable report.

Dismayed by the publicity for their rival, the National conspired with George Creel, the head of the Committee on Public Information, Wilson's new censorship office, to keep the pickets out of the news. Creel not only arranged for National lobbyists to make their case to leading news agencies and newspapers, but he also circulated a statement from the National deploring "the tactics of the isolated handful of suffragists" and urged press and public alike to ignore them.[37]

Wilson chimed in, agreeing "that nothing that they do should be featured or put on the front page but that a bare colorless chronicle of what they do should be all that was printed. That constitutes part of the news but it need not be made interesting reading."[38]

A reporter approached Jeannette Rankin, the newly minted Montana congresswoman, with a question. "How do you stand on the banner question?"

Her reply: "Deaf and dumb."[39]

In the beginning it seemed like a lark. Everyone got arrested; no one went to jail; everyone came back with stories.

On June 23, 1917, a policewoman arrested Dora Lewis and Gladys Greiner, who were carrying the old tried-and-true banners. She commandeered a passing car and ordered them in. The vehicle was so crowded that the elderly Lewis rode in the matron's lap.

When, that same day, police arrested Mabel Vernon and Virginia Arnold at the Capitol and demanded their Russian banner, the pair protested that it was private property and had cost $20. The police took it anyway.

The following Monday, Mabel led eight women from headquarters with rolled banners tucked under their arms. By the time they reached Pennsylvania Avenue, police were flanking both sides of the procession and two hundred people trailed in its wake. At the White House the women abruptly turned away and walked west, then turned again and circled back over their route, keeping their banners rolled during the entire roundabout walk. Throughout the day others streamed from Cameron House, taunting the police with the same maneuver.

At 4:30 P.M. that same day, when the sidewalks filled with homeward-bound government workers, some twenty women marched briskly to the White House and occupied the space between the two gates. Like the finale in a chorus line, they suddenly unfurled their banners. Police rushed the line. The demonstrators scattered like pigeons. The men in uniform collared a dozen; the rest escaped.

The next day, nine more pickets were arrested, some for the second and third time, and a Georgia congressman introduced a bill that would prohibit picketing at all government buildings and adjacent streets.

The first trial opened on June 27. Mabel Vernon, Virginia Arnold, Anne Arneil, Katherine Morey, Mabel Dock, and Maud Jamieson were charged with violating section five of the District's Peace and Order Act, which made it a crime "to congregate and assemble in any street, avenue, alley, road or highway, or in or around any public building or enclosure or any park or residence, or at the entrance of any private building or enclosure, and engage in loud and boisterous talking or other disorderly conduct, or to insult or make rude or obscene gestures or comments or observations on persons passing, or in their hearing, or to crowd, obstruct or incommode the free use of any such street."[40]

The three-hour proceeding featured a technical discussion of just how much space the protestors had occupied and how close to the White House palings they had stood. The defendants produced photographs that showed the sidewalk empty of pedestrians at the time of the arrest. No matter. There had at one point been a crowd. Therefore, said Police Court Judge Alexander R. Mullowney, "you must realize that your being there was the proximate cause of this idle curious crowd. . . . It is a principle of law that if you are the proximate cause you take the consequences."[41]

The prisoners were convicted and sentenced to either a $25 fine or a three-day jail term. All chose jail. A Black Maria swept them away to the Washington Asylum and Jail, known simply as "District Jail." The *New York Times*, mindful of the martyrdom British suffragists had achieved with hunger strikes, rejoiced at the short sentence. "Militants Get 3 Days; Lack Time To Starve."[42]

The jail, according to a United Press dispatch, was "a gloomy old-fashioned prison at the end of a marsh and overlooking a branch of the Potomac, about three miles due east of the Capitol building."[43]

The *Washington Post* painted a rosier picture. "The berths and corridors are clean, the walls are white and in the corridor windows overlooked a green courtyard, where potted geraniums bloom, and the Eastern Branch of the Potomac." Breakfast, the *Post* said, was to consist of rice, molasses, bread, and coffee, and for supper, beef stew.[44] The *New York Times* reported that the prisoners occupied six of the best cells, each with running water and bath facilities.[45]

Upon their arrival on June 27, Mabel Vernon had spied a small organ. With the warden's permission, as her fellow protestors gathered round, she pounded out the mournful strains of "God Be With You Till We Meet Again." Huddled on a stairway beyond a barred partition, thirty other inmates, mostly Negroes, joined in. After more hymns, Mabel launched into a suffrage speech that prompted one to pipe up, "Well, I tell you, when we gits the vote, we will make the men suffer."[46]

Headquarters had provided the suffrage pickets with nightgowns, towels, toiletries, and snacks. Virginia Arnold's only complaint was the bed. "To make one's bones (never minded being thin before) and the hills and gulleys [*sic*] of a jail bed agree with one another friendly like takes real mental concentration." Her heart went out to some of the prisoners she met. One was an apparently wellborn drug addict who seemed barely sane. "I judge she has had trouble peculiar to unfortunate women oppressed by unprincipled men."[47]

In all, the pickets spent less than forty-eight hours behind bars before they "tripped down the steps of the prison and into taxicabs" under the gaze of motion picture cameras.[48] Back at headquarters they were greeted by some sixty Woman's Party members and ushered into the walled garden of Cameron House, where breakfast was waiting. Surrounded by banners, they feasted on raspberries and cream, bacon, creamed eggs, hot rolls, and coffee. Their voices lifted in the "Women's Marseillaise," with words tailored to the suffrage cause. The version sung by British suffragettes hailed *"Our comrades, greatly daring, through prison bars have led the way."*[49]

To the extent that authorities intended to discourage future picketing, they had failed. On hand in a headquarters storeroom, according to the *New York Times*, were "more than 1,000 purple, yellow, and white banners, a great pile of poles, yards of muslin, and cans of paint—the materials for future demonstrations."[50]

As June drew to an end, the first American soldiers reached Europe. Marking their arrival, reported the *New York Times*, "All France celebrated the Fourth of July." Crowds cheered as an American military band played the Marseillaise and a French band, "The Star-Spangled Banner." Shouts rang out: "Vive les Americans! Vive Pershing."

The scene in front of the White House on July 4, 1917, was less festive though also dramatic. While Wilson was yachting on the Potomac, the *Times* reported that "A suffrage demonstration by members of the Woman's Party . . . resulted in a comedy riot, eighteen arrests and much amusement for a holiday crowd." Lucy Burns, in the front ranks with Vida Milholland, fought back when a policeman grabbed her banner and "triumphantly wrenched the pole from his hands."[51] In a nod to the holiday, one banner carried a quote from the Declaration of Independence: Governments derive their "just powers from the consent of the governed."

In Washington on Independence Day the strains of the Marseillaise resounded as well, sung by women as they were carted off to jail.

CHAPTER 15

PARDON TO PRISON

Sixty days in the workhouse!

The sixteen defendants were stunned. Previous jail terms had been for only three days, and the July 14 picketing that had led to this harsh sentence was so very tame that reporters, who now measured success or failure by the outrage of spectators, pronounced it a flop. It had taken place on a Saturday, Bastille Day, and perhaps because the sightseers strolling past the White House in the fierce summer heat did not include ultra-patriotic government workers, or perhaps because a sign the women carried, "LIBERTY, EQUALITY, FRATERNITY"— the motto of the French Revolution—was more vague than provocative, there had been no disorder, nothing approaching the arrests of thirteen women in a near riot just ten days earlier, on the Fourth of July. *That* was the sort of demonstration reporters liked to see. And the same Judge Mullowney had levied sentences of only three days.

On Monday morning, July 16, the defendants took seats in the stuffy police courtroom filled with supporters sitting hip to hip with the human flotsam and jetsam of Saturday night revelries. "I've never seen but one other court in my life and that was the Court of St. James," quipped Florence Bayard Hilles, the daughter of a former ambassador to Great Britain. "But I must say they're not very much alike."[1]

It was no accident that this most recent crop of prisoners included some of the party's most distinguished members. In planning the Bastille Day demonstration, Lucy Burns had intentionally fielded a cast that reporters could not ignore. Besides the aristocratic Hilles, head of the Woman's Party Delaware chapter, there was New Jersey chairman Alison Turnbull Hopkins, whose husband was a Progressive Party leader and Wilson loyalist. Nevada's Anne Martin was the Woman's Party's vice-chairman. The well-connected Elizabeth S. Rogers was present, and also Eunice Dana Brannan, the daughter of the late Charles A. Dana, distinguished editor of *The Sun*. Matilda Hall Gardner's husband Gilbert was a respected Scripps Howard journalist. Doris Stevens was known to have attracted the admiring eye of Dudley Field Malone, a Wilson intimate appointed collector of the Port of New York. Although Malone was married to the daughter of a former New York senator, he had been writing mash notes to Stevens—"Beautiful girl of mine" and "Dearest Loved One"—since the previous summer.[2]

For two days the defendants protested their innocence to Judge Mullowney, whom they were getting to know, and not in a pleasant way. Spectators applauded each speech with such noisy enthusiasm that the judge grew irritated. On the second day he allowed himself to be drawn into an argument over the Russian banner, although it had not been displayed since the first arrests and had nothing to do with the Bastille Day demonstration. From the bench he proclaimed it "treasonable and seditious."

In the final speech of the unruly proceeding, Doris Stevens charged that Wilson and his people "gave the orders, which caused our arrest and appearance before this bar. We know and you know, that the District Commissioners are appointed by the President, that the present commissioners were appointed by President Wilson. We know that you, your Honor, were appointed to the bench by President Wilson, and that the district attorney who prosecuted us was appointed by the President."[3]

All the speeches, all the eloquence, all to no avail. Mullowney himself, or the powers behind him, had decided to curb these women. The defendants were prepared for a guilty verdict. They had arrived with bags packed.

But sixty days!

The overly harsh sentences dramatized once again the capricious nature of suffrage justice. Lucy Burns had raised the issue at the trial of the Fourth of July offenders. Why, she asked, had she been arrested for doing exactly what pickets had done without repercussions on June 21? How was she to know, Vida Milholland inquired during the same trial, that "what was perfectly legal" in March would be illegal four months later on Independence Day? "How could I possibly tell what was right and what was wrong?"[4]

And why did behavior that merited a three-day sentence on July 5 deserve sixty days on July 17?

After conferring with Malone, the women said they would accept the sentences rather than pay a fine. The lawyer went off to see his friend the president to lodge a protest, and the sixteen prisoners were taken to Union Station for a twenty-mile journey down the river to the Occoquan Workhouse.

Built to relieve the deplorable conditions in the District of Columbia jail, Occoquan in rural Virginia was a Progressive Era showplace, designed for access to nature, light, and clean air. Its twelve-hundred-acre farm produced fresh vegetables, and a dairy herd yielded milk. Prisoners were housed in dormitories rather than cellblocks, and no walls or watchtowers surrounded the site.

The superintendent of Occoquan, however, was an old-school tyrant with political connections who had left a previous post in Indiana under a cloud of corruption. None of this was known to the suffrage prisoners, who were puzzled when Superintendent Raymond Whittaker greeted them with overt hostility. On his behalf, Matilda Gardner invented an apology. "We felt that he was probably sorry to be obliged to take us, and possibly embarrassed in carrying out his duty."[5]

Most refused the food served on their arrival: a thin, unappetizing soup accompanied by rye bread and water. Talking was prohibited during the meal. Afterward, they were taken to a large room and told to undress before an ill-tempered white matron and two black attendants, who seemed annoyed at having to work past quitting time. Once stripped, the suffragists were instructed to walk across the room to a bank of open showers. Under prevailing standards of modesty this was the archetypal naked-in-public nightmare come true. Wrote Doris Stevens, "No woman there will ever forget the shock and hot resentment."[6]

Despite the stifling July heat, they were given thick stockings and coarse muslin underwear, a petticoat, and a loose-fitting Mother Hubbard dress of heavy dark gray cotton topped by a dark blue apron. The ensemble included a small rough towel, to be folded and tucked in the waistbands of their aprons. Whittaker told them they would be permitted to write one letter a month to their families, "and of course, we shall open and read all letters coming in and going out."[7]

That night, the suffrage prisoners slept on cots lined up side by side with Negro offenders, even though there were empty beds in the white dormitory. "Understand, we did not object to the Negro women," Eunice Brannan later told reporters, in a studied show of tolerance. In fact, she said, there were many friendly conversations. Her statement notwithstanding, the suffragists were as prejudiced as the next American, as Brannan unwittingly revealed in her next remark. What truly rankled, she said, was that Whittaker had deliberately chosen, she said, "the most offensive thing that can be done to white women in the South."[8]

Readers of the next day's *Washington Post* would learn of the suffragists' treatment from a reporter who clearly delighted in seeing high-born women brought low. Their reception, he wrote, "was an awkward ordeal. Nearly all the ladies, being of wealth and distinction, usually had maids to attend to or help them out in such important details as dressing and undressing. But maids are not included in the Occoquan service, and the occasion was unceremonious."[9]

When they realized they would not be wearing their own garments for sixty days, wrote the reporter, "For the first time the ladies who have defied the police and braved the police court seemed to blanch. By then the clothes will be out of style."[10]

Back in Washington, the Woman's Party pressed its network into action. Angry telegrams flooded the White House. The Newark branch held a rally in support of Hopkins, its jailed leader. Margaret Sanger, the birth control crusader, who knew something about prison, congratulated the prisoners "for taking the sentence rather than paying the fine."[11]

Josephine du Pont, of the Delaware du Ponts, wrote that "I am so boiling hot, that if I thought my neuritis and sixty-four years could stand imprisonment, I would go to Washington and picket myself."[12]

Meanwhile husbands and allies were working to spring the women. Malone's scheduled five minutes with the president on July 17 had lasted forty-five. Clearly upset when he left the White House, the New York port collector dodged reporters and walked rapidly toward his hotel, forgetting his waiting taxi.[13]

One voice was missing from the furor. Alice Paul had not been heard from in public since before Bastille Day. The typewriter that clattered out her voluminous correspondence had come to an abrupt halt. The thirty-two-year-old leader was in a clinic under the care of her physician, combating a debilitating illness.

When they heard the diagnosis, the women in Cameron House remembered the death of the president's first wife, Ellen Wilson, and felt despair. The nation had not been told that the First Lady was gravely ill until just before she died. Only in the obituaries did they learn what had killed her. Defined in 1827 by

English physician Richard Bright, the modern term would be acute or chronic nephritis, an umbrella label for kidney inflammation. When Ellen Wilson succumbed, it was known as "Bright's Disease." Greatly feared, it was often mentioned in the same breath as cancer, stroke, heart failure, and diabetes.

In the case of Alice, fatigue, digestive problems, and especially urine tests pointed in one direction. She, too, had Bright's Disease. Alice Paul's friends were told she could live a year—if she radically changed her lifestyle. Perhaps three weeks if she didn't. Lucy Burns stepped in as acting chairman; Dora Lewis took over the fundraising.

Though ill, Alice was as eager as ever to know what her organizers were doing. Hazel Hunkins begged field rep Elsie Hill to write more frequently, with more details. She could not bear to read Hill's letters to Alice over the phone and hear the leader reply, "in a little querulous voice, 'Is that all she says?'"[14]

"Everyone I meet is so concerned over the health of Miss Paul," Elizabeth Stuyvesant, a dancer and settlement house worker and veteran of the July 4 arrests, wrote from New York. "I wonder if she knows how much people care?"[15]

After three days, Wilson yielded to pressure to pardon the Occoquan suffragists. Superintendent Whittaker bade them farewell with an unsettling remark. "The next lot of women who come here won't be treated with the same consideration that these women were."[16]

Even if Wilson hadn't explicitly said so, the Cameron House suffragists believed a presidential pardon was a tacit admission of their innocence. Hazel Hunkins wired a member of the advisory council the good news. "Picketing declared lawful no further arrests."[17]

There was more to celebrate. Alice had been moved to Johns Hopkins in Baltimore, where, Hazel said, she was "progressing nicely."[18] A few days after the pardon came the surprising report that she did not have Bright's Disease after all. "She has nothing at all wrong with her except accumulative fatigue," Hazel wrote Elsie Hill joyfully. A letter to Elizabeth Kent explained that Alice's "physical habits of eating and sleeping are bad, and her nerve cells are exhausted so that she is easily tired. She will be all right after a summer's rest."[19] When Anne Martin and Lucy Burns went to Johns Hopkins on July 25, 1917, they found Alice's bed empty. She had left for the Home Farm.

The pardon ushered in a period of relative calm. A little too much calm, it seemed, for some. Lillian Ascough urged Lucy Burns to "think of some ripping

big stunt to keep the good work going, and if so, send for me." Lucy wrote a
Connecticut supporter that they were on the lookout for "hectic ideas." And she
cautioned one prospective picket to "be prepared for arrest and imprisonment."[20]

On August 10, 1917, the Woman's Party fired a fresh salvo, the most
provocative yet. Lucy Burns marched to the White House gates carrying a new
banner:

KAISER WILSON: HAVE YOU FORGOTTEN HOW YOU SYM-
PATHIZED WITH THE POOR GERMANS BECAUSE THEY
WERE NOT SELF-GOVERNED? TWENTY MILLION AMERI-
CAN WOMEN ARE NOT SELF-GOVERNED—TAKE THE
BEAM OUT OF YOUR OWN EYE.[21]

Kaiser Wilson! James Delaney, a Navy Department clerk, sprang forward,
grabbed the banner, shot back through the crowd, and disappeared. The next
day, when Delaney answered his office phone, Katherine Morey was on the other
end, demanding its return. As reported in the *Suffragist*, the conversation went
like this:

Delaney: "I'll give it back to you if you promise never to carry it again on
    the picket line."
Morey: "We are making no conditions. We are simply demanding the re-
    turn of our property. The last man who destroyed one of our flags was
    given his choice between a twenty-five-dollar fine or sixty days in the
    work house."
Delaney: "I'll bring it over as soon as I can get off."

After she had hung up with Delaney, Katherine's phone rang. The offender's
boss was calling to report that the miscreant was on the way over. "Please take
him in the back room and spank him."[22]

The next day, two more Kaiser Wilson banners were ripped down. On the
third day, three Kaisers were destroyed, one by a sailor in uniform, and two others by government employees. It happened just as the president and his wife
were leaving for an engagement. The couple, reported the *New York Times*,
"smiled and bowed to the crowd."[23]

Coming after the Russian banner, the Kaiser banner all but eliminated any
dregs of sympathy for the Woman's Party. The protests against it were many and

heartfelt. It made "everyone I had got turn on me," wailed organizer Joy Young in the hills of Vermont. "I can get no opportunities to speak."[24]

The rage built. A mob of several thousand, many of them servicemen whose emotions had reached a tipping point, descended on Cameron House on August 14. When a suffragist exited with her Kaiser banner, a sailor grabbed it. She fetched another but got no farther than the corner before she was attacked. Two more women's banners were snatched. Two policemen did nothing.

During the ensuing melee, three sailors seized Lucy Burns and dragged her to the curb. Freeing herself, she raced into the house and up to the second floor, where she and others defiantly draped more banners over the balcony rail. Incensed by the rectangles of cloth dangling out of reach, three sailors fetched a tall ladder from the Belasco Theatre next door, leaned it against the facade, and climbed up and over the iron railing. They tore down the suffrage banners and an American flag that had flown there since the declaration of war.

Then a bullet from a .38 revolver struck a second-floor window, passed eighteen inches over the head of a member from Montana, and lodged in the ceiling. Defiant suffragists hung a fresh banner from the balcony. Protestors hurled eggs and tomatoes. Finally police dispersed the crowd. But that was not the end of it. Women streamed from headquarters with more banners. All were destroyed by lingering remnants of the mob.

The next day, with no police in sight, the pickets marched out the front door of Cameron House, led by a familiar figure, who appeared even more fragile than usual.

Alice Paul was back.

A mob waiting at the White House needed no encouragement to attack when the women arrived. Fifty banners were snatched, and women were flung to the ground. Alice was knocked down three times. A trophy-seeking sailor dragged her across the sidewalk, grabbing at her suffrage sash.

One woman, it was reported, wrapped herself in a banner after most of her clothing was ripped from her body. Another delighted onlookers by pulling a replacement banner from her white stocking. When journalist and Wilson stalwart William Bayard Hale chatted sympathetically with a picket, he was pelted with rolled-up newspapers and pushed and shoved by sailors.

Six days had passed since the first Kaiser Wilson banner, and two since the riot at Cameron House. Finally, the police acted, but not in the manner the women had hoped. A reporter witnessed police, including an inspector and a captain, carrying out what seemed to be orders to destroy the flags. One hundred forty-eight were seized. Cut from silk and linen, some with scallops and fringe, and lettered in colors, the banners were beautiful and expensive. At six dollars apiece, the loss was considerable. Six dollars would buy ten organdy blouses, forty loaves of bread, twenty-four matinee theater tickets, or two maple porch rockers. Woman's Party secretary Virginia Arnold gripped hers so fiercely that she required a doctor's care after officers twisted her arms. Two men were arrested, one a reporter who had tried to shield the women.

Afterward, Major Pullman informed Alice in person that the presidential pardon was no protection. Continued picketing would trigger arrests. For the second time, she ignored his warning. That same day a new banner declared "THE GOVERNMENT ORDERS OUR BANNERS DESTROYED BECAUSE THEY TELL THE TRUTH."[25] At 4 P.M., as a tide of government workers from nearby offices flooded the sidewalk, the threatened arrests took place. In a proceeding that lasted forty minutes, six pickets were tried and sentenced to thirty days in the Occoquan Workhouse.

This time, Major Pullman announced, there would be no pardons.

The food was dreadful. Sour hominy, tainted meat. No sugar. No milk, unless ordered by the doctor. Worms in the oatmeal and the cornbread, more worms floating in the soup. In the course of a month, wrote Mary Winsor, a Bryn Mawr student and by nature a tabulator, "we found worms ten times—the largest collection of worms at one meal being fifteen worms." The meat was foul seven times. The soup served at supper was brewed from the midday leftovers, thus "merely dinner over again, only much more horrid." When stirred, a "greenish-gray sediment rose from the bottom. . . . Everyone hated the soup. Scarcely a night went by that some woman in our dormitory was not ill from constipation, pain in the stomach, vomiting or diarrhea."[26] Among the prisoners was Maud Malone, the New York suffragist who had interrupted Wilson's 1912 campaign speech. In her ginger cake she found a dead fly and a piece of newspaper.

From her prison cell, Mary Winsor penned a "prayer."

O, good Lord, we pray thee to put it into the hard hearts of the people in charge of this workhouse to send us a good breakfast. We ask thee for three slices of toast apiece and a poached egg and real coffee with cream and sugar, and a large dish of oatmeal with no worms in it.

We have been hungry for a long time, O Lord, we pray thee to soften the heart of Mr. Whittaker so that he may allow us to have some of the fine vegetables growing in the garden instead of rotten canned tomatoes.

We also pray thee Lord to allow us to have milk for supper from the fine fat cows which graze around the workhouse instead of dreadful soup made of spoiled meat and raw peas which makes us very sick.

And O Lord, please remember that we have not had a taste of sugar in any thing for a month, and do not forget the real coffee with sugar and cream and some clean oatmeal without any worms or mouse dirt in it.

Amen.[27]

Penicillin had not been invented, but hygiene was a known prophylactic against disease. Still, the prisoners had no choice but to drink from the open pail where water was ladled into a single cup, shared by all. There was no soap except for the weekly bath; a single bar was passed from hand to hand.

Whittaker ordered his charges to paint dormitory walls and lavatories in the Negro women's barracks. Weak from hunger, the suffragists found it difficult to climb stepladders or even hoist big brushes heavy with paint. A friendly congressman introduced a resolution in mid-August demanding an investigation. It went nowhere.

In late August, Whittaker fired a matron, Virginia Bovee, and gave her two hours to get out. She promptly went to the Woman's Party with still more appalling details. The suffragists' mail was often destroyed, she said. Sheets were not changed between prisoners, and blankets were washed once a year. The one worker who handled bedding always wore rubber gloves for protection. Unless they had open sores, women with syphilis were housed with the general population. Two Negro inmates were known to have tuberculosis. The prisoners never saw the cream yielded by the farm's cows; it was turned into butter and sold for profit. She had heard the cries of female prisoners and the sound of blows as they were beaten.[28]

On September 7, 1917, dismayed by the treatment of the pickets, Malone wrote the president an emotional four-page letter of resignation from his plum patronage post as collector of the Port of New York. Stumping for Wilson in 1916, Malone reminded him, he had pledged to use his influence to secure the president's backing for the federal amendment. The president had let him down. "The present congress shows no earnest desire to enact this legislation for the simple reason that you, as the leader of the Party in power, have not yet suggested it."[29]

Not only that, but the man he had so loyally served was now "permitting splendid American women to be sent to jail." Concluded Malone, "I think it is high time that men in this generation, at some cost to themselves, stood up to the battle for the national enfranchisement of American women."[30]

His resignation earned Alice's "sincerest gratitude and admiration,"[31] and brought a stream of speaking invitations for the Woman's Party's male martyr. In the months ahead he would seldom turn down a request for help.

When it became clear there would be no congressional investigation into Occoquan, Malone pressed for action from the District Board of Charities, the overseer for the Washington prisons. To supplement the suffragists' accounts of harsh treatment, Malone gathered affidavits from former guards and prisoners, in whose testimony Whittaker took shape as a tyrant who ran Occoquan for his profit and pleasure.

The superintendent horsewhipped male prisoners for infractions as minor as smoking or talking after hours, chained them together and forced them to run laps around a stockade, handcuffed them to trees and beat them, kicked an elderly man for refusing to break a rock, and chained prisoners to a fence overnight in rain and snow. When male prisoners wore out their shoes, they worked without soles, in snow and slush.

An escapee was caught and beaten until he couldn't walk. Another was captured, then shot in the arm, then placed in a punishment cell for eight months. One guard came on duty to find a prisoner had been shot in the leg, then forced to stand for two hours. A matron saw Whittaker punch a woman till her mouth filled with blood. She saw him beat another, then lock her in the "booby—which is only like a cupboard—for two weeks on bread and water."[32]

Inmate Susie Washington was punished by being given bread and water; her bed was a cement floor. The letters of inmates who mentioned sickness were destroyed. Often the men tried to escape. "We have heard shots and screams many times at night. They shoot them like dogs," wrote Susie.[33]

Malone would allow his witnesses to testify only if the inquiry was public. "The people of Washington and Virginia should publicly know what kind of prison they have in their midst." But the Board of Charities instead met privately and concluded that suffragists, not Whittaker, were the problem. "The officers and guards at Occoquan are worn out by overwork and inmates excited by the conduct of the members of the National Woman's Party, and this is seriously threatening the enforcement of discipline and endangering the usefulness of the institution."[34]

Whittaker was cleared of wrongdoing.

While Malone pressed his case, Alice Paul was arrested on October 6, 1917. She was holding a banner with Wilson's words: "THE TIME HAS COME TO CONQUER OR SUBMIT; FOR US THERE CAN BE BUT ONE CHOICE—WE HAVE MADE IT." Her sentence was suspended, but after she was detained again on October 20, she was sentenced to seven months in the district jail. Two days later she began serving her term.

Just before leaving headquarters Alice quickly dashed off a note telling her mother not to worry. "It will merely be a delightful rest."[35]

CHAPTER SIXTEEN

NIGHT OF TERROR

WASHINGTON, Nov. 12.—A harassed and unhappy judge, sighing and clasping his soggy brow, astonished Washington yesterday by suspending sentence on the forty-one naughty "suffs" who picketed the White House Saturday.

—New York Evening Mail, *November 12, 1917*

Over a span of five months, beginning June 17, 1917, Judge Mullowney had jailed scores of suffragists from the National Woman's Party. It seemed to make no difference what they did. Whether they stood on the sidewalk or marched on the sidewalk, carried banners that quoted the president or ones that insulted the president. Attracted a crowd, or didn't. Were mauled by mobs or ignored. No matter their conduct, the judge always pronounced them guilty of obstructing traffic. And no matter the punishment—suspended sentences, three-day terms, thirty days, sixty days, even, most recently, *seven months* meted out to the leaders—they kept on picketing. The fifty-three-year-old judge, a Richmond native, didn't know what to do. Nothing like this had occurred in his twelve years on the bench, nor in the years before when he had been a police court prosecutor.

And now, on Monday, November 12, 1917, they were again in his courtroom, their faces turned toward him like all-knowing cats waiting for food. Here were the pedigreed Eunice Dana Brannan and Dora Lewis, pardoned in July by

President Wilson, both gray-haired and as spirited as the twenty-year-olds. And here, too, was the party's redheaded troublemaker Lucy Burns, the veteran of British street fights, chalker of sidewalks. How many arrests for her? A glance at the record would have showed this was number six (not counting the chalking). The oldest defendant at seventy-three, Mary Nolan, up from Florida, had limped into the courtroom. A bad foot had not prevented her from picketing. She peered at him from under a cap of white hair.

Doubtless their crafty leader Alice Paul would have been here as well, and Rose Winslow, the Polish worker girl, but he had already sent them to jail. According to the newspapers, they had gone on a hunger strike and now doctors were forcing food down their throats.

This particular saga, a finale of sorts, had begun two days earlier, on Saturday, November 10, with what Dora Lewis, the chief recruiter in Alice's absence, had announced as "our last picket line." And the biggest. As a tactic, leaders agreed that picketing was losing its impact. In an effort to counter the arrests once and for all, Alice had decided even before she herself was convicted to crowd the jails with "such numbers that government cannot handle situation."[1]

Dozens of pickets glided out of Cameron House in waves, each from a different quadrant of the country. "One of the quietest and at the same time most sedately spectacular of all the picketing affairs yet staged," proclaimed the *New York Times*.[2] Sedate, perhaps. But all forty-one women were arrested anyway. They posted bail and went free for the weekend.

On Sunday, those women, reinforced by fifty others who had come down on a midnight train from New York, made their way to the district jail where Alice Paul was imprisoned to let her know, as one put it, that they were intent on "taking their medicine."[3] She was forbidden to have visitors, but they knew the location of her cell. From below they called out to the slight figure that appeared in silhouette at the window.

"West Virginia greets you!" they called. "Oklahoma is with you." "New York salutes you."

"How are you?"

"Oh, I'm all right," their leader called back. "I am being forcibly fed three times a day. It is worse than in England. There they feed you only twice."

"Hold on," they called.[4]

Immediately after that, authorities took steps to ensure that Alice would no longer hold court from her window. They transferred Alice to the jail's psychiatric ward and held her incommunicado. The prison physician, Dr. J. A. Gannon, ordered one of her two windows nailed shut from top to bottom and an iron-barred cell door installed. One morning, through the second window, she spied the face of an old man who was standing atop a ladder. He explained apologetically that he had instructions to cover the opening with boards. As he pounded nails, she watched his face gradually disappear and her room grow darker.

Intrepid Alice experienced an unfamiliar sensation. "I confess I was afraid of Dr. Gannon." He visited each day with a threatening message: "I will show you who rules this place."[5] A nurse entered hourly and beamed an electric light full onto her face. Mental patients peered constantly through the bars. The prison alienist, as psychiatrists were then called, visited often. The forced feedings continued.

One day, a young intern arrived to take a blood test. When Alice protested, he told her with a sneer, "you know you're not mentally competent to decide such things." She wondered if indeed she was going crazy.[6]

Through the night she heard shrieks and moans. She told herself, "I'll pretend these moans are like an elevated train, beginning faintly in the distance and getting louder as it came near." She was grateful to friendly nurses who reassured her that she was not insane.[7]

After Alice's note that she was headed for a "delightful rest," Tacie and Helen, not reassured, hurried to Washington. The prison turned them away.

As Judge Mullowney grew increasingly frazzled, the trial of the suffrage incorrigibles went on for six interminable hours, punctuated with the usual defiant speeches, delivered over the click of knitting needles dipping in and out of khaki yarn, growing sweaters to keep doughboys warm. Some of the defendants had sons or brothers or nephews fated for the muddy trenches on the Allies' side of No Man's Land, a fact that came in handy when their patriotism was questioned.

What the judge did then took everyone by surprise. After saying he regretted that the court lacked the power to deal with the situation—no one was sure what he meant by that—Mullowney figuratively threw up his hands, pronounced the whole thing "puzzling," and let the women go. They were to come back when summoned.

The "naughty 'suffs'" left the crowded courtroom and proceeded directly to Cameron House, clutching their bags and suitcases. They were as puzzled as the judge, but they displayed not the slightest doubt about what to do next.

Less than two hours later, thirty-one sign-toting pickets stood in front of the White House—twenty-seven veterans of the earlier courtroom proceeding plus four fresh faces. No one had expected them to return that same day, and the women held the stretch of sidewalk between the gates for close to an hour before a mob gathered, ripped down banners, and roughed up the banner bearers. As usual, police ignored the attackers, but hustled the pickets off to the station house.

They spent that night in the District House of Detention, sleeping on mats.

On November 13, the suffragists were back in Judge Mullowney's courtroom. That same day lawyer Dudley Field Malone wrangled a visit to his notorious client in the psychiatric ward. Miss Paul, he told the press afterward, was "more sane than any of the administration officials who have been responsible for this outrage." He demanded that "this malicious attempt to discredit Miss Paul's leadership and to reflect on her sanity in placing her in a psychopathic ward, surrounded by maniacs, cease at once, and that she be removed forth with."[8]

On November 14 a more resolute Mullowney imposed sentences. Mary Nolan received just six days, in deference to her age. The majority were given fifteen- and thirty-day terms. He sentenced repeat offenders Eunice Brannan and Dora Lewis to sixty days. Labeling Lucy Burns the "ringleader," Mullowney dealt her a six-month penalty.[9] They were to do their time in the district jail, where Alice Paul and Rose Winslow were already locked up.

It was a varied group. All white, to be sure, but separated in age by as much as fifty years. Twenty were single. New York accounted for the largest contingent—eleven. Among them was Dorothy Day, barely twenty, erstwhile reporter for Socialist publications and future founder of the Catholic Worker Movement. Sisters Betty and Alice Gram had come from Oregon; Minnie Quay and Mrs. C. T. Robertson were from Utah. And two southerners had flouted Dixie's anti-suffrage, anti-picketing sentiment to join the demonstration—"little" Julia Emory of Maryland and Alice Cosu, a carpenter's wife from Louisiana. In all, the Woman's Party's canny effort to recruit pickets from around the country had paid off. Newspapers in eleven states would surely carry reports of what was happening to their hometown prisoners.

And what happened wasn't pretty. Their first night in jail would forever be remembered in suffrage history as the "Night of Terror."

Travelers in Union Station stared as police officers herded women in fine wool coats and furs across the marble expanse to the 5 P.M. train that steamed south to Virginia. The suffragists realized they were not going to the nearby district jail after all, but to Occoquan, and that was bad news. Repeat offenders like Lucy Burns had brought back alarming first-hand accounts of the despotic Raymond Whittaker and his tough, right-hand matron, Minnie Herndon.

The train car was crowded, and the prisoners stood for most of the hour-long journey. Herndon was waiting for them in the reception room in the women's prison. All had agreed that Dora Lewis would act as their spokesman. A widow since 1890, when her husband was killed by a train, she had raised three small children alone. The door of her four-story brick Philadelphia town-house, not far from fashionable Rittenhouse Square, was always open to a suf-frage sister passing through, and she also rented a permanent room in Cameron House for her frequent visits. In the past year, she had emerged as a principal fundraiser, second only to Alice.

Dora spoke out in a resolute voice. They would not give their names, she told the matron, until they saw Mr. Whittaker. He wouldn't be back that night, Herndon answered. Or perhaps not for two or three days, or perhaps not for two or three weeks. "You'll sit here all night," she warned. "We will await his return," the suffragist leader said calmly.[10] She had heard the superintendent was to at-tend a meeting in New Orleans, but suspected he had not yet left.

Dora's refusal prompted one of the guards to make a threat so odd that none would forget it. "If you don't give your names we will put you in the sardine box," he said. "And we will put mustard on."[11] Was he joking, or was it the nickname of some particularly vile enclosure?

Under the watchful eyes of five male guards, as well as a contingent of sev-eral dozen others on the verandah who glared through the windows, the women waited quietly in chairs lined up in front of the matron's desk, as if in school. The room was brightly lit and not unpleasant. Like a teacher, Herndon called the roll, but no one in this class answered. She allowed several women to use the lavatory, but then denied further requests. She also ignored a plea for water from Eunice Brannan, who had a severe sore throat. An hour passed, then another. Two exhausted young women nodded off.

Mrs. Henry Butterworth had just finished her knitting and was putting away her glasses when a stout man burst through the door, trailed by a retinue of guards. Even those who had never seen him knew instantly he was the su-perintendent. "He has stiff white hair, blazing little eyes, and a dull purple birth-mark on the side of this face," wrote Kathryn Lincoln, who kept a diary during her imprisonment.[12]

Dora Lewis rose. "Mr. Whittaker, I am authorized by my companions to say that we wish to be treated as political prisoners."[13] Alice had been researching privileges granted such prisoners in other countries. It was her contention that Woman's Party violators should be allowed to receive mail, visitors, and gifts of food; wear their own clothing; and read books and newspapers.

Recently exonerated by the Board of Charities, Whittaker clearly felt no obligation to behave with courtesy or even professional restraint. "Shut up. Sit down," he barked. As Dora tried to continue, he turned to two guards and snapped out an order. "Take her." The other women watched in dismay as the men grabbed their leader, one on each side, and forced her out through a door— "like a dressmaker's dummy," wrote Lincoln.[14]

Julia Emory started after Dora. Two guards grasped her and dragged her across the room, tossing aside furniture, then through the outer door, across the front porch, and down the front steps. "Take that woman," Raymond Whittaker repeated over and over, signaling to the guards to seize first one and then another.[15] The room filled with men armed with clubs.

As the guards hauled Dorothy Day from the reception room, another woman's bag caught on her arm. The woman hung onto it, and the guard, thinking that Dorothy was resisting, "began to twist my wrist and pull me violently." The bag's cord broke and she was free. But the twisting and pinching continued. Three guards leaped on her "so that I felt that I was in the midst of a football scrimmage. . . . My feet were completely off the floor, my arms and shoulders were almost twisted out of joint and my back was bruised. One man's hand was at my throat."[16]

The men half-pushed, half-dragged the stumbling women over a grassy expanse to the men's prison, a long low building. Previous suffrage prisoners had slept in large dormitories, but here there were individual cells, usually reserved for prisoners undergoing severe punishment. The dormitories would have been preferable. Never had these refined women seen a place so foul. Or a public official so enraged.

"The dungeon I was in was very filthy, tobacco spit on the floor and all along the side of the filthy bunk; dirty horse blankets, open dirty toilet, no water, dark and damp," Minnie Quay testified afterward. "I was so cold my teeth chattered all night. Superintendent Whittaker ran up and down the corridor screaming to the guards to bring the handcuffs, straight jackets and gags."[17]

Phoebe Scott spent the night with a pair of other pickets. Two shared a single bed and one slept on the floor. With the arrival of daylight, she saw the sheets

and pillowcases for the first time. Her stomach churned. "Evidently the last occupant had been a dirty person or had used the bed a long time."[18]

A guard grabbed the elderly Mary Nolan by the shoulder. "I remember saying, 'I'll come with you; don't drag me; I have a lame foot.' But I was dragged
down the steps and away into the dark. I didn't have my feet on the ground. I
guess that saved me."[19] The last thing Nolan saw before she was forced inside the
men's prison was an American flag atop the roof, glowing in the refracted light
from a window. As she was shoved into a cell, the bed broke her fall. Following
just behind, Alice Cosu was thrown against the stone wall.

Hurled into a cell at the far end of the corridor, Kathryn Lincoln fell to her
knees. The red iron gate clanged shut behind her. As she staggered to her feet
and looked out, she saw Eunice Brannan across the corridor, offering a smile of
encouragement. And then: "Mr. W. suddenly appears wild with fury, his fists
clenched. Abuse rains from his crooked mouth and ends with 'or I'll gag you and
put you in a straight jacket for the night. Now get away from that door.'"[20]

There would be neither food nor water all that night. Nor could they flush
the open, waste-filled toilets, which were operated from outside the cell. To their
embarrassment, they were forced to ask the very guards who had manhandled
them to do it. And only male guards were on duty, prowling the corridor.

While her companions were being dragged away, Dora Lewis was locked in
a small room where she could hear "shrieks, cries, heavy bodies falling and then
quiet once more." Left behind, Mrs. Robertson was literally frozen with terror.
Someone fetched water and ammonia and told her a doctor was on the way. As
she waited, she heard Whittaker say that "Mrs. Lewis and Miss Burns ought to
be locked up in solitary confinement for the rest of their lives, and he was not sure
but that they should be taken out and shot."[21]

When all her companions had been removed, the superintendent pushed
open the door to the room where Dora sat. "Are you going to give your name or
not?" he demanded, raising his arm and clenching his fist. "If you don't I will
put you where the others are." She shook her head "no," and he ordered his men
to take her away. "I was lifted from my chair and dragged down the corridor
through the reception room out into the night."[22]

Mary Nolan and Alice Cosu watched as their cell door opened and a guard
tossed Dora's limp body onto a mattress on the floor. They thought she was dead
and shouted desperately for help. Reviving, Dora called out to everyone that she
was all right. The superintendent, face twisted in anger, appeared instantly and
threatened to put her in a straight jacket and gag if she didn't keep quiet.

A frigid breeze blew through a high ventilation slit. In the commotion, Dora had left her coat behind, and she shivered through the night with just a thin piece of cotton blanket for warmth. Alice Cosu had worried about her, and now Dora worried about Alice, who had begun to vomit and was clearly in pain. Perhaps she was having a heart attack. Every few minutes for two hours, Dora cried out for a doctor until Alice was finally taken to the prison hospital.

One by one, Lucy Burns called the names of the other prisoners, to ask if they were all right. Whittaker materialized once again, shaking his fist. "Shut up there, you."[23] The angrier he got, the redder his face, the more purple his birthmark. When Lucy paid no attention, a guard produced handcuffs, yanked her hands through the bars, and chained her to the cell with her arms above her head. Julia Emory raised her hands in sisterhood and held the position until hours later, when the superintendent had left for good, and an aging guard released Lucy's arms.

Clad in a bulky overcoat, her hands still cuffed, Lucy shared a single cot with Dorothy Day. Sleep wouldn't come, and they lay awake talking of Joseph Conrad's novels. In the morning, Lucy's wrists were bruised and red. Dorothy's shoulder and back were so stiff that she could neither turn her head nor bend.

Through that long night, playwright Paula Jakobi was haunted by the male shades gathered at one end of the corridor, their bodies outlined by the illumination of a feeble light, nightsticks swinging like pendulums. The next morning, she was taken before Whittaker. She was surprised to find him courteous and businesslike. His attitude changed instantly when she insisted she would neither work nor wear prison clothing. Well, then, he said, she would be taken to the *male* hospital—emphasis on the word—and placed in solitary confinement. When she still refused, he made good on his threat. A trusty led her away. On the second day, still playing both roles in a good cop/bad cop routine, Whittaker offered to personally drive her back to Washington if she promised never again to picket. She turned him down.

Having decided to follow the example of their hunger-striking leader in district jail, Dorothy Day and fifteen others found it easy to refuse the cold milk and stale bread left in their cells that first morning. But that night brought "hot milk and fragrant toast that came to tantalize us for the next ten days."[24] When no one came to take away the full plate, rats crept into the cells, empty bellies low to the floor and eyes fixed on the food. Flies flitted through the bars, their presence in winter an indication that somewhere something was dead.

"Keep the strike," Dorothy heard a woman call out. "Remember, if it's broke we go back to worms in the oatmeal, and the workshop." Better the workshop, Dorothy reflected. Time passed so slowly. "Those first six days of inactivity were as six thousand years. To lie there through the long day, to feel the nausea and emptiness of hunger, the dazedness at the beginning and the feverish mental activity that came after. I lost all consciousness of any cause. I had no sense of being a radical, making protest against a government, carrying on a nonviolent revolution. I could only feel the darkness and desolation around me."[25]

After four days without eating, Kathryn Lincoln huddled next to the faint heat of the radiator and wrote in her diary that "My back seems to be breaking and the dull pain in my head becomes unbearable." She longed for fresh air and exercise. As she gazed around her cell, she noticed the corners seemed to be moving. "Why, they are coming together!" The next day, clearly suffering, she was taken to the prison hospital, where she found other suffragists also being treated for illnesses. Or was there another reason they were there? In the room next to hers, which she knew to be Lucy's, she heard sounds of a struggle and then someone gagging. She recognized instantly the sound of forced feeding. "I cannot write about it." Footsteps in the corridor sounded threatening. "The door opens. The light is flashed on. Two doctors appear and look us over. We plead that we are all right and they finally decide that we 'can wait.'"[26]

The superintendent continuously moved the women about, transplanting them at will from this room to that, a tactic known to disorient prisoners. "We were in the same room scarcely two consecutive nights," Paula Jakobi wrote afterward. "One was never sure when she would be searched and when the few remaining treasures would be taken." She was forced to strip down before two matrons and two trusties, shower, and don the long blue prison dress, which was clean but so rough it chafed. Shoes came in two sizes, "large and small."[27]

For two days Paula refused to eat the milk and toast brought to her room. On the third day, fried chicken and a salad appeared. A penciled note worked its way along the steam pipe that ran between the cells. It was from Lucy Burns. "They think there is nothing in our souls above fried chicken."[28] One night Paula dreamed of a rabbit, held up by a hospital intern who volunteered to prepare it. "The women—our women—did not wait for him to cook it, but rushed toward it, pulled it from his hands, and tore the living animal into pieces and ate it."[29]

She woke, sobbing.

Eunice Brannon had been in prison two days when a matron decided to lead an outing through nearby woods. Exhausted from their travails, the group asked frequently to rest. On the way back they could hear the ominous baying of bloodhounds. At times the dogs seemed to be close, at times more distant. "You must hurry," the matron said. "The bloodhounds are loose."

Would they attack us? asked a young prisoner.

"That's just what they would do," the matron replied.[30]

In Washington, Malone's insistence to the press following his visit to Alice had its intended effect. On November 18, she was removed to the prison hospital. But the forced feedings went on as before.

"Don't let them tell you we take this well," wrote Rose Winslow in a smuggled note. "Miss Paul vomits much. I do too, except when I'm not nervous, as I have been every time but one. The feeding always gives me a severe headache. My throat aches afterward, and I always weep and sob, to my great disgust, quite against my will. I will try to be less feeble minded."[31]

Word of the brutality at Occoquan began to seep out. Armed with a court order, Malone's co-counsel, Matthew O'Brien, visited and found Lucy Burns lying on a cot in a dark cell, wrapped in blankets, stripped of her clothing as punishment for refusing to wear a prison uniform. He was able to speak briefly with her, Dora Lewis, and Eunice Brannan before being barred from further visits.

John Brannon, president of the Board of Trustees of Bellevue Hospital, succeeded on his third attempt to see his wife, Eunice. But Whittaker had warned Eunice not to discuss conditions and refused to allow questions about her treatment.[32] As the physician walked through the workhouse accompanied by the superintendent, he said he could not help noticing "the look of terror which came into the faces of all the women prisoners when Mr. Whittaker stepped near them."[33]

The most complete description of conditions came from Mary Nolan. Released after serving her six-day term, she stunned the women at headquarters with her first-hand report on all that had happened that first dreadful night.

A week into the hunger strike, Raymond Whittaker could not be sure that one of the women would not somehow perish in a death that would be laid at his doorstep. His career would be ruined. He blamed Lucy Burns and Dora Lewis for leading the others. And Dora, who was growing weaker with each passing day, might herself be the first to die. On November 21, he decided to transfer the pair back to the district jail. So they wouldn't be quite so frail on arrival, Whittaker first ordered a round of forced feeding.

Dora Lewis's nourishment was forced through her mouth while she was held down by five people. Lucy Burns refused to open her mouth, and the doctor pushed a tube up her left nostril, succeeding even though she twisted her head from side to side. Afterward, she smuggled out a description. "It hurts nose and throat very much and makes nose bleed freely. Tube drawn out covered with blood. Operation leaves one very sick. Food dumped directly into stomach feels like a ball of lead."[34]

Having gone six days without food, Dorothy Day was moved to the Occoquan hospital, where she discovered that her friend Peggy Baird was next door. They were able to pass notes back and forth through a hole surrounding the radiator that heated both cells. When on the eighth day the usual offering of milk and toast arrived, Peggy lost her resolve. Whispering through the opening, she urged Dorothy to eat some as well. At first Dorothy refused. "Don't be a fool," Peggy told her, poking a sliver of bread through the hole. "Take this crust then and suck on it. It's better than nothing." To Dorothy this seemed a reasonable compromise. She knew that at least two or three of her companions were sticking to the fast, and that was sufficient, she decided, to keep up the pressure. Besides, she thought to herself, she should support her friend by sharing her crust.

"With what intense sensual enjoyment I lay there in my cot, taking that crust crumb by crumb."[35]

Since early November Woman's Party heavyweights Maud Younger and Mabel Vernon had been touring the heartland, fanning a flame of sympathy for the pickets whose brave leader was herself now a prisoner. At least a thousand people thronged a hall in Mobile, Alabama, on November 6, including "three commissioners two judges bank president all city department fifteen prominent lawyers spirit friendly much applause," wired organizer Rebecca Hourwich. In little Pensacola, Florida, three hundred came to a meeting, "newspapers very generous friendly."[36] In Mitchell, South Dakota, women appealed to Vernon to send "the girls from Washington" whose experiences had filled the pages of the *Suffragist*.[37]

As news of Occoquan brutality reached readers, the flame burned ever brighter, until the "great wave of sentimentality" sweeping the country was almost more than Anna Shaw could bear. "They refuse to eat the food and then say they are starving," declared the former head of the National. "If I were going to be a martyr I'd martyr—I wouldn't spend my time complaining about conditions."[38]

Shaw refused to use her influence to soften their treatment, even though Dora Lewis was a longtime friend, and Dora's son had implored Shaw to help his mother. She wrote Shippen Lewis, a Philadelphia lawyer, that "in my opinion the Government has been more mistreated in this whole matter than the pickets, and especially the President of the United States," who, she said, "has been most patient and courteous."[39]

"Ostracism is what they deserve," editorialized the *LaCrosse (WI) Tribune and Leader-Press*.[40] On a swing through Tennessee with Joy Young in the last week of November, Maud Younger wired that mayors in three cities refused to let them speak. In Knoxville, chilly air greeted them both inside and outside the courthouse, where they had been scheduled to appear at a formal gathering. Backed by ten deputies, the sheriff barred their way. In evening dress, the pair remained on the steps and delivered their speeches.

In one piece of good news, members of the National at last were working for the federal amendment. Fears that the picketing would sour the New York electorate on suffrage had proved unfounded. The state had given women the vote in a November 6 referendum, dramatically improving prospects for a pro-suffrage Congress.

Because Judge Mullowney had sentenced the women to the district jail within city limits, not distant Occoquan where they ended up, the two Woman's Party attorneys decided they had grounds for a writ of habeas corpus that would spring the prisoners from Occoquan. The women's crimes were committed in the District of Columbia; therefore they should serve their time in the District. To be sure, the error was a technicality that would, at best, do no more than return them to another jail, and not a nice one. Just that March, the district jail warden's wife, Mary Zinkhan, had begged Congress to find a new site at least for the prison hospital, calling the present one a "disgraceful blotch of inflammable buildings."[41]

The jail itself was cold and so filled with vile air that on arriving Alice Paul had hurled the sole book she brought for entertainment during her imprisonment, a volume of Robert Browning's poems, through a high closed window in a common room, breaking the glass and letting in some ventilation. Her unerring aim drew cheers from the other prisoners. Elsewhere drafts of stale air ricocheted through the cells as if searching for victims huddled under blankets. When inmates in upper tiers wielded brooms, clouds of dust rained down on their companions below.

When suffragists refused to enter the stifling cells unless windows were opened, guards strong-armed them in. The women waited overnight until breakfast arrived, then threw the dishes through the windows, broke the electric lights, and tore up bed clothing. The Woman's Party press secretary Beulah Amidon covered up the incident. A lurid story about her fellow members on a rampage was not one she cared to see in newspapers.[42]

In the jail's hospital, Rose Winslow encountered a Negro woman with syphilis who had lost a leg; it had "rotted so that it was alive with maggots when she came in." Her remaining leg was now as bad. Children, apparently wards of the state, were among the patients—one young girl waiting for a tonsillectomy, another whose mother refused to care for her, and another with syphilis. Rose was horrified to learn that she and Alice had been taking baths in the same tub used by afflicted children.[43]

All the prisoners shared their quarters with bedbugs, roaches, and rats as big as rabbits.

As bad as conditions were at the district jail, a court order for a transfer there from Occoquan would be a symbolic victory over the government. The case was originally scheduled for trial on November 27. Fearful that his hunger-striking clients would not survive that long, attorney O'Brien prevailed on the court to move the date up to November 23.

The prospect of starving women, some too weak to walk, on display in a federal courtroom crammed with reporters filled officials with panic. Whittaker repeatedly dodged a subpoena requiring him to testify. Finally, O'Brien came up with a ruse to catch the superintendent. On the night of November 21, subpoena in hand, the Woman's Party lawyer visited Whittaker's home and was told, as he had anticipated, that the superintendent wasn't there. O'Brien left, and then called from a nearby phone saying he would return in the morning. Instead, he went back immediately. Whittaker had surfaced. The subpoena found its mark.[44]

On the eve of the trial, the Occoquan staff made a last-minute effort to fatten up the hunger-striking plaintiffs, who now had been without food for eight days. The prison doctor told diarist Kathryn Lincoln that if she did not eat, she would not be permitted to testify the next day. He pledged to bring her a baked apple from his own kitchen. With cream. She was suspicious of the threat, but conflicted.

"I cannot give in lest he think it is because of the baked apple. To sell one's soul for a baked apple! . . . What shall I do? They have brought my supper. I stand over it about to begin. I feel guilty! Guilty! Yet I know perfectly well I am not. There is no doubt that the best thing to do for the Party is to get to court. My spoon sinks into the baked apple. I have eaten."[45]

The next day, feeling ill—she was sure it was the apple—she struggled to court in Alexandria, Virginia, where Cameron House friends and counsel were waiting to offer joyful greetings. Bedraggled as war refugees, wan as the winter sun, some prisoners came armed with bottles of smelling salts. Several stretched out on the wooden benches, using their coats as pillows. Eunice Brannan collapsed in the courtroom and was allowed to rest in a nearby office.[46]

Lucy Burns and Dora Lewis were conspicuously missing—too ill to appear, district jail warden Louis F. Zinkhan told U.S. District Judge Edmund Wadill Jr. In response to a question from Malone, Zinkhan acknowledged that Burns and Lewis were being forcibly fed.

"How many men does it take to hold Miss Burns?" the lawyer asked.

"Four."

"Then, your Honor, don't you think that if it takes four men to hold Miss Burns to give her forcible feeding, she is strong enough to appear in Court?"[47]

The proceedings focused narrowly on why the women had been taken to Occoquan. In explaining that such moves had been a routine practice since the workhouse opened, Zinkhan helpfully dug himself a trench big enough to hold an opposing army. He said he sent "all the able bodied prisoners to Occoquan—women able to perform useful work," adding that he was guided by "humanitarian motives."

Malone pounced.

"Were you actuated by humanitarian motives when you sent Mrs. Nolan, a woman of seventy-three years, to the workhouse? Did you think that she could perform some service at Occoquan that it was necessary to get her out of the District Jail and down there?"

Zinkhan looked everywhere but at his interrogator.

"Mrs. Nolan, will you please stand up?" Malone said.[48]

In the front row, a small figure rose. Mary Nolan wore a plain black dress that set off her pale skin. She looked impossibly fragile, like a china doll.

Three days after the trial, on November 26, Judge Mullowney suggested to Zinkhan that among the prisoners in his custody were some "committed by this Court, whose physical conditions are such that further imprisonment might be dangerous to the health."[49] Indeed, there were such prisoners, Zinkhan replied the next day. *All of them.* "All the suffragists" should be released, he wrote back. The jail wasn't equipped for their care.[50]

Though not an impartial observer, Doris Stevens, the former Ohio organizer who had been on the Woman's Party payroll since 1913, most surely got it right in the history she would eventually write. "With thirty determined women on hunger strike, of whom eight were in a state of almost total collapse, the Administration capitulated. It could not afford to feed thirty women forcibly and risk the social and political consequences; nor could it let thirty women starve themselves to death, and likewise take the consequences."[51]

It was just as Alice had planned. The mass arrests had pushed the district's penal system to its limit. And so, all went free, including Alice herself. She was lighter by a few pounds, and so thin that three fingers could slide beneath her once snug watchband, but no weaker in resolve. She hoped, she said, there would be no more need for further demonstrations. "But what we do depends entirely upon what the Administration does."[52]

CHAPTER SEVENTEEN

STALEMATE

The astonishing news jumped by telephone from one end of Pennsylvania Avenue to the other and streaked around the country by wire. Newspapers bannered the story: "President Champions Suffrage Amendment."[1] On January 10, 1918, the U.S. House of Representatives would vote on the Susan B. Anthony amendment. And it seemed that Wilson wanted his fellow Democrats to vote "aye."

Wilson had conveyed his change of heart in a private meeting on January 9 with a dozen pivotal Democrats, who confessed their fears about the next day's vote in light of the swelling female electorate. What should they do? In November, New York had given women the ballot, adding an estimated one million voters to the roles and bringing the total to twelve states where women had full suffrage. And five state legislatures had granted presidential suffrage to their women since 1913—a relatively simple process that was likely to be replicated in other states. Republicans were rallying around the amendment. Should it fail, women voters would blame Democrats and might well seek revenge at the polls.

John Raker, chairman of the House suffrage committee, claimed he had known all along which way the president was leaning. But his companions were amazed when Wilson told them of his about-face. What about states' rights, they asked. Well, yes, said Wilson, but in the end, wasn't suffrage a constitutional question? And that Democratic Party platform he had pledged to follow? Well, times had changed. Exigencies had arisen. Slavish adherence could no longer be expected. Just that day over lunch, the governor general of Canada had informed him that his country was on the verge of giving women the vote. It would not do, the president said, for the United States, as a foremost leader in the family of nations, to be reactionary on any great world question.

Edward Taylor from Colorado jotted down a statement for the press: "The committee found that the president had not felt at liberty to volunteer his advice to members of congress in this important matter; but when we sought his advice he very frankly and earnestly advised us to vote for the amendment." Then the president himself reached for a pencil and added this powerful phrase: "As an act of right and justice to the women of the country and the world."[2]

Raker stepped outside the White House, where Alice Paul and her suffragists were waiting in the snow with reporters. Not only had the president declared himself in favor of the amendment, Raker told the shivering group, but he was prepared to sacrifice his morning golf if other congressmen wished to speak to him.

Carrie Catt was celebrating her fifty-ninth birthday in the National's Washington headquarters when one of her lobbyists burst in with the news, crying, "It's over. We've won." The women waved their water glasses in a toast to "President Wilson—the best friend suffrage ever had." Catt issued a statement saying they were "thrilled."[3]

Alice too had a comment for the press: "It is difficult to express our gratification at the President's stand. For four years we have striven to secure his support for the national amendment for we knew that it and perhaps it alone, would insure our success."[4]

Assuming the House passed the amendment by a two-thirds majority, it would next go to the Senate, where a two-thirds majority was also required for passage. Afterward, the legislatures in three-quarters of the states—thirty-six in all—would have to pass the amendment by simple majorities before the U.S. Secretary of State could sign it into law. It was Alice's goal to have all that take place by the next presidential election in 1920, and preferably in time for the primaries.

By the suffragists' count, three weeks before the announcement of Wilson's change of heart, the amendment had been sixty votes short of passage. Lobbying hard during that time, they had pared the number to twenty. It remained to be seen if by tomorrow sufficient Democrats in Congress, as Alice put it, "will follow their great leader."[5]

Scrubwomen were still wielding brushes and buckets of soap suds in the halls of the Capitol when spectators, fortified with knitting, sandwiches, and apples for a long day ahead, lined up at the entrance to the House gallery. The food they were allowed to keep, but guards insisted they abandon their knitting.

"We aren't taking any chances," a guard told a woman who protested. "You folks make an awful lot of camouflage with them there bags. We don't know what's in them."[6] The woman obediantly added her satchel to the mound of pink, purple, and green bags climbing toward the ceiling.

The National leaders—Shaw, Catt, and others—as usual occupied privileged seats on the speaker's bench as guests of Speaker Clark, who had pledged to vote yes in the event of a tie. Alice's people filled the gallery to the right of the press. Every available inch of standing room was taken.

Appointed acting floor leader for the Republicans, Jeannette Rankin swept in on a wave of applause, holding a bouquet of yellow rosebuds tied with a yellow ribbon, a black stole tossed over her shoulder. Hers was the first and lengthiest speech of the day, the war she once opposed now a touchstone for justice.

"The boys at the front know something of the democracy for which they are fighting," she said. "These courageous lads who are paying with their lives testified to their sincerity when they sent home their ballots in the New York election and voted two to one in favor of woman suffrage and democracy at home."

She continued, "How can we explain if the same Congress that voted for war to make the world safe for democracy refuses to give this small measure of democracy to the women of our country?"[7]

Representatives defeated two measures that would have strangled the amendment. One imposed a seven-year time limit on ratification, and another required approval by state conventions.

Republican James Mann of Illinois appeared at the speaker's door in time for the final vote; he had just emerged from a six-month hospital stay in Baltimore, pale and trembling but determined to vote yes. Indiana Democrat Henry Barnhart, another yes vote, arrived on a stretcher, having just had his appendix removed. Another Democrat, Thetus Sims, limped into the chamber. He had refused to have a broken shoulder set after slipping on ice two days earlier, lest the procedure prevent him from voting in favor. New York Representative Frederick Hicks Jr. had lost his wife the night before. She was a suffragist, and he honored her memory by coming to Washington just long enough to offer his assent.

Suffragists were in high spirits. As the roll call began, however, and nays boomed from the mouths of Democrat after Democrat, the faces of the antisuffragists brightened while those of the true believers grew grim. "We are defeated," one murmured in anguish. Hands twisting, they listened helplessly as opponents fought to disallow the vote of a pro-suffrage legislator from Missouri who had not responded when his name was called. The man pushed through a scrum at the speaker's rostrum and insisted he had been present. His vote provided the two-thirds majority. But it was too soon to celebrate; opponents called for a second roll call. A hush fell over the House as tension mounted for a second time.

The result was the same as the first: 274 to 136 for suffrage. The Anthony amendment had squeaked through with the required two-thirds majority and not a vote to spare.

Women in the galleries jumped to their feet, shouting Hallelujah and waving handkerchiefs as congressmen saluted them from the floor. In the corridor, other women broke into solemn song, "Praise God, from Whom All Blessings Flow."

Alice was not there to witness the triumph. Well beforehand, she had returned to headquarters. As her exuberant troops entered, she looked up from her desk.

"Eleven to win before we can pass the Senate," she announced, handing Maud Younger a list of names. "Will you see these to-" She glanced at the clock. It was nearly 8 P.M. "morrow."[8]

What had turned Wilson around? Was it because, as he told Tumulty, he feared his party would suffer if Democrats defeated the amendment?

Or was it the pickets?

As it happened, the House victory came exactly a year after the Silent Sentinels had first marched to the White House. Newspapers seized this timely moment to weigh their impact.

"Picketing accomplished two things, and accomplished them thoroughly well," editorialized the *Hartford Globe*. "It kept the cause of woman suffrage everlastingly to the front and it awakened first compunction and then support in the mind of the President, who is the leader of his party, as well as of the nation."[9]

Given the "possibility of having the annoyance growing continuously worse," said the *Faribault News-Republican*, "and confronted with the utter impossibility of ever breaking it up without making a crop of martyrs, it may be that [Wilson] was brought to a state approaching desperation and concluded that this was the best way to end it all."[10]

But perhaps there was another reason. For weeks, Wilson had been contemplating an end to the Great War. Two days earlier he had made a surprise address to Congress, outlining his far-reaching Fourteen Points, a foundation for present and future peace that was rooted in an association of nations. Among other points: open seas, an end to secret covenants, and the restoration of national sovereignty to war-torn nations. Better, he likely thought, that a messy domestic struggle over votes for women not interfere with his historic crusade to save the world.

In the six months since the first American troops arrived in France at the end of June 1917, war-induced austerity had descended on America like a joyless new season. The signs of a downcast mood were evident on New Year's Eve in Times Square, where few revelers were on hand to watch the electric light ball plummet from the Times Tower and the electric sign flash 1918. The *New York Times* said, "The New Year slunk in with rubber shoes on, coming upon a lightless, noiseless, and frigid Broadway."[11]

It was extraordinarily cold that January. Transportation delays snarled coal deliveries, and much of what arrived in the Northeast was frozen into solid blocks. To the fuel shortage was added a milk shortage and a bread shortage. The nation's food czar, Herbert Hoover, called for meatless Tuesdays, wheatless Mondays and Wednesdays, a couple of porkless days, and "Victory Bread" made from grains other than wheat. Rice throwing was banned at weddings. Whale meat swam onto menus.

Fashion models vamped in cloth-saving silhouettes so slim, said the *Times,* that "the fashionable lady of the moment is but one straight line with hardly an interruption. . . . What with war menus and war styles there will be no seeing us at all after awhile."[12]

For working women, there was a bright side. Waitresses, seamstresses, and domestics traded their low-wage jobs for bigger paychecks doing work once claimed by the men who ran machines, collected trolley fares, and counted out money in banks. The new factory workers in long skirts and hair tucked into caps were first objects of curiosity and then of study. It turned out that in the metal trades women had a particular affinity, claimed the National Industrial Conference Board, for work of a "repetitive" character, in which one simple operation was performed over and over. In fact, they did it better than men, were more careful with their tools, and more steady and dependable. In banks, offices, and factories alike, they seldom asked for time off and they always came to work on Mondays.[13]

A newcomer to the factory floor was Paul loyalist Florence Bayard Hilles, Delaware aristocrat, ambassador's daughter, senator's sister, lawyer's wife. At fifty-three, she was older than most of her co-workers. But to the teenage girls and the young mothers with whom she stood side by side wearing a cap and sleeve protectors, filling shells in a munitions factory, she was "Florence," not "Mrs. Hilles," and her skin turned yellow and her hair orange with "powder poison" as theirs did. She didn't need the money, but she craved a patriot's satisfaction. The unexpected bonus, she told the *Suffragist*, was a "lesson in democracy."[14]

In December 1917, the Woman's Party had been forced to vacate their cherished Cameron House after it was purchased by the Cosmos Club. Following an unsettling two months in temporary quarters, Alice and her crew moved into a handsome, four-story mini-mansion at 14 Jackson Place on the west side of Lafayette Square.

Alice loved the new building, which had a ballroom that would seat three hundred. In addition, she had long dreamed of opening a tearoom, a gathering place for suffragists, reporters, and friendly bureaucrats, and here there was space to do so. Soon, the *Suffragist* was carrying ads for "The Grated Door," which served a 25-cent breakfast, 50-cent lunch, and 85-cent dinner. But unlike Cameron House, 14 Jackson didn't come furnished, and it required extensive repairs. The end of the struggle in Congress was surely so close. Dora Lewis, now the party's treasurer, questioned the wisdom of spending hundreds on a furnace and steam pipes, for surely "we shall use them only a short time." Alice disagreed and pledged that not a cent of "suffrage" money would go for furnishings.[15] Members contributed furniture, some of it valuable antiques. Betty Gram made rugs out of paper towels to take the chill off the floors. The new tenants picked up paintbrushes. Alice's office was done in purple, white, and gold; she hung a favorite watercolor of Susan B. Anthony.

On February 11 the *Washington Post* published a small news item saying that the Woman's Party was pressing for the appointment of a female to fill the top post at Occoquan Workhouse. Raymond Whittaker, it seemed, had resigned as superintendent to go into the hotel business.

"The path of the lobbyist is a path of white marble. And white marble, though beautiful, is hard."[16]

Maud Younger, the author of those words, had trod the Capitol's white marble path too many times to count. To circle all five floors of the House office building required a mile of walking. Now the battleground was the Senate, where the marble path was shorter but the distance to victory more daunting.

Eleven votes short.

Maud paid her first call to a potential yes vote, Sen. James Reed, a Missouri Democrat. She took down his fulmination word for word. "Women don't know anything about politics. Did you ever hear them talking together? Well, first they talk about fashions and children and housework; and then, perhaps—about churches, and then, perhaps about theaters; and then perhaps"—Reed ended on a note of triumph—"And then, perhaps—about literatoor! Yes, and that is the way it ought to be."

"At each 'perhaps,'" wrote Younger, "he gazed down at his finger tips where his ideas appeared to originate, looking up at me at each new point."[17]

She had an easier time with Sen. James Phelan, a dapper Californian in a cutaway coat, who greeted her warmly. A Democrat, he had resisted suffrage only because the president had. He seemed happy to have a reason to change his vote.

So then, ten senators short.

Sen. Porter McCumber of North Dakota, who had been against the amendment in 1914, allowed that a resolution from his state legislature would give him political cover to change his mind. That night, Beulah Amidon telegraphed her contacts back in her home state, who included her father, a federal judge. Within days, the North Dakota legislature passed a resolution calling on its senators to vote for the amendment.

Nine senators.

When their respective state legislatures endorsed suffrage, Sen. Peter Gerry of Rhode Island and Sen. Charles Culberson of Texas, both Democrats, jumped to the "yes" column. Telegrams, newspaper editorials, and resolutions from diverse organizations bombarded Sen. William King, a Utah Democrat. "I'm as much opposed to suffrage as ever," he told colleagues several weeks later. "But I think I'll vote for it. My constituents want it."[18]

Six to go.

Keeping abreast of the Senate during those weeks was like trying to scale a sand dune. In all, ten senators died during the 65th Congress, seven of them friends of suffrage. Each death required a new toehold.

When New Jersey's pro-suffrage senator, Democrat William Hughes, died, the state's governor, also pro-suffrage, appointed a fellow Republican, David Baird, an Ireland-born lumberman and party boss from south Jersey. At first Baird refused to take a stand. Next he confided to suffragists that he would vote for the amendment so long as his position remained a secret. Word leaked out and he turned negative. Alice despaired. Without his vote, she thought passage was "hopeless."[19]

In February, the anti-suffrage senator from Wisconsin, Democrat Paul O. Husting, was shot by his brother in a duck-hunting accident. His elected replacement, Republican Irvine Lenroot, had voted for suffrage as a congressman, but was less than friendly in his new post. When Younger waylaid him, he snarled at her. "Nagging. If you women would only stop nagging!"[20]

And what about Senator Borah?

One of the most influential senators, Borah had a square, honest face, a dimpled chin, and his hair, parted in the center, fell to each side in a little wave. He was known for his integrity, his independence, and his splendid oratory, polished in Idaho's country courtrooms. Reporters and spectators hurried to the Senate gallery when word circulated that "Borah is up."[21] Beloved by miners and farmers, he leaned Progressive, though he was too much of a Republican loyalist to side with Teddy Roosevelt in 1912.

In 1910, Borah had introduced a suffrage amendment substantially like the one now before the Senate. But something had caused him to become an avowed anti-suffragist. Three years ago he had defended his opposition before a large gathering of Idaho suffragists plus Mabel Vernon. The Anthony amendment would never succeed in winning the thirty-six states required for ratification, he told them, and moreover it ought not to, owing to the distressing "burden" the "race question" placed upon the southern states that did not want Negro women to vote. Those states would stubbornly block Negro women from voting, just as they had Negro men, and the amendment would thus amount to a false promise, "a pledge to those people knowing it is not to be kept." He believed so strongly in that principle "that there is no possibility of my changing my views."

The Idaho women were stunned. Asked one, "Are you, then, more concerned about fulfilling a 'pledge' to black folk, Senator Borah, than you are about seeing justice done to all women?"

"But you can gain suffrage through the states," he protested. He turned to Mabel. "Why, you can have it in Delaware when you want it."[22]

Mabel was amazed at his seeming ignorance of Delaware politics. That spring, the legislature in her home state had defeated a suffrage bill.

Aside from New York's James Wadsworth, who was married to a leading anti-suffragist, Borah was the only senator from a suffrage state to oppose a federal amendment. But his states' rights position was filled with inconsistencies.

Along with many southern senators, Borah had supported the federal Prohibition amendment shutting off the flow of liquor the country over. How could he insist that each state had the right to determine who could vote but not the right to determine whether alcohol was legal? His stand required another contortion. Idaho voters had approved suffrage. As their elected representative, should he not respect their position, asked one letter writer. Replied Borah, were he to abandon his convictions, "what possible respect or admiration could you have for me under such circumstances?"[23]

According to Alice's count in mid-June 1918, they now needed the votes of just three senators, and she was not about to give up on the Lion of Idaho. Borah had flip-flopped once; perhaps he could be persuaded to flip-flop again.

In Idaho, organizer Margaret Whittemore proclaimed the situation "hopeless." Borah appeared immovable. "Senator Borah seems exceedingly difficult to win," Alice conceded. "But all of the remaining thirty-five men from among whom we must get the three votes which are still lacking, seem almost equally difficult."[24]

The National, too, had a corps of lobbyists, based in "Suffrage House," a twenty-six-room mansion on Rhode Island Avenue six blocks from the White House. And the National had its own "Maud" as well. Maud Wood Park was a longtime suffrage leader from Boston who had focused much of her energy on organizing college women. Reporters called the group the "Front Door Lobby," in recognition of its decorum. In contrast, Maud Younger and her cohorts, who often included Alice, thought it quite all right to "pre-empt all of the nooks and corners in the corridors about the Senate and buttonhole Senators going in or out of the chamber. They pay little attention to precedents," reported the *New York World*. They could often be found using "the space between the office of the Sergeant-at-Arms of the Senate and the Senate Chamber as temporary headquarters. There they surround Senators."[25]

In an article for *McCall's*, "Revelations of a Female Lobbyist," Younger described a conversation with Democratic Sen. Thomas Martin, who "would not sit down and talk suffrage, nor would he stand up and talk it. The only way to discuss suffrage with Senator Martin was to run beside him down the hall.

"'The good women of Virginia do not want suffrage,' said he, breaking almost into a trot, with eyes on his goal, which was an elevator." Younger concluded, "It was interesting to talk suffrage with Senator Martin, and very good exercise."[26]

As chief lobbyist, for two years Maud had tended the Woman's Party's burgeoning card index on representatives and senators, pruning old entries, planting new ones, and cultivating sources. By 1918 it occupied a room the size of a small pantry and its fame had spread.

When the Senate battle was at its most heated, the *New York Times* sent a reporter to investigate rumors that such a file existed. He arrived in a suspicious mood. The reporter asked if they used detectives. No, said Maud. The facts came from Woman's Party members and sometimes from other congressmen.

She gave him a taste of how the party drew on information. Suppose a congressman had said, "Women in my state don't want it." That was a signal to flood him with letters and telegrams demanding suffrage. One man promised a "yes" vote if only they would halt the deluge; answering the mail left his staff little time for anything else.

On one occasion they had deliberately dispatched a female constituent to a congressman who had vowed never to vote for the amendment, no matter how many voters asked him. Outraged at hearing his refusal first-hand, the woman gave $100 to the Woman's Party.

It helped to know if their target was a golfer. The greens might be the perfect place for a suffrage supporter and fellow golfer to apply sportsmanlike pressure. It helped to know if he had a weakness for alcohol. "One of our lobbyists may go to him and not know what is the matter with him." If he was always in his office at 7:30 A.M., that too was helpful. He might find a suffragist waiting for him. And it also helped to know as much as possible about his mother. "Mothers continue to have strong influence over their sons," Maud told the reporter. "Some married men listen to mothers more than to their wives."[27]

After the *Times* story was published on March 2, 1918, and word of the card index spread, so too did Maud's notoriety. Elsie Hill, eager to have her speak in New Hampshire, wrote, "The story of her 'card index' has carried up here and she would be a political power and a charmer."[28]

While success in the Senate remained a question mark, the U.S. Court of Appeals in the District of Columbia on March 4, 1918, threw out the convictions of a dozen White House pickets for "obstructing traffic." Under common law, said the Court, "the mere act of assembling was not unlawful, unless it was for an unlawful purpose."[29] It was a hugely important victory, for the suffragists and for posterity.

Henceforth the women might not be able to vote, but they could picket.

It could not have pleased Alice when in March Anne Martin announced her intention to become the country's first female U.S. senator, representing her home state of Nevada. Now? In the throes of the Senate battle? Not only would Alice lose a political workhorse, but the candidate was absconding with Mabel Vernon, and wooing others as well.

Alice stalled for several months after organizer Alice Henkle sought permission to join the Martin campaign. Finally Alice wrote her an unusually revealing letter. "My feeling about our movement, you see, is that it is so pregnant with possibilities that it is worth sacrificing everything for, leisure, money, reputation and even our lives. I know that most people do not feel this way about it but since I do you can see that it cost me a pang to think of anyone abandoning suffrage for any other work."[30]

In the absence of Martin and Vernon, Lucy Burns and Doris Stevens came down from New York to help with the campaign for Senate votes. Woman's Party organizers in the field churned up resolutions in favor of the amendment: the Working Girls' Club and the National Zionist Mass Meeting in Richmond. The State Implement Dealers in North Dakota. In Maine and Florida they canvassed state legislators, pressing for passage of a resolution directed at their senators in Washington. Vida Milholland sang for suffrage. And Dudley Field Malone spoke; turnout was huge for the lawyer who had defied the president, defended the militants, and relinquished a plum job.

None of it was enough. They were stuck, two to four votes short, depending on who was counting and on what day.

The chairman of the Senate Suffrage Committee was Andrieus Aristieus Jones, a freshman senator from New Mexico, a lawyer, and former mayor of Las Vegas. But the new senator was not as adroit as his adversaries. Twice in the months following the House victory, he announced a date for a vote and twice he backtracked.

On May 10, 1918, suffragists came early with lunches, packed the galleries, and offered silent prayers. By their count they were still two votes short. But Jones had assurances that the anti-suffrage senators would not muster. Instead they turned out in force, and he was forced to withdraw the resolution.

On June 27, circumstances again appeared favorable. Then a fight broke out over pairing, the custom by which an absent legislator of one stripe joins his opposite number, so that their votes cancel each other. A southern senator claimed the floor and began to pontificate with no sign of halting. Confronted with the unexpected filibuster, Jones again withdrew the suffrage motion.

And where was the president? Other than write a few wavering senators, he had done nothing to help since the House vote. Like boiling milk, resentment against Wilson built to a froth. The suffragists were certain that victory would be theirs with the president's wholehearted support. The *Washington Herald* agreed. "There is no doubt that if the President insists, the Senate will obey."[31]

In late May, Florence Hilles brought a half dozen of her sister munitions workers to tweak Wilson's conscience. For two weeks the women with coppery hair and yellow-stained fingers came daily to the White House, knitting as they waited quietly in an outer office lined with pictures of the president, watching prominent people stream in and out, arousing curiosity and even indignation from employees who told them they were wasting their time.

"You can't expect to see the President at this hour of the morning," fumed presidential secretary Joe Tumulty. "He plays his game of golf at 10:30." But when could they see the president? What about never? On May 25, newspapers carried a one-paragraph story. Tumulty had sent the petitioners a note stating "that nothing they could say could increase his interest in the matter, and that he had done everything he could with honor and propriety do in behalf of the passage of the amendment."[32]

On July 4, 1918, soldiers and sailors in dress uniforms massed with ten thousand other spectators at Mount Vernon to hear Wilson's Independence Day address. American troops in France now numbered a million, and a summer offensive was under way to wrest back territory held by Germany and to push the war to a victorious conclusion. Though perceived as a visionary for peace, in the eyes of the public Wilson had proved himself worthy of his title as commander in chief.

As he stood at Washington's tomb on the banks of the Potomac, the president called with full-timbered eloquence for "the reign of law, based upon the consent of the governed." He spoke of people's longing "for justice and for social freedom and opportunity."[33] Suffragists read the words the next day and fumed. Nowhere was there a reference to the amendment that would give *them* freedom.

"I think it high time we took drastic action," Connecticut's Lillian Ascough wrote Alice.[34] There was little enthusiasm for another round of arrests, but they *had* to do something. Lafayette Square as a venue for demonstrators appeared to pose no legal obstacles. Letters went out over Alice's signature to "Dear Suffragist," announcing an open-air meeting on August 6, the birthday of Inez Milholland. She would have been thirty-two. Alice cautioned that arrests were possible but not likely.[35]

Just hours before the demonstration, the mail brought formal notices from both Col. C. S. Ridley of the U.S. Army Corps of Engineers and Major Pullman, saying that a permit was indeed required to make a public speech in a public space.[36] Too late. Alice ignored them.

Gowned in white, a solemn procession of close to a hundred women bearing shimmering tri-colors marched across the park, heading for the three-story marble statue of Lafayette that faced the White House. They carried two lettered banners. One asked the familiar question, "HOW LONG MUST WOMEN WAIT FOR LIBERTY?" The other bore a sterner message, aimed directly across Pennsylvania Avenue. "WE PROTEST AGAINST THE CONTIN-UED DISFRANCHISEMENT OF AMERICAN WOMEN FOR WHICH THE PRESIDENT OF THE UNITED STATES IS RESPONSIBLE."[37]

Standing at the statue's base, her backdrop a bare-breasted maiden extending a sword to Lafayette atop his perch, Dora Lewis opened the meeting. "We are here," she said, "because when our country is at war for liberty and democracy—"[38]

As police seized her, Dora's last word lingered, suspended in the August heat, an irony not lost on listeners. After a moment of stunned silence, banner bearer Hazel Hunkins took her place and began to speak. Police arrested her too. One after another, women rose to speak and were led away by men in uniform. The respected nurse and social reformer Lavinia Dock began to sing "America." The song was cut short by her arrest. When some of the banner bearers began to march around the statue, the police hurriedly consulted a book of regulations, then arrested them all. An officer spied Alice watching from the middle of the street and shouted, "That's the leader. Get her."[39] In all, forty-eight women were whisked away in patrol wagons.

Opponents' reactions followed the usual script. Once again, the Woman's Party militants had "brought the cause of woman suffrage into disrepute," said Mary Garrett Hay, the influential leader of the New York City Woman Suffrage Party. "Purely pathological," fumed the *New York Times*. On Capitol Hill, Sen. Thomas suggested that some legislators might reconsider their support "if this keeps up."[40]

In police court the next day, the women faced a new judge, the old one, Alexander Mullowney, having retired after the court of appeals threw out his rulings in March. His replacement, John McMahon, seemed no less sympathetic to the prosecution than his predecessor. When a flustered district attorney confessed that he had no grounds for a case, McMahon helpfully suspended proceedings twice to give the government time to figure things out. When the trial finally opened on August 15, 1918, there had been four more demonstrations in Lafayette Park and repeated arrests. Several of the accused limped into court, and others displayed bandaged wrists and arms from a tussle with police who had attempted to seize their sashes. The women had resisted "so vigorously as to cause the police to treat them rather roughly," the *Times* reported, ever generous to the authorities.[41]

Meanwhile, the district attorney had come up with two charges. The women who had spoken were accused of "holding a meeting in public grounds"; those who had not, with "climbing a statue."[42] Those charged with doing both could receive a double penalty.

Women knit and dozed as overhead fans pushed the stale air in circles. When their turn came for trial, the prisoners refused to recognize the jurisdiction of the court. "Women cannot be law breakers, until they're law makers," declared Hazel Hunkins. During the lunchtime recess, Helena Hill Weed ignored the extended hand of Captain Carl Flather, who had arrested many of the White House pickets. She told him he was a "willful, premeditated and deliberate liar."[43] His genial manner faded and he threatened to arrest her.

On August 15 McMahon sent twenty-four women to jail for ten to fifteen days, among them Alice Paul, Lucy Burns, Dora Lewis, Lillian Ascough, Lavinia Dock, Hazel Hunkins, and sisters Elsie Hill and Helena Hill Weed. But the waiting Black Marias would rumble off neither to the district jail, nor to Occoquan. Days earlier, Louis Brownlow, chairman of the Board of Commissioners, had ordered cosmetic repairs to a never-occupied district workhouse.

A journalist who had found a calling in local government, Brownlow favored suffrage, but his sympathies lay with the National. He was married to the president of the local affiliate; his father-in-law was Thetus Sims, the congressman with the injured shoulder who had voted aye for the Anthony amendment. An adviser to National lobbyist Maud Wood Park, Brownlow had enthusiastically backed every punitive measure against the Woman's Party pickets, disgusted with what he believed was their quest for martyrdom. When they finally achieved it, he had no way to retaliate.[44]

Until now.

The workhouse was a narrow brick building as tall as a church steeple with windows fourteen feet off the floor. The prisoners were supplied with straw pallets for mattresses. The cells reeked of sewer gas from open toilets, and something was terribly wrong with the drinking water. It smelled foul and tasted just as bad. At night, the prison's fetid air turned as damp and cold as winter fog.

Because the mechanism that locked the cells was jammed, the women were free to wander. They moved their pallets to the corridor and huddled together for warmth. By the second day, many complained of nausea, stomach cramps, and pains throughout their bodies. Several broke out in small red spots. They were convinced they were being poisoned.

Louis Zinkhan, the district jail warden, a man only slightly less reviled than Occoquan's Whittaker, was nominally in charge, though Brownlow was running the show. Zinkhan barred visitors, but when Senator Jones arrived with Maud Younger, he could scarcely turn them away. The pair found the women on their pallets wrapped in blankets, bedraggled and listless. Jones struck a match and held it aloft. It did not flicker in the motionless air.

When the prisoners refused food, as he had been certain they would, the commissioner launched a novel form of torture. He positioned two gas stoves in one of the jail corridors and deployed six cooks, hired for the task ahead. "I kept those cooks busy day and night frying ham," Brownlow wrote with evident satisfaction years later. The ham would not go to waste, because it could be fed to prisoners in the district jail. Why ham? "I was convinced that the fragrance of frying ham was the greatest stimulus to appetite known to man. It was terribly hard on the women."[45]

So hard, Brownlow suggested, although there is no evidence to confirm it, that the prisoners had begged to leave prison, driven almost mad by the tempting odor.

Brownlow doesn't say whether his boss knew about the ham torture. But Wilson evidently disapproved of what looked much like suppression of free speech. After five days, on August 20, authorities released the prisoners and issued them a permit to demonstrate in Lafayette Square whenever they chose.

With none of the Woman's Party flamboyance, Carrie Catt was at last pushing for the federal amendment. Members of the National had the kind of access to the president denied yellow-tinged munitions workers. "I shall do all that I can to urge the passage of the amendment by an early vote," Wilson assured a September 16 delegation. But the congressional session was almost over. Even allies were saying that time had run out.

Two hours after that meeting, Woman's Party loyalist Lucy Branham climbed to the base of the Lafayette statue, her feet at head level with a large crowd waiting to see what the suffragists would do next. She held aloft a slip of paper bearing the president's freshly made pledge to the National. A baby-faced twenty-six-year-old with a jumble of curly hair, whose mother, also Lucy, was a Woman's Party suffragist, she had worked in Utah during the 1916 western campaign and done time in Occoquan for White House pick-eting. She also had a hero's medal for saving a drowning swimmer. And now Lucy would be the first to burn Wilson's words, igniting yet another firestorm of criticism.

Standing by with a torch was Julia Emory. "We want action," cried Lucy, taking the torch from Julia. She touched it to the paper. The words flamed and turned to ashes. Lucy faced the crowd. "The torch which I hold symbolizes the burning indignation of women who for a hundred years have been given words without action."[46]

Two weeks later, as the session neared an end, suffrage supporters in the Senate counted noses. At last they had the votes—three more than necessary—for suffrage.

Not so, said the anti-suffragist senators. *They* held a one-vote margin.

The showdown was scheduled for September 26, a Thursday, "unless a fil-ibuster develops," hedged the *Times*.[47] And a prolonged debate did develop as senators rose to loudly proclaim their opposition. Meanwhile, a pro-suffrage sen-ator from each party sat in a corner making hourly tallies. Two "yes" votes, John-son from California and La Follette from Wisconsin, had not arrived. When Gore of Oklahoma, a supporter, entered, spirits rose. Then McClean of Con-necticut, a bitter anti-suffragist, turned up for the first time in weeks.

By Friday, the amendment appeared stalled, one vote short of the sixty-four required for passage. Itchy to adjourn, the senators jousted. Charges and coun-tercharges flew around the chamber like bats. Democrats and Republicans charged each other with lying about their tallies. Anti-suffragist James Reed ac-cused Senate leaders of behaving like little boys, taking orders from the "petti-coat brigade" outside the chamber.[48]

On Saturday, one of the newest senators, Democrat Christie Benet of South Carolina, thought to be pro-suffrage, defected from the cause. "I do not think woman suffrage is necessary at this time," he said. "I cannot regard it as a war measure."[49] Supporters lost hope but filibustered anyway. The session was held over till Monday, September 30.

And on that day the president of the United States finally did as suffragists across the spectrum had been urging. Appearing in person before the Senate, he pronounced passage of the federal suffrage amendment "vitally essential to the successful prosecution" of the war.[50] Suffragists were surprised and delighted to see Edith Wilson, her mother, and her sister in the Executive Gallery, loyally mirroring Wilson's conversion.

"It is my duty," the president said, "to win the war and to ask you to remove every obstacle that stands in the way of winning it."[51] By the time he was done—fifteen minutes later—Wilson had called for passage of the amendment as a war measure, as a measure of justice for women, and as a measure by which the rest of the world could judge the country's commitment to democracy.

His plea changed not a single vote. On October 1, the Susan B. Anthony amendment was defeated, two votes shy of the required two-thirds majority.[52]

CHAPTER EIGHTEEN

VICTORY!

WE PROTEST AGAINST THE 34 WILFUL SENATORS WHO HAVE DELAYED THE POLITICAL FREEDOM OF AMERICAN WOMEN. THEY HAVE OBSTRUCTED THE WAR PROGRAM OF THE PRESIDENT. THEY HAVE LINED UP THE SENATE WITH PRUSSIA BY DENYING SELF-GOVERNMENT TO THE PEOPLE.[1]

Six days after the Senate vote, on October 7, 1918, a quartet of suffragists wrestled the big banner and a complement of purple, white, and gold tri-colors up the Capitol's marble steps and stationed themselves at its portals. Minutes later, the Capitol police herded them into a subterranean guardroom.

It was a pattern that would repeat itself throughout the month of October, as the suffragists shifted their protests from the man in the White House, who had finally lent a hand, to the Senate's obdurate males.

The women picketed the Capitol when the Senate was in session and the Senate Office Building when it wasn't. As quickly as they were released, they reappeared. Soon their captors were waiting till after the Senate had adjourned, as late as 6 P.M., to let them go. Once, 11 P.M.

The banners named names. Wadsworth, whose New York regiment was fighting in Europe while he was "FIGHTING AGAINST DEMOCRACY IN THE SENATE." Shields of Tennessee and Baird of New Jersey, who had pledged to stand by the president's war program, then denied his appeal for suffrage as a war measure. And Borah, yes, Borah, who once said of Germany,

"They don't know over there what a free Government is." But Germany, cried the banner, had established universal suffrage. "DOES IDAHO WANT A SENATOR WHO VOTES TO PLACE THE UNITED STATES BE- HIND GERMANY AS A DEMOCRACY?"[2]

In yet another legal victory for the pickets, a federal judge ruled that the suffragists couldn't be held without being charged. The Capitol police now al- lowed the women to stand, but grabbed their banners, valued at $500. The women went to see the judge again. The police returned the banners.

As pickets spread across the Capitol's pristine facade, a deadly virus known as "Spanish influenza" drifted like poison gas across America. In Washington alone, health authorities estimated ten thousand had been sickened, with an un- certain number of deaths. Hospitals were so full that even people with ill rela- tives were being asked to stay away from the city. Too few doctors were available to conduct army physicals, so the draft had been suspended.

The campaign to elect the Sixty-Sixth Congress was entering its final weeks, but the epidemic hobbled candidates and suffragists alike. In Idaho, all public meetings were canceled. Theaters and schools were shuttered; stores closed early, and no more than ten people were allowed to gather in one spot, indoors or out. Many towns were quarantined against anyone coming or going.

Influenza also put the brakes on an encore to the 1916 Suffrage Special. Alice had to abandon her plan for two dozen former prisoners, uniformed in Occoquan's striped Mother Hubbards, with aprons and rags circling their waists, to whistle-stop across the country, speaking and soliciting funds on a train she had christened "Democracy Limited."

On the morning of October 21, 1918, a Sunday, a distinguished male visitor ap- peared at the Jackson Place headquarters. Alice greeted him with her political op- erative, Abby Scott Baker, at her side. She would need a witness to this exchange.

Ever since the Senate defeated the amendment, William Borah had been dropping hints that he might change his vote. He had the perfect cover in the Republican Party's endorsement of federal suffrage. He had merely to say that he felt honor bound to carry out the party platform. As Alice related their con- versation to a supporter, "He said that he could not make a promise to vote for the federal amendment before the election because this would seem as though he were attempting to catch votes, but that as soon as the election was over he would make a public statement as to his position."[3]

The senator from Idaho agreed to put his pledge in writing, as long as its source seemed to be the Woman's Party. As the two women watched, he wrote the following statement: "We have talked over the suffrage situation with Senator Borah, especially as to his view of the binding obligation of the platform of his party and our understanding from the interview is that he will carry out, by voting for the National Suffrage Amendment, the platform, if elected." Then came the quid pro quo, penned by Borah himself. "For this reason we no longer oppose his election." The senator said he would not publicly own up to his pledge, but the Woman's Party was allowed to say he had made it.[4]

Alice only half-believed that Borah would follow through on his promise. But she thought she could outwit him. After he left, she instructed Margaret Whittemore to release the statement, then have their Idaho supporters demand of Borah whether it was true. "I do not feel at all certain that he is going to vote favorably after the elections," Alice told Margaret, "but I feel that it is quite possible that he can be pushed into such a position during these next two weeks in which he will be committed beyond retreat."[5]

Borah tried to have it both ways. When questioned by voters, he denied making the pledge. But he admitted to Republican leaders in Idaho that the story was true, and he wired a copy of the statement to his campaign manager. Word of its existence spread, and many women believed he would vote for the amendment if reelected.

Disgusted with Borah's two-step, Alice wrote him off. With just a week remaining until voters went to the polls, she wired Whittemore to forge ahead with an anti-Borah campaign. "Only self respecting course we can pursue is to cast all our strength against him."[6] Within the Woman's Party, the Lion of Idaho acquired a new nickname: Knight of the Double Cross.[7]

Whittemore promptly slung a banner across a main street in Boise. "Vote against Senator Borah. He defeated the National Suffrage Amendment." It vanished in broad daylight. A replacement was torn down as well. The suffragists made the most of the crime, reporting it to police, the mayor, the governor, and newspapers. They restrung the banner, reported Whittemore, and the next night came "more excitement."

"A band of men climbed to the roof of the building and shot at it. . . . We have now given out the statement that we will have kites made and float them, so they cannot be taken down." There was only one problem with this plan. "Unfortunately no one knows how to make a kite in this town."[8]

The congressional winners would not take their seats until March. Suffrage supporters would thus have four months to pry an additional vote from the lame-duck Congress that would convene immediately after the November 5, 1918, election. Should they fail, they would have to begin anew, with a vote in an all new House and another in the Senate.

In New Jersey and New Hampshire, voters would fill two vacant seats in the outgoing Senate, exactly the margin of victory needed to pass suffrage. Running for reelection, David Baird, the south Jersey Republican boss, had held one of the seats as an appointee and voted against suffrage.

Suffragists poured into New Jersey, defying a flu epidemic that had felled 4,400. Siphoned off by the war, doctors and nurses were scarce. Hospitals were overrun. Dead bodies piled up so fast that teams of horses ploughed mass graves. However risky the campaign, women were determined to defeat Baird. Lucy Burns, Vida Milholland, and Elizabeth Rogers came down from New York, and Elsie Hill from Connecticut. Dora Lewis led a Pennsylvania contingent. Dudley Field Malone and Harriot Stanton Blatch teamed up with the Democratic candidate, Charles Hennessey. Alice put her sister Helen to work in Burlington County. For once there was a measure of cooperation with the local National affiliate, whose volunteers canvassed voters.

In New Hampshire, the suffrage position of Republican George Moses, Taft's onetime minister to Greece, was a mystery. Inez Milholland's father, John, who had nurtured Moses's senatorial ambitions, told the candidate he was "heading for defeat and disastrous defeat" if he did not speak out in favor.[9] But Moses waffled.

Alice waited hopefully for Wilson to step in. She thought the least he could have done was to ask New Jersey voters to oust Baird. Finally she wired her organizers out West to campaign against Democratic candidates, as the president and the party "seem to be doing nothing to win two additional votes still needed in Senate."[10]

On November 5, obliging policemen kept an eye on baby carriages, while New York women went to the polls for the first time and voted for forty-three representatives, who would henceforth be accountable to female constituents if they wished to stay in office. Suffrage, on the ballot in a few states, carried in Oklahoma, South Dakota and, at last, in Michigan; Louisiana voted it down.

From Washington, Maud Younger polled the incoming members of the Sixty-Sixth Congress. A New York delegation newly tuned to the siren call of female voters was solidly in favor of suffrage, and Maud calculated the amendment would win easily in the House and squeak through in the Senate. But prospects were poor for passage by the outgoing Sixty-Fifth. Baird had won, and Moses, who appeared to be leaning anti, had also been elected.

Failure to approve the bill before March would not only mean beginning anew but would also bode ill for ratification. If it passed in early 1919, the legislatures in forty-three states would still be in session and able to ratify. But if the amendment was delayed until after the new Congress convened in May, all but eleven would have adjourned. For women to vote in the 1920 primaries or even in the 1920 general election, governors would have to call special sessions, an expensive prospect fraught in many instances with political risks and few apparent benefits.

Everyone knew the amendment, once approved, would eventually become law. Unlike the Prohibition amendment, which gave states only seven years to ratify, no time limit was attached. But failure to ratify by 1920 would require that a rapidly unraveling movement somehow regroup and soldier on.

At 3 A.M. on November 11, 1918, sirens screamed and church bells pealed. The *New York Times* building lit up like a giant lantern, and the searchlight atop its tower swept golden beams over the peaks and valleys of the sleeping city. Word had just reached American shores that the Great War had ended. Within minutes Times Square echoed with the cheers of revelers. Drivers left their milk wagons, taxicab drivers and streetcar conductors abandoned their conveyances, people on their way to work detoured. Men hoisted soldiers and sailors on their shoulders and bounced them around like children.

Across America, dawn ushered in a day of celebration for the common folk who had loyally sent their boys off to fight a distant, costly, and little-understood war. Mayors in every city and hamlet declared a holiday. Factories and schools closed, spilling workers and children into the streets for impromptu parades that grouped, disbanded, and regrouped throughout the day and into the night. Wash boilers and frying pans, tin horns, and whistles were pressed into service to produce a cacophony punctuated here and there by gunshots. More than one person was injured by random bullets. Churches overflowed with joyful worshippers eager to offer prayers of gratitude. Confetti rained down and fireworks shot upward. Kansas City prudently closed its saloons.

In Washington, Wilson read aloud the terms of the armistice to Congress, concluding in a memorable understatement, "The war thus comes to an end."[11]

Alice delivered her own victory address, a thumping speech rich with cadence, published in the November 16 issue of the *Suffragist*.

At this very time a year ago we were eighty votes short of a favorable vote; this time a year ago both majority parties believed suffrage should come state by state; this time a year ago the President believed suffrage should be won by the states, and this time a year ago suffrage was not before either the House or the Senate as a practical political subject.

This year we have seen the old views of the Administration crumble—even to the point of going up to the Senate to plead for Suffrage. During this year we have seen the opposition in the House disappear. During this year we have seen both political parties endorse national suffrage. And during this year, finally, we have seen every single one of the votes necessary to pass suffrage in the Senate secured—except one.[12]

One vote. Four months.

On December 16, as dusk approached, three hundred women in full regalia marched from the Jackson Place headquarters toward the Lafayette statue. First came state delegations, with fluttering flags and flickering torches, then row after row of women bearing the familiar tri-colors. One by one, women tossed the words of the country's leader into a cauldron at the statue's base and touched them with a torch—"all the words," said the *Suffragist*, "he has ever uttered or written on the subject of democracy."[13] With each offering, flames burst upward, stabbing the darkness.

Once again, Alice had demonstrated her talent for pageantry and ability to shock. After speaking so forcefully for the amendment in September, the president had fallen silent in October. Anti-suffrage Democrats coasted to victory in November, unimpeded by the party's leader. Suffragists had been abandoned again by their president. From flaunting Wilson's utterances on banners, Alice had ratcheted up her disdain by burning them.

Christmas found Alice holed up at headquarters with other holiday orphans, away from home for the third year. On December 25, 1916, she had staged the Milholland memorial. In 1917, Tacie Paul was evidently expecting her, but Alice wired on Christmas Eve that she would not be coming. "I have been saving my present to thee until thee came," her mother answered, "but will send it now for thee to get something thee wants." She wished her daughter "a pleasant day."[14] As 1918 drew to a close, Alice and her housemates shared dinner around the fire in the drawing room, doubtless deep in speculation about what 1919 would bring. They knew how it would begin, on the sidewalk in front of the White

House, with a New Year's Day conflagration. And from that date on they would keep their fire, a "watchfire," burning.

In the suffragists' opening parry of 1919, with the White House as a backdrop, a new banner denounced the nation's leader for "deceiving the world when he appears as the prophet of democracy."[15]

A crowd gathered, morphing into a mob as the soldiers and sailors on the scene absorbed the message. It was too much. A melee ensued. Alice and four others were arrested.

For five nights, despite freezing temperatures, more arrests, and sporadic mob attacks, the suffragists defiantly kept the fire going in the park, hiding wood under their coats as they furtively made their way toward the urn. In headquarters, fumes seeped from the room where the wood marinated. The entire building reeked of kerosene and so did the keepers of the flame.

On January 4, Dora Lewis drew the 2 A.M. to 5 A.M. shift. "So many interesting things happened during those quiet hours," she wrote her friend Mary Burnham. A man appeared with a large bundle of faggots that he placed at her feet "to help keep our liberty fire burning. Was not that quite beautiful of him?" A young *Washington Post* reporter arrived at 3:30 A.M. with the story that would appear in the morning edition. He told Lewis "with great conviction, 'The way I figure it out is this, men are more important than women.' So you see, our night world is like our day world; even when there are only a few there are still divided opinions."[16]

During another tour of duty that afternoon, Dora was arrested, along with Alice Paul and a third member of the Woman's Party.

The authorities knew the women had done something wrong. People just couldn't go about randomly setting fires. But as the trial opened on January 6, they once again had trouble finding a law to fit the crime. They settled on "lighting bonfires after sundown." But when was sundown? The judge sent for an almanac, delaying the trial an hour and a half until they could check the hour the sun made its exit. Observed Dora, "I suppose if it had been a cloudy day and if it could not have risen or set at all, we would not have been convicted."[17]

In the courtroom, Alice dictated thank you letters to women who had contributed wood. She dashed off a note to her mother, who had planned to visit. "Was sentenced to prison this morning for five days so cannot see you tomorrow. Sorry to miss you."[18] When Tacie and Helen came anyway, Warden Zinkhan turned them away. Zinkhan's days were numbered. By July he had been "dismissed," according to the *Washington Post*.[19]

Demonstrations, arrests, convictions and hunger strikes continued through the month; many women were arrested over and over. During their previous trials, the suffragists had refused to answer questions. Now they refused to behave. Julia Emory rose from the dock to chat with a friend at the rail, ignoring whispered pleas from a bailiff to return to her seat.

The judge sentenced thirteen women for contempt, including Florida's white-haired Mary Nolan, star of last year's federal picket trial, whom Alice had imported when reporters' attention began to flag. During Nolan's fifth trial that month, she cried out, "I am guilty if there is any guilt in the demand for freedom."[20] There was no stopping the applause for the woman who signed her letters, "the oldest picket."

From jail, Mildred Morris, a federal worker, reported that the food hadn't improved. "Not one worm is wasted." The cells had been scrubbed down, however. "One may now clearly distinguish cockroaches and bedbugs as they crawl up and down the walls."[21]

In the field, organizers worked to marshal the missing Senate votes. Joy Young was keeping a death watch on Tennessee Democrat John S. Shields, a Senate opponent. "He had some bad disease in his gums and had to have all his teeth pulled and a very bad infection got into his veins from that operation, so that he is now suffering from blood-poisoning." She dared not target him in his condition. In South Carolina, her home state, Anita Pollitzer's sources told her that Sen. William Pollock was very close to making a pro-suffrage statement. Without Pollock's commitment, Jones, the head of the suffrage committee, was refusing to schedule a vote. Alice fretted. "Pollock's indecision will soon kill the bill for this session."[22]

On January 23, with thirty-nine days left in the session, Lucy Burns stepped up efforts to recruit protestors for one last big demonstration. They needed "to gather in jail all the women who are willing to go there."[23]

On February 9, 1919, a procession of a hundred women armed with fluttering flags, tri-colors, and accusatory banners aimed at the president, plus two women carrying an urn, and a twenty-six member cotillion of wood bearers, marched in formation to the White House. The next day, the Senate would vote on the amendment. By all counts, supporters were still one vote shy, but they were banking on the possibility that one of two men would come through in the final hour.

The honor of dropping the effigy of Woodrow Wilson into the flames fell to Sue White of Tennessee, a recent convert from the National. The *New York*

Times described it as "a huge doll stuffed with straw ... slightly over two feet in height." But Alice, who surely knew, maintained the "so-called effigy" was merely a "little paper cartoon from the *Suffragist*." She defended herself. "It did not seem to be any more serious than burning his speeches, while it had the advantage of being something different and, therefore, getting more publicity where another burning of the speeches would not have had any particular news value."[24]

Thirty-nine women were whisked away by police. Twenty-five went to jail.

When the amendment came up for a vote, just two senators took the floor. South Carolina's Pollock, a son of secessionists, spoke long and eloquently. "What could give to any citizen of a country a right to vote except a stake in their country? Who could have a greater stake in a country than a wife, a mother, a mistress of a home?" He spoke for the "new South," he said, "the real south," and the "American South." "We want this privilege. We feel that the women are entitled to it, and we know that we can handle any race question that comes up in this enlightened age."[25]

But the old South had its say, in the person of Sen. Edward Gay of Louisiana, who offered up the familiar argument, "the right of the States to decide this matter for themselves."[26]

The amendment lost by one vote.

Hope flared anew just before the end of the session when Gay offered a compromise resolution that gave women the ballot but granted states the right of enforcement. Alice decided she could live with it. But New York's Wadsworth blocked it on a technical maneuver, and the chance for federal suffrage fell under the weight of his petulance.

Afterward, old hands Dora Lewis and Maud Younger went up to the Hill "to see Congress on its dying night." In the aftermath of defeat, the words of a southern congressman offered sufficient solace that Dora quoted them at length to a friend. "Your being so annoying and persistent and troublesome and being just like that sand that gets into your eyes when the wind blows, is what has put the suffrage amendment on the map. It is like a cinder in your eyes, you have to get rid of it. What your organization has done means this amendment is going through ten years sooner than it ever would have done without you." He laughed as he spoke. If they ever quoted him, he said, he would deny it.[27]

On February 15, with the influenza epidemic in abeyance, the Prison Special steamed across country. Everywhere crowds turned out to hear the war stories of genuine militants dressed in baggy Mother Hubbards.

The final demonstration against Wilson, and one last attempt to burn his words, was March 4, 1919, in New York, when Alice Paul led twenty-five pickets to the Metropolitan Opera House, where the president was to speak on the eve of his departure for Europe. Before a fire was lit, police rushed, beat, and trampled the women and destroyed their banners, assisted by members of an instant mob. Alice was arrested with five others, held briefly, and released without explanation.

The suffragists did not know then that the violent scene was the dénouement to two years of protest that began January 10, 1917, with the first picket line, and that theirs were the last arrests. During that time, some 2,000 women had picketed, 500 had been arrested, and 168 served jail time.[28]

When the Sixty-Sixth Congress convened on May 19, 1919, prospects for a favorable vote were again good in the House but still shaky in the Senate, where four men refused to reveal their intentions. After an April poll showed the amendment stuck, one vote shy of passage, Alice deployed her organizers to scrounge for votes, and found one with Georgia's new senator William Harris, who had served in the administration for the past six years. Half a dozen pro-suffrage Democrats came to the rescue and convinced Wilson to confer with Harris, and shortly thereafter, they had their vote.[29]

The endorsement of New Hampshire Senator Henry Keyes gave them a margin of safety. When yet another Senator converted, Frederick Hale of Maine, they were home free.

Every year since 1913, at the dawn of each new Congress, suffragists had implored the president to support the amendment in his opening day message. At last he did so, but the text cabled from Paris and read aloud by clerks on May 20 lacked drama. Wilson said only that "every consideration of justice and of public advantage" called for the "immediate adoption" of the suffrage amendment. It was scarcely a bugle call to action, but he sounded a grace note, albeit in tortured wording: recognition to the "women and men who saw the need for it and urged the policy of it when it required steadfast courage to be so much beforehand with the common conviction."[30]

The following day, the amendment sailed through the House with little debate, passing 304 to 89—42 votes more than the required two-thirds majority.[31]

Days passed, however, with no movement toward a Senate vote. Finally, on June 3, suffragists again packed lunches and trudged to the Capitol for what now appeared certain to be the last debate. Missing were their two leaders. After the last painful defeat, Carrie Catt had vowed never again to listen to Congress ponder suffrage. And Alice felt sure enough of passage to embark on a fundraising tour. Overcoming a $10,000 deficit from the Prison Special took precedence over the momentary thrill of victory.

A shopworn amendment to limit the extension of suffrage to white women was defeated; likewise another, greatly feared by suffragists, that would have referred ratification to state conventions rather than legislatures.

The vote was called on June 4. Suffragists waited on the edge of their seats as the first senator, Henry Ashhurst of Arizona sounded an "aye," followed by four intransigent B's: Bankhead, Beckham, Borah, and Brandegee. Then came anticipated "ayes" from five C's: Capper, Chamberlain, Culberson, Cummins, and Curtis. The voting hopscotched through the alphabet; listeners ticked off the names. With the last aye, James Watson of Indiana, they knew they had won.[32]

A roar went up from the galleries. The vote was 56 to 25 in favor.

On the trail of money, Alice missed the jubilee dinner party at headquarters. "Most everybody of the real family is here but you and the circle seems very incomplete," wrote Julia Emory to "Dear little leader."[33] Congratulatory letters and telegrams piled up.

"Your place in History is assured," wrote an admiring jurist, Walter Clark, chief justice of the North Carolina Supreme Court. "There were politicians, and a large degree of public sentiment, which could be won only by the methods you adopted."[34]

"Your unconquerable soul in that frail little body has done it all," scribbled Elizabeth Rogers. "I can hardly believe it is really true. I had so little faith in men. I feared they would play tricks at the end."[35]

And congratulations to the National Woman's Party from "Colonel" Ida Craft, of the 1913 Pilgrims brigade, which "put pep into the work for the federal amendment."[36]

Alice's single-minded crusade had allowed no room for romance, but she had attracted admirers. Passage of the Nineteenth Amendment prompted two to write letters with fond memories of personal encounters. "My dear Miss Paul," began "Howard G. Brownson, Ph.D." from Des Moines, upon reading of her in the magazine *Everybody's*. He recalled "some pleasant experiences in Philadelphia and even a trip to the Paul home a few years ago." He had "not yet been persuaded" about the wisdom of suffrage, he said, but "ever since we were first introduced your pluck and heroism has [*sic*] interested me. Somehow you have grasped, as few have done in this age, the power of suffering, of non-resistance, of meekness." He wished that he, too, could "break away from the bonds of dead custom and convention, and dare to live the life of heroism and complete self surrender you have lived."[37]

Another fan, himself a well known zealot, was artist Frank Stephens, the founder of Arden, a Utopian colony on a wooded Delaware farm. In a voice as humble as Brownson's, he wrote to "Dear Alice Paul" that he understood what it meant to be committed to a cause, in his case land reform: "every available effort bound to that one thing." But he, too, could not meet her measure. He was "without the ability that has brought suffrage under your leadership—and without the personal courage you women have shown." He ended his letter, "I wish with all my heart that I could see you again in peace and find another time like that one good summer evening when you were all kindness."[38]

Perhaps the most satisfying reaction was that of the *New York Times.*

For six years the newspaper's editorial page had openly reviled suffrage. But the view from the Times Tower underwent a distinct change in 1919 after the newspaper featured Maud Younger's card index in a lengthy Sunday story. The catalogue was suddenly famous. From the Russell Sage Foundation came a request to examine the cards for a study of publicity and organization. The *Literary Digest* called it "an elaborate, powerful, and hitherto little-known instrument" that was "cleverly conceived" to put pressure on Congress.[39]

The files provided the *Times* with an acceptable explanation for how the women had wrested victory from a recalcitrant Congress. It was not the demonstrations, deputations, petitions, and electioneering that had turned the tide. "Triumph of the Index" proclaimed an editorial following the House victory.

And when the suffrage resolution prevailed in the Senate, the *Times* came as close to a compliment as it could muster. The writer gave credit to the much larger National for its "sagacity" and "habitual moderation." Yet it was the National Woman's Party that was "bolder, more original, implacable. . . . In the hands of determined women a full card index of politicians is mightier than pen or sword."

The *Times* had not gone over to the other side. Ratification, the paper noted hopefully, offered formidable obstacles. Likely more than thirteen states were negatively inclined, the number that would spell defeat. But the card index had instilled doubt in the writer's mind.

"Yet Legislatures are weak and politics and women powerful persuaders."[40]

CHAPTER 19

FORWARD INTO LIGHT

Six days after the amendment passed, Wisconsin became the first state to ratify, just ahead of Illinois and Michigan. Before June was out, nine states had
voted in favor. But fully twenty-eight governors would have to call special sessions to ensure ratification by the 1920 election. In addition to cost, there were
as many other reasons not to do so as there were governors.

Woman's Party organizer Vivian Pierce wrote from California that the governor was in no hurry to act. Fully "a score of disgruntled factions [were] anxious
for an extra session to repeal legislation the Governor has signed." [1] Potatoes
were the root of the problem in North Dakota, where the legislature was dominated by farmers. Fargo-based Ella Riegel said it would be suicidal to meet before the harvest, whenever that was. The potato crop "*may* be ready to gather
the end of Sept. *or* may not be ripe before the middle of Oct."[2]

Given the obstacles, "It scarcely seems probable" that the amendment would
take effect by 1920, opined the *Washington Post*. The *Waterloo Times-Tribune*
predicted 1924.[3] Four more years! How could Alice hope to hold the Woman's
Party together for that length of time? No sooner did a state ratify than its branch
disbanded. Already the National had held a "Victory Convention" and voted to
become a new organization, the League of Women Voters.

Where once they had spent years negotiating with a single body of colorful
and opinionated lawmakers, now Alice Paul and her operatives had just over one
year to tame a dozen or more recalcitrant state legislatures, populated by hundreds of small-bore politicians, whose actions were as likely to be governed by

historic grudges, family feuds, secret deals, masked motives, cravings for power, and all around misogyny as they were by reasoned judgments susceptible to argument. Since 1913 she had raised and spent a half million dollars. The final phase would require at least $50,000.

Alva Belmont was less visible these days, and also less generous. Her attorney had embezzled more than $120,000 from her sister's estate; as one of the executors, she had to make good. An even greater drain on her income was a wartime income tax that climbed to 75 percent for people in her bracket.[4]

By 1919, however, Alice had acquired a network of friendly officeholders, government appointees, influential politicos, and well-placed newsmen, who fed her information and did her bidding when it was mutually advantageous. She would need them all. She had lost several valuable operatives. Lucy Burns was back in New York; Mabel Vernon was headed for Nevada, where Anne Martin was again seeking a Senate seat. And Maud Younger, lobbyist extraordinaire, had sailed for Paris to care for her ailing father.

In her favor, the political parties were mindful of the role women would play in the 1920 election. Even without the amendment, seventeen million would be able to vote for president, though just seven million for Congress. With the amendment, the number climbed to twenty-eight million and women could choose candidates for every federal office. Democrats were desperately seeking ways to steal credit from the Republicans, who had pushed the amendment through Congress and spearheaded ratification in those state legislatures where they outnumbered Democrats, a majority. At every opportunity, Wilson, new friend of women, urged Democratic governors and legislators to work for ratification.

Alice refused to write off any state, even those in the suffrage-averse Deep South. She appointed Dora Lewis national ratification chairman and sent her to Georgia. On her first day in Atlanta, Dora learned all the influential men were at something called a "barbecue." "I do not know exactly what a barbecue is, but I strongly suspect that the governor is doing it too."[5]

As expected, Alabama and Georgia trounced the amendment, the first of eight southern states to do so. California ratified in November, the Dakotas and Colorado in December. The year 1919 ended with twenty-two of the required thirty-six. But instead of speedy victories in the western states where women could vote, a wall of resistance rose up like the Rockies. Among the holdouts were Oregon, Washington, Arizona, Oklahoma, and even Wyoming, the first state to enfranchise women. Oklahoma's governor inveighed against "he-women from the north."[6]

In the nation's capital no one was at the helm. Wilson spent much of the year at the Paris peace conference, and on his return he was embroiled in opposition from congressional conservatives to the League of Nations, a mechanism for resolving international disputes and fostering peace, incorporated largely at his insistence into the Treaty of Versailles. On October 1, 1919, Wilson suffered a debilitating stroke. For the remainder of his term, the president remained largely hidden from public view; his physician, wife, and secretary conducted state business behind a screen of secrecy.

On January 16, 1920, Prohibition took effect. Two things then happened. A crime wave of astonishing proportions swept the country as lucrative opportunities opened up for smugglers, bootleggers, and illegal purveyors of alcohol. And the liquor lobby immediately sought to reverse the ban, or at least turn it into something less potent. Denying women the vote became a high priority.

In New Jersey, the political bosses who had opposed prohibition now united to combat suffrage, which the state's foremost politico, Democrat James Nugent, labeled "the mother of all isms," threatening the stability of the American government.[7] No tactic was too petty. The owner of a Trenton hotel was forced to evict suffragists after Nugent threatened to withdraw his patronage. But a pro-suffrage address by Senator Selden Spencer of Missouri to the Republican caucus helped turn votes, and on February 10, New Jersey became the twenty-ninth state to ratify, followed by Arizona and Idaho.

In Oklahoma, the governor had finally yielded to demands for a special session. When Lillian Kerr arrived on February 23, the state senate was tied fifteen to fifteen, with ten uncommitted lawmakers. She could almost hear the meshing of gears and the warning whistle as the Washington crew fired up its locomotive. "Before six hours elapsed we were conscious of the fact that the National Woman's Party Headquarters at Washington was in action," Kerr wrote Alice. "Telegrams began to pour in from the leaders there to the leaders here." Both senators wired messages. "Telegrams from the Oklahoma Congressional Delegation followed promptly." Wilson wired his desire for passage. The debate that followed, Kerr wrote, was "a terrible ordeal—'blood, thunder, riot and sudden death' type of argument from our opponents," but in the end the suffrage supporters prevailed.[8]

Where was Jesse Bloch?

Under the gold dome of the West Virginia capitol, on the banks of the stately Kanawha River, one half of the senate was holding the other half hostage until its vacationing member, a bespectacled forty-year-old tobacco millionaire from Wheeling, could charge to the rescue of the Susan B. Anthony amendment.

The House had passed the bill but the state senate had tied, 14 to 14, then refused to reconsider. Still, the session could not end without a majority of both houses voting to adjourn. And so the fourteen pro-suffrage lawmakers signed a pact to wait for Jesse, a like-minded Republican, said to be sunning himself somewhere in California.

When Bloch surfaced, in Pasadena according to one report, he jumped on a train, still in his swimming suit. It made good reading—and by now the newspapers were full on the story—but the senator would later say he was in San Francisco when he read that his colleagues needed him.

By March 4, Bloch and Mrs. Bloch were speeding east. A front page editorial in the *Charleston Daily Mail* fumed that the senate was running up a bill of $1,500 a day to stay in session—"a wicked perversion" that promised "untold evils for the future."[9]

The West Virginia lawmaker arrived in Chicago at 11:30 A.M. March 9. A one-car special booked for $5,000 by the Republican National Committee panted in a train shed, ready to spirit him to Cincinnati and a connection with the 7:00 P.M. train for Charleston.

After a journey already being compared to the historic ride of Paul Revere, the Wheeling legislator entered the Senate on the afternoon of March 10 to a standing ovation. A suffragist pinned a yellow flower to his lapel. The Senate voted to reconsider. At 6:10 P.M. the thirty-fourth state ratified.

The state of Washington followed on March 22.

Thirty-five. One to go.

The Republican state of Delaware could not, would not fail. A century of struggle would come to a triumphant end in a diminutive, red-brick statehouse, the seat of power in a largely rural state with three counties and 223,000 residents. The ratification banner in Woman's Party headquarters would sprout its thirty-sixth star.

To Alice's dismay, however, the pro-suffrage head of the Republican Party, Alfred I. du Pont, lost his wife in January, 1920, and resigned from politics just before the Delaware campaign. But he would have no peace. For the next three months, the Woman's Party pressed the grieving widower to drive ratification home, appealing "through members of his family, his political friends, his personal friends, national Republican leaders and all other avenues of approach that we could find."[10]

On March 22, a special session opened and suffragists swarmed over the tiny state like bees, vying with anti-suffragists to pin a yellow jonquil or tri-colored badge on every lapel before their rivals arrived with a red rose. Alice threw her nine available organizers into the fray. Then she arrived herself to take charge.

But Delaware shared a peninsula with Maryland and Virginia, and its downstate Democrats were just as opposed to suffrage as their southern neighbors. When they threw in with the anti-suffrage Republicans, the coalition in the House was strong enough to crush the ratification resolution, 26 to 6. The Senate passed it 11 to 6, but the House refused to reconsider, even after Alfred du Pont lent his support. The *Times* posted an epitaph on May 29, 1920. "Suffrage Dead at Dover."

Still one state short. Meanwhile, two stubborn New England governors, both Republicans in states with pro-suffrage legislatures, were preventing millions of American women from voting. Five times had suffragists gone to Connecticut's Marcus Holcomb asking for a special session, and five times he had said no. Vermont Governor Percival Clement insisted that only voters, not legislators, could endorse ratification.

As Republicans gathered in Chicago to nominate a presidential candidate, they were met on June 8, 1920, by Alice and her followers holding aloft a new crop of banners. "VOTE AGAINST THE REPUBLICAN PARTY AS LONG AS IT BLOCKS SUFFRAGE," shouted one. Stopping to chat with pickets, Corinne Roosevelt Robinson, Teddy's sister, told them her brother "always believed in you. I admire your courage."[11]

The Ohio legislature had ratified, but the state constitution required a popular referendum as well. Voters—all men—could still reject the measure. But on June 1 the U.S. Supreme Court ruled that the decision of the Ohio state legislature was final. Tennessee also required what amounted to a referendum: a legislative election after an amendment was passed by Congress but before it was voted on by the state legislature. For that reason suffragists had ruled out the state as a candidate for ratification before 1920. Suddenly, thanks to the Court's ruling, Tennessee was open territory.

The Republicans had nominated Ohio Senator Warren Gamaliel Harding for president and now the Democrats put up the state's governor, James Middleton Cox. Alice was determined to drag both candidates into the Tennessee fracas. Thanks to geographical proximity—their headquarters were less than a hundred miles apart—Woman's Party leaders were able to play one off the other with relative ease. Abby Scott Baker bounced between the two, demanding Cox and Harding rally their respective party members in Tennessee, where Alice was opening a new front in an inhospitable universe.

The antis were already revving up, and the state's two biggest papers opposed the amendment. Tennessee's mountainous terrain made it difficult to track down legislators. Sue White wanted fifteen organizers plus Alice. Alice could afford to send only nine, while she stayed in Washington. "I will come to Tennessee the moment I can raise enough money to keep work going while I am away," she wrote. But there was never enough. In June Dora Lewis borrowed $5,000 from her bank to lend to the campaign.[12]

Contributions dribbled in, scrimped from household budgets. From Mildred Hicks in Bainbridge, Georgia, $2.50, "Send it where it will do the most good." Five dollars from Mrs. M.C. Barnard in Emlenton, Pennsylvania, "Wish it was $1,000—Am also passing your letter along—hope you may hear from others." From Gertrude Achilles of Ossining, New York: "$5 for myself, $5 for my daughter, $5 for my housekeeper. Here's to success!"[13]

On August 9, 1920, the curtain rose on the last great suffrage drama. Fully six groups of suffragists and anti-suffragists had opened headquarters in Nashville. Largely absent from the ratification battle until now, Carrie Chapman Catt had slipped into the Tennessee capital in mid-July, booked herself into the elegant Beaux Arts Hotel Hermitage, and taken charge of a deeply divided National chapter. The political landscape was filled with traps. Everywhere she looked, Catt said, she saw "suspicion, animosity and uncompromising hate."[14]

Monitoring events from Washington, Alice realized that a supposed majority for ratification in early June was dissolving like ice in the August heat. Speaker Seth Walker, who had introduced the ratification resolution and vowed his support, suddenly did an about face, leading a stampede to the other side

When the Tennessee Senate ratified on August 13, by a vote of 25 to 4, the lopsided margin thrilled even the most optimistic suffrage supporters. Insiders, however, knew that the house loomed as the real test, and its members were backpedaling.

In the Hermitage Catt took note of the presence of "mysterious men in Great Numbers" who were escorting off-duty lawmakers up to the eighth floor, awash in bottomless quantities of bourbon and moonshine. By evening, supporters and opponents alike were reeling through the corridors. Wrote Catt afterward, "The Legislature was drunk!"[15]

Alice's moles reported a complicated new plot, engineered by Connecticut Sen. Frank Brandegee, an arch-conservative believed to be behind the refusal of Holcomb, the Connecticut governor, to hold a special session. Lobbyists for the influential Louisville and Nashville Railroad were nudging Tennessee lawmakers to vote "no." L&N's opposition suddenly made sense when Alice learned that its owner was the Atlantic Coast Line Railroad Company, with roots in Connecticut. Atlantic's chairman, she was told, had a close relationship to Brandegee. And Brandegee, standing for reelection that year, had good reason to fear the wrath of newly enfranchised women.[16]

The house debate began on August 17 in a hilltop capitol modeled after a Greek temple, draped for drama with yellow bunting. The vote came the next morning. Walker, the house speaker and suffrage turncoat, offered a motion to table, proclaiming full-throttle: "The battle has been won, and the measure has been defeated." But his motion lost on a 48–48 tie. A surprise "nay" came from Banks Turner, a Democrat not allied with the suffragists. Anti-suffragists immediately called for a vote on the ratification resolution itself. Suffragists despaired. Another tie would mean failure.

Just before the vote Febb Burn had written her son Harry, at twenty-four the house's youngest member, "Hurrah and vote for suffrage and don't keep them in doubt." [17] But Burn, a Republican, voted to table the first time around. As the roll call began on the resolution, his mother's words nagged at him. When his name was called, he voted aye. Suffrage had won! Or had it? What would Turner do? Later in the roll call, Turner passed. The anti-suffragists cheered. But before the roll call ended, he asked to be recorded as voting yes. Ratification had been approved, 49 to 47.

Women screamed. Women jigged in a jostle of bodies. Women waved suffrage banners and threw yellow flowers. And women wept. In Washington, Alice stitched the thirty-sixth star on the ratification banner and draped it over the second floor railing of headquarters, as a dozen of her workers on the ground applauded with upraised hands.

A motion by the Tennessee antis to reconsider flopped. When a county judge issued a five-day restraining order forbidding the governor to certify the ratification results, Governor Albert H. Roberts chose to ignore it. On August 24, he signed the ratification certificate and sent it by train to Washington. At 3:45 A.M. on August 26, an aide awakened Secretary of State Bainbridge Colby at home. Colby thought it would be unseemly to sign a constitutional amendment "in the wee morning hours of the night."[18] He sent the certificate to his department's solicitor for review, then settled down with a cup of coffee to await its return by 8 A.M.

By prior arrangement, according to an account by suffragist Emma Wold, Colby was to summon members of the Woman's Party for a ceremonial signing and photograph. Alice and her co-workers sat up waiting. Finally, at 8 A.M. they received word to come to the State Department. Once there, however, they were not invited into Colby's office. After staying for as long as felt "compatible with our dignity and with the dignity of women in general," said Wold, they returned to headquarters, whereupon they learned Colby had already signed the proclamation.[19]

Afterward he invited Alice to return. She did so reluctantly but by then Carrie Catt had arrived with a delegation from the National. Catt was photographed on leaving Colby's office, looking victorious, while Alice was kept waiting again. Alice's session with Colby never took place.

Said Wold, "It was not so much the disappointment about which we felt bitter as it was the indignity placed upon Miss Paul, and the fact that the Secretary deliberately broke his word and behaved cowardly. That, and the continuation of the bitter hostility of the other organization, has sunk very deeply into our souls."[20]

Alice remained characteristically silent. But Abby Scott Baker declared the denouement "quite tragic. This was the final culmination of the women's fight, and women, irrespective of factions, should have been allowed to be present when the proclamation was signed."[21]

The national turnout for the presidential election on November 2, 1920, was 26,765,180, eight million more than in 1916. In New York City, where 90 percent of registered voters cast ballots, women frequently outnumbered men. So heavy was the voting in certain New Jersey precincts that barrels were substituted for ballot boxes.

What happened in Savannah, Georgia likely occurred all too frequently in the South. When Negro women attempted to cast ballots, authorities turned the would-be voters away, citing a law that required registration six months in advance. Moreover, said newspapers, "no white women presented themselves at the polls."[22]

In a decisive rebuff to Wilson and the League of Nations, Harding won a sweeping victory over Cox, carrying all but eleven states. Despite opposition from suffragists, Wadsworth was reelected in New York as was Brandegee in Connecticut.

Well in advance of the election Alice Paul had decided to file an absentee ballot rather than travel to Moorestown. Her signature required verification by a notary public. A photographer snapped a picture of Alice with her hand upraised, capturing a moment she and the notary must have relished. Taking her oath was Catherine Flanagan, a three-year soldier in Alice's army, who had done time in Occoquan. She was among the first female notaries appointed after the suffrage proclamation. Outgoing President Wilson had signed her certificate.

At some point after that, Alice's long-suffering mother opened a scrapbook she had started in 1919, when she and Helen moved from the Home Farm into town. In it, Tacie Paul penned a brief entry:

"During the summer Suffrage was granted to women & we voted for the first time for the President Nov. 1920.

"Alice at last saw her dream realized."[23]

EPILOGUE

The executive committee of the National Woman's Party met to ponder its future on September 10, 1920, when the Nineteenth Amendment was just two weeks old. The setting was Alva Belmont's latest luxury abode, Beacon Towers on the north shore of Long Island, a 140-room full-scale replica of an Irish castle; a dazzled journalist described one fireplace as "big enough to live in."[1]

While Doris Stevens took notes, some of the biggest names in feminism held forth. Alva Belmont favored a full-fledged political party, and Harriot Blatch, back in the fold, agreed that the world needed an independent feminist force. Author Charlotte Perkins Gilman spoke loftily of an organization with mass power and a flexible program in the hands of a party with brains. Socialist Crystal Eastman called for a feminist movement focused on education, freedom in occupational choice, and birth control.

Lucy Burns attended the meeting, but she heard nothing there to tug her back to Alice's side. The ideas were commendable, she said, but her fear was that they "would take until eternity to translate into fact."[2]

In the end, it was Alice Paul who set a concrete goal: equal rights for women, shaped by legislation at both the state and national levels. Suffrage alone would not convey the right to serve on juries or give women equal standing in cases involving children and property or grant a myriad of other entitlements. Alice had planned the new tack all along. Following the election, she and Maud Younger had moved into a small apartment, while Alice raised money to pay off the $10,000 debt from the ratification campaigns. But she also enrolled in the George Washington University Law School and the Washington College of Law, attending one by day and one by night. By doing "double work," she wrote Tacie, "I can graduate next summer, I think."[3] Before the decade was out, she had earned three law degrees.

Soon it became obvious why Alice believed she needed a legal education. Over the next two decades, the Woman's Party drafted 600 pieces of legislation and saw 300 passed. Alice wrote the original version of the Equal Rights Amendment (ERA) in 1923 and revised it in 1943.[4] The narrow legal reforms, however, did not tap the springs of emotion unloosed by the suffrage struggle, nor did they lend themselves to pageantry or demonstrations. As for the ERA, many women were conflicted by the opposition of powerful women's organizations that seemed to hold dear their best interests.

Between the two world wars, the National Consumers League, the Women's Trade Union League, and the National American Woman Suffrage Association in its new incarnation as the National League of Women Voters blocked the ERA at every turn, arguing that it would eradicate hard-won protections for women against exploitive wages and hours. They had an ally in Eleanor Roosevelt, beloved by American women.

The Woman's Party membership plummeted from its peak of sixty thousand during the late teens. By the 1960s only a few hundred women remained on the rolls. Though hampered by a shrinking membership and a perpetual shortage of funds, the party never ceased its quest. The ERA was first introduced in 1923 and in every Congress thereafter for almost fifty years. Gradually more and more organizations concluded it would help rather than hinder women, American presidents fell into line, and congressional opposition dwindled. The National Organization for Women spearheaded the drive anew, and in 1972 the amendment finally passed. It was never ratified.

After the Nineteenth Amendment became law, the women warriors scattered. A dozen of the younger ones quickly married. Doris Stevens became Mrs. Dudley Field Malone, the wife of the crusading Woman's Party attorney who had resigned his administration post in protest against Wilson's treatment of the pickets. The marriage lasted just seven years. Dudley Malone's 1929 Christmas gift to Alice was a collection of his speeches, *Unaccustomed As I Am—*. He signed it, "In happy memory of great days—affectionately Dudley Field Malone."

When in 1923 her youngest sister died in childbirth, Lucy Burns acquired a new cause. She and her two older sisters stepped in to care for their motherless niece, Janet Burns Appleton, whose father was a distant presence. In 1931, when she was fifty-two and her red hair had faded to a rich gold, she wrote in her Vassar class report that she had "taken on the care of a niece . . . thinking it would be rather lovely to have a child growing up in a corner of our home, only to find out as the years fly past, that it is I who am in the corner, while the child occupies the center and nearly all the circumference of our lives. I have become an impassioned baby-minder. I really need someone to come along and emancipate me."[5]

Maud Younger, the onetime "millionaire waitress," contributed her lobbying talents to the ERA until her death in 1936.

After a leave during which she earned a master's degree in political science from Columbia University, Mabel Vernon returned to the Woman's Party. She worked for the ERA until 1930, when she joined the Women's International League for Peace and Freedom. She devoted the years until her retirement in 1955 to the twin causes of peace and disarmament.

Dora Lewis remained loyal to Alice, but age increasingly limited her activities. She spent her sixty-seventh and last year in New Haven, Connecticut, where her son Robert was a physician.

Alva Belmont died in 1933. Her funeral, for which she had left precise instructions, tapped the spirit of the suffrage years for one last pageant. A thousand mourners gathered for the service in Saint Thomas Church on Fifth Avenue, where she had married off her daughter Consuelo to the Duke of Marlborough in 1895. Robed in traditional purple, white, and gold, women bearing matching tri-colors marched solemnly up the side aisles as a cadre of honorary pallbearers in the center aisle, including Alice Paul and Christabel Pankhurst, preceded a coffin draped in rose velvet and blanketed with flowers. A banner bearer carried Susan B. Anthony's last pronouncement, "Failure Is Impossible," which accompanied Alva to her grave.[6]

In 1938, deeply disturbed by the plight of women under repressive totalitarian governments in Spain, Italy, and Germany, Alice founded a World Woman's Party with headquarters in the stately, nineteenth-century neoclassical Villa Bartholoni on Lake Geneva, Switzerland, today a museum dedicated to the history of science. Until war doomed the League of Nations, she lobbied its diplomats for guarantees of female equality. As the decade ended in desolation and despair, refugees poured into Geneva seeking asylum in whatever country would have them.

Alice opened the villa and her heart. During the summer of 1940, she gave up her large front room to a Jewish family that had fled Austria: Alice Muller, her husband Felix, and their two small children. Felix Muller, a linguistics professor, had been hounded from his job by the Nazis and briefly imprisoned in Buchenwald. Forty years later, interviewed in America by oral historian Amelia Fry, Alice Muller could still picture Alice Paul on the phone with the American consul in

Zurich ("She called him quite often"), ordering him to intercede on their behalf. "One day she stamped her foot. She was quite annoyed. 'I *know* these people; I can *vouch* for them. They will make *good* citizens. They *must* get to America.'"[7]

Life at the villa, even in those early war years, was quite formal. Diplomats frequently came to high tea, served on a lawn that stretched down to the lake. Dinner prepared by another refugee, Erika Lowenstein, was served by candlelight on elegant china with polished silverware. Regardless of the occasion, said Alice Muller, Alice Paul wore purple. "I don't think she wore any other clothes but purple. Everything was purple! Everything!"[8]

Alice used her connections to rescue at least eleven Europeans, most of them Jews. She would have helped more, but time ran out and she herself left Geneva.

In 1945, thanks in large measure to Alice's continuing efforts in the international field, the United Nations incorporated equality provisions into six different sections of its charter, including the preamble, which affirms faith "in the equal rights of men and women and of nations large and small."[9]

Twenty years later, her party rent by schisms, Alice nevertheless scored another important victory: a prohibition against sex discrimination in employment in Title VII of the 1964 Civil Rights Act.[10]

ERA historian Susan Becker, reflecting on the party's post-suffrage legacy, wrote, "In fighting for its vision of women's equality, the NWP [National Woman's Party] kept feminism alive during the interwar years, alerted women to the legal and economic discriminations against them, and I think, prevented many of these discriminations from becoming worse. Finally, in formulating the Equal Rights Amendment, NWP feminists pointed the way to a future equality before the law that, unfortunately, women do not yet enjoy."[11]

When in 1965 Letha Mae Glover first noticed the rundown house overrun by vines on Constitution Avenue, she wondered who lived there, if anyone. After she glimpsed a group of elderly women sitting in the rear patio, she concluded it was an old folks' home. Glover was thirty, the mother of small children, and had a home nearby. Learning that the occupants needed someone to clean, she applied. Alice Paul interviewed her and gave her the job.

Alice, now eighty, had no secretary. She pressed Glover into action. "Miss Paul told me what she wanted me to do for her on the ERA. I told her, 'I know nothing about the ERA.' And she said, 'I'm going to teach you. You can read, can't you?'"

"I can read,'" Glover assured her.[12]

And from then on, Glover was more than a housekeeper. "A Senate paper came out every day, and whenever there was the name of a senator or congressman introducing the ERA, she said, 'I want you to call his office and thank him.'" Glover had never been inside the Capitol, but soon Alice was giving her material to deliver to members of Congress. "Everything was ERA."[13]

In those days the Woman's Party took in boarders to make ends meet. Among them was Christopher Hanson, a twenty-year-old volunteer for Sen. George McGovern's 1972 presidential campaign. The ERA would pass that year, and the house had filled with college students and equal rights pioneers who sallied forth daily to lobby. Sometimes Hanson would return late at night to find Alice still up. She would press him to make certain that McGovern would be on hand to vote favorably on some aspect of the amendment. His heart went out to the small, fragile old woman. When he protested that he was merely a lowly volunteer with no control over the senator's schedule, she would fix her blue eyes on him and say, "Please try."[14]

The day the ERA passed, recalled Glover, Alice did not join in the celebration. Congress had imposed a seven-year deadline, which ultimately choked off ratification. "She was just as unhappy as she could be."[15]

Alice moved to a small frame cottage in Ridgefield, Connecticut, that she had inherited from her sister Helen. In 1974, she was hospitalized for a head injury suffered during a stroke. She spent the next two years in a Connecticut nursing home, while her brother Parry's son, Donald Paul, her closest living relative, plundered her estate. He was removed as conservator and replaced by a court-appointed guardian, but it was too late. The money was gone.

On November 4, 1975, a small story appeared on page twenty-one of the *New York Times* under the headline "Mother of U.S. Equal-Rights Measure Nearly Penniless in Nursing Home at 90." It began:

> RIDGEFIELD, Conn., Nov. 3—On the eve of the vote on Equal Rights Amendments in New York and New Jersey, the author of the original Federal version is near destitution, recovering from a stroke at a nursing home here.
>
> Dr. Alice Paul, now 90 years old, nevertheless continues to push for the amendment that she drew up in 1922 and keeps abreast of the states that have ratified the equal rights amendment to the Federal Constitution.

Alice Muller's sister sent her a copy from France, where she had read the story in the *International Herald Tribune*. Muller went in person to the Quakers in Moorestown, New Jersey, Alice's old hometown, to ask that they help her erstwhile benefactor. The Quakers responded. "The next thing I learned," she told Amelia Fry, "was that Alice Paul is no longer in Connecticut but at the Greenleaf nursing home in Moorestown."[16]

As it happened, Alice's cousin Beulah Parry provided funds in her will to cover indigent Quakers. Sixty years earlier Beulah and her sister Susannah had been staunch opponents of Alice's suffrage campaign. Now, Alice was Beulah's beneficiary, and shared a room with Susannah.

When the Mullers visited Greenleaf, Alice Paul listened intently to all that had happened since she rescued them in Geneva. They had been resettled as egg farmers in New Jersey. Then Felix Muller began teaching. Six years earlier, when his hearing failed, his wife took his place.

"Do you get the same pay?" Alice asked.

"Yes, I do," replied Alice Muller.

Alice Paul patted her arm. "Praise them! Praise them!"[17]

Alice Muller noticed that her old friend was wearing a purple scarf.

When Alice turned ninety-two on January 11, 1977, the governors of Pennsylvania and New Jersey proclaimed "Alice Paul Day." Reporters called, television crews appeared, and the White House made arrangements for a telephone message from Betty Ford. Alice fretted for hours. What would she say to the First Lady, and more to the point, could she reach the hall telephone from her wheelchair? The call seemed to go well enough, however. Alice even laughed at herself, telling a reporter that "It was almost the most awful thing that ever happened to me."[18]

In her final months, her mind dimmed, but occasionally she would speak of the suffrage struggle to Carol Mullin, a young student nurse hired for private duty. When she talked about the ERA, however, the mists lifted. She badgered the young nurse. "What was I going to do to further the cause of women? You, you, you young people are the ones who should take up the mantle," Alice would say. And she would stare at the nurse with piercing "crystal blue eyes," unfaded by age. Said Mullin, "If I didn't have a good response, she dropped it. I could tell that I had let her down."[19]

Alice Paul died on July 9, 1977.

At a memorial service in Washington's august National Cathedral, her old ally Hazel Hunkins-Hallinan recalled the suffrage years for the benefit of younger mourners. She told them how "women came from all over the country, willingly and at their own expense, to take part in the picketing. And the paper carried headlines daily back in the hometown of the picketers. Alice Paul had made suffrage the burning issue of the day."[20]

Alice's contribution to the theory and practice of political protest can hardly be exaggerated. For six years, she devised one strategy after another to keep the cause of suffrage in the headlines, and in front of the president and Congress. Polite but incessant letters and petitions demanding the vote wore them down. In their white-domed preserve, lawmakers could not hide from female invaders armed with individual dossiers, who had elevated lobbying to a science. Back in the lawmakers' home districts, women from local chapters of the National Woman's Party hunted them down. No one was safe, neither Democrat nor Republican, from campaigns that stressed party responsibility.

It was part of Alice's innovative genius, too, that she targeted the White House. In doing so, she recognized what no one else had, that the mounting press of official business and the presence of journalists had changed that building's character forever. It was no longer merely the president's home, but a political nerve center.

The legal precedents set by the Woman's Party protected later generations who took their protests for civil rights, an end to the Vietnam War, and other causes to the streets, sidewalks, and parks around the White House and the Capitol. But more than that, Paul and her party virtually invented the modern tactics of nonviolent civil disobedience that those later protestors would use. Hunkins-Hallinan said, "We were attacked by mobs. We were clubbed by the Police. But Alice Paul never allowed anyone to retaliate." It was precisely the tactic used decades later by Dr. Martin Luther King Jr. and his followers.

"You may well wonder," Hazel continued, "how one young woman, slender, frail, modest, retiring, even shy, could have managed all this. She had the secret of all great leaders. Within her spirit was a flame forcing her to make right what she thought to be wrong to her sex and she communicated this in full strength to others. After a talk with Alice Paul about what had to be done, one left her presence twice one's size and ready to do anything for a cause she made you feel so deeply."[21]

NOTE ON
MAJOR SOURCES

For Alice Paul's childhood and the years she spent in Germany and England, I drew heavily on the Alice Paul Papers at the Arthur and Elizabeth Schlesinger Library, Radcliffe Institute for Advanced Study, Harvard University, Cambridge, Massachusetts. Also at Schlesinger and also useful were the papers of Doris Stevens and Hazel Hunkins-Hallinan. The oral histories conducted by Amelia Fry of Alice Paul, Mabel Vernon, Sara Bard Field, and Rebecca Hourwich Reyher were another major source. They are included in the Suffragists Oral History Project, Oral History Collection at the Bancroft Library, University of California at Berkeley, and available online at http://bancroft.berkeley.edu/ROHO/projects/suffragist/index.html.

The material involving the Congressional Union and the National Woman's Party is drawn primarily from the microfilm edition of the National Woman's Party Papers: The Suffrage Years, 1913–1920, and the National Woman's Party Papers, 1913–1974 (Sanford, NC: Microfilming Corporation of America, 1981). I used the copy owned by the Alexander Library at Rutgers University in New Brunswick, New Jersey. Because the papers are arranged chronologically, I cited reel numbers only where no date was available.

For back issues of the *Suffragist*, I read copies that were initially lodged at the Mt. Laurel, New Jersey, public library and were moved midway through my research to the Alice Paul Institute, housed in Alice's childhood home, also in Mt. Laurel.

The account of the 1913 suffrage parade owes much to the report of the Senate Committee on the District of Columbia, *Suffrage Parade*, May 29, 1913, Washington, D.C.

Especially helpful were two books written by contemporaries of Alice Paul and members of the National Woman's Party, *Jailed for Freedom* by Doris Stevens (New York: Schocken Books, 1976, reprint of 1920 edition) and *Up Hill With Banners Flying* by Inez Haynes Irwin (Penobscot, ME: Traversity Press, 1964).

Two newspaper databases were indispensable: the *New York Times* Archive for both its news and opinion pieces, and newspaperarchive.com, which reflects what Americans in scores of cities and towns around the country were reading about suffrage, and what their newspapers had to say on the subject. Other newspaper articles from the period can be found in the Alva Belmont Scrapbooks, in the National Woman's Party Papers, reels 164 through 169.

NOTES

ABBREVIATIONS

API—Alice Paul Institute
APP—Alice Paul Papers
APP/API—Alice Paul Papers at Alice Paul Institute
DSP—Doris Stevens Papers
HHHP—Hazel Hunkins-Hallinan Papers
NAWSAPP—National American Woman Suffrage Association Party Papers
NWP—National Woman's Party
NWPP—National Woman's Party Papers
NYT—New York Times
PWW—Papers of Woodrow Wilson
SL—Schlesinger Library
VULSC—Vassar University Library Special Collections
WP—Washington Post

PROLOGUE

1. www.usconstitution.net/sentiments.html.
2. Elizabeth Cady Stanton, *Eighty Years and More*, chapter 2 (www.gutenberg.org/files/11982/11982-h/11982-h.htm).
3. For a state-by-state discussion see *The History of Woman Suffrage*, (1888–1900), vol. 4, ed. Susan B. Anthony and Ida Husted Harper (Indianapolis: The Hollenbeck Press, 1902), 450–1011. Not until 1975 did the U.S. Supreme Court rule that excluding women from juries was unconstitutional.
4. *New York Times* (hereafter *NYT*), 21 May 1920.
5. *NYT*, 20 December 1908.
6. Ibid.; *NYT*, 27 November 1907.
7. Eleanor Flexner, *Century of Struggle: The Women's Rights Movement in the United States* (New York: Atheneum, 1974), chapter 22, 294–305.
8. Harriot Stanton Blatch and Alma Lutz, *Challenging Years: The Memoirs of Harriot Stanton Blatch* (New York: G. P. Putnam's Sons, 1940), 92.
9. *NYT*, 25 September 1917.

CHAPTER 1

1. *Conversations with Alice Paul: Woman Suffrage and the Equal Rights Amendment*, An Interview Conducted by Amelia R. Fry, Suffragists Oral History Project, The Bancroft Library, University of California, Berkeley, 1976, 15–16.
2. Ibid., 16.
3. Ibid.

4. Margaret Hope Bacon, *The Quiet Rebels: The Story of the Quakers in America* (Wallingford, PA: Pendle Hill Publications, 1999), 12.
5. Quoted in Norma Jacob, *Introducing Elias Hicks: A Condensation of Bliss Forbush's Original Biography* (Friends General Conference, 1984), 8.
6. John Bowie Associates, unpublished report, *Paulsdale: An Historic Structure Report*, for the Alice Paul Centennial Foundation, Inc., Mount Laurel, NJ, 1999, chapter 2, 30–32; Biographical Sketch, "Hon. William Parry," Major E. M. Woodward, *History of Burlington County* (Philadelphia: Everts & Peck, 1883; Reprinted by the Burlington County Historical Society, 1983).
7. Richard J. Walton, *Swarthmore College—An Informal History* (Swarthmore College, 1986), 4; ibid., 12–13.
8. *Diary*, September 21, 1901, and April 17, 1901, Alice Paul Papers (hereafter APP), Arthur and Elizabeth Schlesinger Library on the History of Women in America (hereafter SL), Radcliffe Institute for Advanced Study, Harvard University, Cambridge, MA, box 1: folder 14.
9. *Conversations with Alice Paul*, 7.
10. Alice Paul, "Sketch of the New York College Settlement School of Philanthropy, 1905–06," thesis, n.d., 1–2, APP, 2: 20.
11. Henry Roth, *Call It Sleep* (reprint of 1934 edition, New York: Penguin Books, 1976), 9.
12. Ibid., 141.
13. Alice Paul to Tacie Paul, October 1905, APP, 2: 31.
14. Certificate of The School of Philanthropy conducted by The Charity Organization Society of the City of New York, 105 East 22nd St., NY, awarded to Alice Paul in 1906, APP, 2: 20.
15. *Conversations with Alice Paul*, 20.
16. Alice Paul to Tacie Paul, 4 August 1907, APP, 2: 27.
17. Alice Paul to Tacie Paul, 21 July 1907, APP, 2: 27.
18. Ibid.
19. Alice Paul to Tacie Paul, 4 August 1917, APP, 2: 27.
20. Alice Paul to Tacie Paul, 26 August 1907, APP, 2: 27.
21. Emmeline Pankhurst, *My Own Story* (London: Eveleigh Nash, 1914), 38. Quoted in June Purvis, *Emmeline Pankhurst: A Biography* (London: Routledge, 2002), 67.
22. Bacon, *The Quiet Rebels*, 127.
23. *Conversations with Alice Paul*, 33–34.
24. Purvis, 104.
25. E. Sylvia Pankhurst, *The Suffragette* (New York: Sturgis & Walton Company, 1911), 246.
26. *NYT*, 22 June 1908.
27. Alice Paul to Tacie Paul, 22 October 1908, APP, 2: 28.
28. *Conversations with Alice Paul*, 39.
29. Alice Paul to Tacie Paul, 27 June 1908, APP, 2: 28.
30. Alice Paul to Tacie Paul, 14 January 1909, APP, 2: 29.
31. Alice Paul to Tacie Paul, 22 January 1909, APP, 2: 29.
32. Alice Paul to Helen Paul, n.d., APP, 11: 159.
33. Maria DiCenzo, "Gutter Politics: Women Newsies and the Suffrage Press," *Women's History Review* (March 2003), 24.
34. Ibid., 23.
35. Ibid., 27.
36. *Conversations with Alice Paul*, 45.
37. Alice Paul to Tacie Paul, n.d., November 1907, APP, 2: 27.
38. Alice Paul to Tacie Paul, 2 January 1909, APP, 2: 29.
39. Alice Paul to Tacie Paul, 5 June 1909, APP, 2: 29.
40. Ibid.
41. *Conversations with Alice Paul*, 47.

42. Pankhurst, *Suffragette*, 109.
43. Ibid., 111.
44. Ibid., 120.

CHAPTER 2

1. Pankhurst, *Suffragette*, 384; Alice Paul to Tacie Paul, n.d. July 1909, APP, 2: 29.
2. Ibid., 385.
3. Ibid., 386.
4. Alice Paul to Tacie Paul, n.d. July 1909, APP, 2: 29.
5. Ibid.
6. Lucy Burns, Seventh Annual Bulletin (1908), Vassar Class of 1902, Vassar University Library Special Collections (hereafter VULSC), 7.
7. Alice Paul to Tacie Paul, n.d. July 1909, APP, 2: 29.
8. Ibid.
9. Ibid.
10. Alice Paul to Tacie Paul, 27 December 1909, APP, 2: 29.
11. Purvis, *Emmeline Pankhurst*, 132
12. Pankhurst, *Suffragette*, 362–363; see also *Marion Daily Star*, 23 February 1909.
13. *NYT,* 22 August 1909.
14. Reprinted in Midge Mackenzie, *Shoulder to Shoulder* (New York: Vintage Books, 1975), 116–119.
15. Pankhurst, *Suffragette*, 392.
16. James D. Hunt, *Gandhi in London* (New Delhi: Romilla & Co., 1978), 102.
17. Ibid., 137–138.
18. Ibid., 139.
19. Alice Paul to Tacie Paul, n.d., APP, 2: 29.
20. Ibid.
21. Ibid.
22. Alice Paul to Tacie Paul, 5 August 1909, APP, 2: 29.
23. Marjorie L. Nickerson, *A Long Way Forward: The First Hundred Years of the Packer Collegiate Institute* (Brooklyn, NY: Packer Collegiate Institute, 1945), 100.
24. Ibid., 94.
25. Burns, Fourth Annual Bulletin (1906), Vassar Class of 1902, VULSC, 6.
26. Burns, Seventh Annual Bulletin (1909), Vassar Class of 1902, VULSC, 8.
27. Lucy Burns's notes for an unfinished article, transcribed by her great-niece, Janet Burns Campbell, and made available to the author.
28. *Brooklyn Daily Eagle,* 18 November 1909.
29. Ibid.
30. Ibid., 19 November 1913; "Epitaphs," Packer Collegiate Institute file on class of 1899.
31. *Conversations with Alice Paul,* 51.
32. Alice Paul to Tacie Paul, 21 August 1909, APP, 2: 29.
33. *Daily Record and Mail,* 21 August 1909, APP, 16: 226.
34. Alice Paul to Tacie Paul, 31 August 1909, APP, 2: 29.
35. Alice Paul to Tacie Paul, 25 September 1909, APP, 2: 29.
36. Purvis, *Emmeline Pankhurst*, 264.
37. *NYT,* 12 November 1909.
38. Ibid.; *Washington Post* (hereafter *WP*), 6 February 1910; Pankhurst, *Suffragette*, 459.
39. Alice Paul to Tacie Paul, 27 December 1909, APP, 2: 29.
40. Ibid.
41. Ibid.
42. *Fort Wayne News,* 27 November 1909.
43. *NYT,* 13 November 1909.

44. Edwin Parry to Tacie Paul, 20 November 1909; Marshall D. Swisher to Tacie Paul, 19 November 1909; Mickle T. Paul to Tacie Paul, 14 December 1909, APP, 13: 210.
45. Alice Paul to Tacie Paul, 9 February 1908, APP, 2: 28.
46. Alice Paul to Helen Paul, n.d., 1908, APP, 11: 159.
47. Alice Paul to Tacie Paul, 4 August 1907, APP, 2: 27.
48. Alice Paul to Tacie Paul, 17 March 1909, APP, 2: 29.
49. *Syracuse Post-Standard,* 29 November 1909.
50. *NYT,* 1 December 1909.
51. *NYT,* 30 November 1909.
52. Whitelaw Reid to Tacie Paul, 30 November 1909, APP, 14: 210.
53. Tacie Paul to Christabel Pankhurst, 2 December 1909, APP, 14: 210.
54. Christabel Pankhurst to Tacie Paul, 30 November 1909, APP, 14: 210.
55. Alice Paul to Tacie Paul, 10 December 1909, APP, 2: 29.
56. Alice Paul to Tacie Paul, 27 December 1909, APP, 2: 29.
57. Ibid.

CHAPTER 3

1. *Logansport Reporter,* 27 January 1910; *Philadelphia Inquirer,* 21 January 1910.
2. *Philadelphia Inquirer,* 21 January 1910.
3. Ellen Carol Dubois, *Harriot Stanton Blatch and the Winning of Woman Suffrage* (New Haven: Yale University Press, 1997), 94.
4. Unidentified news clipping, box 6: folder 46, Alice Paul Papers at Alice Paul Institute (hereafter APP/API), Mt. Laurel, NJ.
5. Ibid.
6. "Woman Suffrage at Moorestown," *Friends' Intelligencer,* 19 February 1910, 121–122.
7. Ibid., 122.
8. "The Church and Social Problems," *Friends' Intelligencer,* 20 August 1910, 514.
9. Ibid.
10. *NYT,* 14 April 1910.
11. *WP,* 15 April 1910.
12. Ibid.
13. Ida Husted Harper, ed., *History of Woman Suffrage (1900–1920),* vol. 5 (New York: National American Woman Suffrage Assn., 1922), 269–271.
14. *WP,* 15 April 1910.
15. *Conversations with Alice Paul,* 62.
16. *WP,* 15 April 1910.
17. *New Castle News,* 15 April 1910.
18. Harper, ed., *Woman Suffrage,* 5: 271–273.
19. Caroline Katzenstein, *Lifting the Curtain* (Philadelphia: Dorrance & Company, 1955), 44.
20. Ibid., 45.
21. Ibid., 49.
22. Ibid., 50.
23. Ibid.
24. Ellery C. Stowell, n.d. APP, 1: 1.
25. Carl Kelsey to Alice Paul, 17 April 1912, APP, 2: 21.
26. Ida Porter-Boyce to Alice Paul, 5 August 1912, and Jane Campbell to Alice Paul, 2 July 1912, APP, 16: 227.
27. Dora Lewis to Paul, 15 July 1912, APP, 16: 227.
28. William Parker to Paul, 15 September 1912, APP, 3: 38.
29. Lynn Sherr, *Failure Is Impossible: Susan B. Anthony in Her Own Words* (New York: Random House, 1995), 94.

30. Mary Beard and Florence Kelley, "Why Women Demand a Federal Suffrage Amendment" (Washington, D.C.: Congressional Union for Woman Suffrage, 1916).
31. Paul to Lewis, 24 October 1912, microfilm edition, National Woman's Party Papers (hereafter NWPP) (Sanford: Microfilm Corporation of America:1979), at Alexander Library, Rutgers University, New Brunswick, NJ; Harper, ed., *Woman Suffrage*, 5: 378.
32. Wilson to Eugene Noble Foss, 17 August 1912, Papers of Woodrow Wilson (hereafter PWW), ed. Arthur S. Link (Princeton, NJ: Princeton University Press, 1966), PWW, 25: 42; Arthur S. Link, *The Road to the White House* (Princeton, NJ: Princeton University Press, 1947), 3.
33. Wilson to Bynner, 20 June 1911, PWW, 23: 160; Wilson to Foss, 17 August 1912, PWW, 25: 42.
34. *NYT,* 20 October 1912.
35. *Evening Bulletin*, 20 November 1912.
36. *Public Ledger*, 23 November 1912.
37. Alva Belmont, "Why I Am a Suffragist," *The World To-day*, 21 October 1911, 1172. Quoted in Peter Geidel, *Alva Belmont: A Forgotten Feminist*, PhD dissertation, Columbia University, 1993, 73.
38. Shaw to Member of the Official Board, 20 March 1909, Laura Clay Papers, Margaret I. King Library, University of Kentucky, Lexington, KY. Quoted in Geidel, 78.
39. *Public Ledger*, 22 November 1912.
40. *NYT,* May 9, 1909.
41. Max Eastman, *Enjoyment of Living* (New York: Harper, 1948), 322, 324.
42. *Public Ledger*, 25 November 1912.
43. *Evening Bulletin*, 21 November 1912.
44. *An Account of the Proceedings on the Trial of Susan B. Anthony on the Charge of Illegal Voting, at the Presidential Election in Nov.*, 1872 (Rochester, NY: Daily Democrat and Book Print, 1874), 159. http://books.google.com/books.
45. Ibid.
46. *Evening Bulletin*, 24 November 1912.
47. Blatch and Lutz, *Challenging Years*, 129.
48. Ibid. 129, 132.
49. *NYT,* 5 May 12 1912.
50. Harper, ed., *Woman Suffrage*, 5:378.

CHAPTER 4

1. *Conversations with Alice Paul*, 66–68, 70.
2. *WP,* 23 January, 1911.
3. Testimony of Richard Sylvester, *Suffrage Parade*, Report of the Committee on the District of Columbia, United States Senate, 29 May 1913, 137.
4. Testimony of Alice Paul, *Suffrage Parade*, 132. Elsie Hill, ibid., 128.
5. Ibid.
6. *NYT,* 5 May 1912.
7. Sylvester testimony, *Suffrage Parade*, 197.
8. Lucy G. Barber, *Marching on Washington* (Berkeley: University of California Press, 2002), 3.
9. Paul to Caroline Katzenstein, 7 January 1913, NWPP.
10. Testimony of John A. Johnston, *Suffrage Parade*, 226.
11. Testimony of Helen H. Gardener, *Suffrage Parade*, 451.
12. Franklin McVeagh to Elizabeth Kent, 2 January 1913, NWPP.
13. Paul to Mary Ware Dennett, 6 January 1913, NWPP.
14. *WP,* 10 January 1913.

15. David Glassberg, *American Historical Pageantry: The Uses of Tradition in the Early Twentieth Century* (Chapel Hill: The University of North Carolina Press, 1990), 105.
16. Paul to Mary E. Bakewell, 18 January 1913, NWPP.
17. Paul to NAWSA board, 16 December 1913, NWPP.
18. *World*, 26 January 1913.
19. *Morning Telegraph*, 11 November 1918.
20. Inez Haynes Irwin, *Uphill With Banners Flying* (Penobscot, ME: Travesity Press, 1964), 14.
21. Ibid.; Crystal Eastman, *On Women and Revolution*, ed. Blanche Wiesen Cooke (New York: Oxford University Press, 1978), 64.
22. Irwin, *Uphill*, 14–15.
23. Ibid., 24.
24. Ibid., 19–20.
25. Ibid., 23.
26. Ibid., 25.
27. *WP*, 2 February 1913.
28. *WP*, 24 February, 1913; *Fort Wayne News*, 16 January 1913; *WP*, 10 February 1913; *WP*, 28 February 1913; *Evening Tribune*, 30 January 1913.
29. *Fort Wayne News*, 24 January 1913; *Oakland Tribune*, 23 February 1913.
30. George Clinton, *Indiana Progress*, 5 February 1913.
31. Affidavit from Wm. Henry Dennis, *Suffrage Parade*, 200.
32. Paul to Dr. Burghardt Du Bois, 12 July 1913, NWPP; Paul to Blackwell, 15 January 1913, NWPP.
33. For coverage of the Green case, see the *WP*, 3 January, 25 January, 2 May, 4 June, 6 June 1913.
34. Paul to Blackwell, 15 January 1913; Blackwell to Paul, 23 January 1913, NWPP.
35. Dennett to Paul, 14 January 1913, NWPP.
36. Nellie Quander to Paul, 15 February, 1913, NWPP; Paul to Nellie Quander, 23 February 1913, NWPP.
37. Mary Beard to Paul, n.d. 1913NWPP.
38. Clara B. Wells to Paul, 27 February 1913, NWPP; NAWSA to Paul, 28 February 1913, NWPP.
39. Anna Shaw to Paul, 24 February 1913, NWPP.
40. *WP*, 21 February 1913.
41. *WP*, 22 February 1913.
42. Caroline I. Reilly to Lucy Burns, 30 January 1913, NWPP.
43. Ibid.
44. Helen Hill, 16 February 1913, NWPP.
45. Elizabeth Hyde to "Ladies," 1 February 1913, NWPP; Dennett to Paul, 27 February 1913, NWPP.
46. Inez Milholland to Paul, 7 February 1913; Paul to Inez Milholland, 12 February 1913, NWPP.
47. Paul to Agnes Ryan, 3 February 1913, NWPP; Ryan to Paul, 6 February 1913, NWPP.
48. *WP*, 1 February 1913.
49. *Fort Wayne News*, 1 February 1913.

CHAPTER 5

1. *New York American*, 2 February 1913.
2. Paul to Caroline Katzenstein, 7 February 1913, NWPP.
3. *New York World*, 13 February 1913.
4. *New York Herald*, 18 February 1913.
5. *NYT*, 28 February 1913.

6. *WP,* 1 March 1913.
7. Paul to the Commissioners of the District of Columbia, 15 February 1913, *Suffrage Parade,* 117.
8. Robert Shaw Oliver to Paul, 20 February 1913, *Suffrage Parade,* 118.
9. *Indianapolis Star,* 3 February 1913.
10. *Fort Wayne News,* 3 March 1913.
11. Doris Stevens, *Jailed for Freedom* (New York: Schocken Books, 1976), 21.
12. Sylvester, *Suffrage Parade,* 203.
13. Mrs. Richard Coke Burleston, *Suffrage Parade,* 496.
14. Ibid., 500.
15. Anson Mills, *Suffrage Parade,* 111.
16. *Chicago Tribune,* 4 March 1913; Sarah Brown, *Suffrage Parade,* 461.
17. Testimony of Helen H. Gardener, *Suffrage Parade,* 437–438.
18. Testimony of Helena Hill Weed, *Suffrage Parade,* 456.
19. Ibid., 67.
20. Testimony of Walter L. Thiesen, *Suffrage Parade,* 459.
21. Testimony of Patricia Street, *Suffrage Parade,* 70.
22. *NYT,* 6 May 1913.
23. Affidavit of Cobb S. Miller, March 5, 1913, NWPP; Jeannette King Gallinger, *Suffrage Parade,* 62–63.
24. *Philadelphia Inquirer,* 4 March 1913.
25. *Chicago Tribune,* 4 March 1913.
26. Nellie Marks, *Suffrage Parade,* 461.
27. *Atlanta Constitution,* 4 March 1913.
28. Winifred Mallon, *Morning Telegraph,* 11 November 1917.
29. Mary U. Foster Baughman, "The Day 'Those Creatures' Shook a City": Recollections of the Woman's Suffrage Procession, March 3, 1913, photocopy, 6: 52, APP/API.
30. Shaw to Paul, 5 March 1913, NWPP.
31. Paul to Phoebe Baily Sherwood, 10 March 1913, NWPP.
32. *Suffrage Parade,* xv.

CHAPTER 6

1. Anna Howard Shaw, *The Story of a Pioneer* (Charlottesville: The University of Virginia Electronic Text Center), etext.virginia.edu/toc/modeng/public/ShaPion.html, 201.
2. Wil A. Linkugel and Martha Solomon, *Anna Howard Shaw: Suffrage Orator and Social Reformer* (New York: Greenwood Press, 1991), 105.
3. Flexner, *Century of Struggle,* 248.
4. *WP,* 9 March 1913; *Fort Wayne News,* 12 March 1913.
5. Irwin, *Uphill,* 34.
6. Stevens, *Jailed for Freedom,* 23.
7. *NYT,* 8 April 1913.
8. Shaw to Paul and Burns, 21 March 1913, NWPP; Dennett to Paul, 22 March 1913, NWPP.
9. Lewis to Paul, 20 April 1913, NWPP.
10. Dennett to Paul, 16 May 1913, NWPP.
11. *Conversations with Alice Paul,* 24–25.
12. Alice Paul, "Ivy Ode," *The Phoenix,* June 1905, Swarthmore College Library, 11.
13. Paul to Vernon, 21 April 1913, NWPP.
14. Hazel Hunkins-Hallinan, "Memorial Service for Mabel Vernon," 16 November 1975, Hazel Hunkins-Hallinan Papers (hereafter HHHP), Schlesinger Library, 64: 8.
15. Paul to Anson Mills, 2 August 1913, NWPP.

16. Dennett to Paul, 5 August 1913; Shaw to Burns, 10 September 1913, NWPP.
17. Paul to Shaw, 27 September 1913, NWPP; Shaw to Paul, 10 October 1913, NWPP.
18. Harper, ed., *History of Woman Suffrage*, 5: 359.
19. Paul to Shaw, 20 November 1913, NWPP.
20. Public Record Office, HO 45/10695/231366/27, transcript by Edward James of Women's Social and Political Union meeting, 19 February 1913, quoted in Purvis, *Emmeline Pankhurst*, 210.
21. *NYT*, 14 September 1913.
22. Burns to Florence Griscom, 4 November 1913, NWPP.
23. Shaw to Burns, 19 November 1913.
24. *Brooklyn Daily Eagle*, 18 November 1913.
25. Ibid.
26. Shaw to Burns, 19 November 1913.
27. Irwin, *Uphill*, 41–43.
28. Shaw to Burns, 19 November 1913, NWPP.
29. Burns to Shaw, 21 November 1913, NWPP.
30. Mary Garrett Hay to Paul, 7 July 1913, NWPP.
31. Shaw to Mrs. M. M. Forrest, 31 March 1914, NWPP.
32. *WP*, 6 December 1913.
33. Shaw to Dear President and Executive Council Member, n.d., reel 7, NWPP.
34. Helen Frances Shedd to Ruth McCormick, 30 July 1914, NWPP.
35. "Opening Meeting for 1914 of the Congressional Union," *Suffragist*, 17 January 1914, 6.
36. Ibid.
37. Antoinette Funk press release, 15 February 1914, enclosure from Ryan, n.d., reel 7, NWPP.
38. Paul to Shaw, 17 January 1914, NWPP.

CHAPTER 7

1. Inez Haynes Irwin, "Adventures," 414, quoted in Judith Schwarz, *Radical Feminists of Heterodoxy*, (Norwich, VT: New Victoria Publishers, Inc., 1986), 19.
2. Eastman to Burns, 9 January 1914, NWPP; Beard to Burns, 9 January 1914, NWPP.
3. Burns to Paul, 15 January 1914, NWPP; Belmont to Paul, 23 January 1914, NWPP.
4. Paul to Jessie Hardy Stubbs, 17 September 1914, NWPP
5. Stubbs to Paul, 21 February 1914, NWPP.
6. Abby Scott Baker to Paul, n.d., reel 8, NWPP.
7. Beard to Burns, 15 March 1914, NWPP.
8. *New York Tribune*, 3 May 1914.
9. McCormick to Mrs. A. H. Potter, 6 May 1914, NWPP.
10. Paul to Upton, 20 March 1914, NWPP.
11. Paul to Rheta Childe Dorr, 22 February 1914, NWPP.
12. Paul to Elizabeth Harris, 3 March 1914, NWPP; Paul to Harris, 4 March 1914, NWPP; Paul to Smith, 27 April 1914, NWPP.
13. Dorr to Paul, 21 April 1914, NWPP; Elizabeth C. Harris to Paul, 8 June 1914, NWPP.
14. Paul to Belmont, 8 June 1914, NWPP.
15. Burns to Beard, 28 April 1914, NWPP.
16. Paul to Beard, 28 April 1914, NWPP.
17. Mrs. George M. Kenyon to Paul, 2 May 1914, NWPP.
18. Helen Paul to Alice Paul, 5 May 1914, NWPP.
19. Funk to Paul, 5 May 1914, NWPP.
20. "Three Views of Mabel Vernon," in *Speaker for Suffrage and Petitioner for Peace: Mabel Vernon*, An Interview Conducted by Amelia R. Fry, Suffragists Oral History Project, The Bancroft Library, University of California, Berkeley, 1976, iv.

21. Mary R. de Vou to Paul, 10 April 1914, NWPP; Paul to de Vou, 14 April 1914, NWPP.
22. Paul to Lewis, 16 April 1914, NWPP; Lewis to Paul, 3 June 1914, NWPP.
23. Martin to Paul, 9 April 1914; 29 July 1914, NWPP.
24. "Campaigning Through Nevada," *Suffragist*, 23 May 1914, 7.
25. Ibid.
26. Ibid.
27. "Record of the Democratic Party on Suffrage," *Suffragist*, 19 September 1914, 6–7.
28. Beard to Paul, 15 August 1914, NWPP.
29. Irwin, *Uphill*, 76.
30. Ibid., 77.

CHAPTER 8

1. Paul to Belmont, 8 September 1914, NWPP.
2. Paul to Caroline Katzenstein, 14 September 1914, NWPP.
3. Paul to Gertrude Hunter, 26 September 1914, NWPP.
4. *Seattle Star*, 24 September 1914, quoted in *Suffragist*, 2 October 1914, 6.
5. McCue to Paul, 2 October 1914, NWPP.
6. Pincus to Paul, 27 September 1914, NWPP; Pincus to Paul, 13 October 1914, NWPP; Hunter to Paul, 14 October 1914, NWPP.
7. *Rocky Mountain News*, 16 September 1914.
8. Stevens, *Jailed for Freedom*, 11.
9. Stevens to Paul, 16 September 1914, NWPP; Stevens to Paul, 21 September 1914, NWPP.
10. Stevens to Paul, 26 September 1914, NWPP.
11. Hunter to Paul, 3 October 1914, NWPP; Hunter to Paul, 22 October 1914, NWPP.
12. Hunter to Paul, 21 October 1914, NWPP; Hunter to Paul, 20 October 1914, NWPP.
13. Pincus to Paul, 13 October 1914, NWPP; McCue to Paul, 16 October 1914, NWPP.
14. Weed to Paul, 15 October 1914, NWPP.
15. Edna Latimer to Lola Trax, 21 October 1914, NWPP.
16. Latimer to Paul, n.d. 1914, NWPP.
17. *Ogden Standard*, 15 October 1914.
18. Ibid.
19. Mickle Paul to Alice Paul, 8 October 1914, NWPP.
20. Paul to Jane Pincus, 12 October 1914, NWPP.
21. Paul to Hunter, 16 October 1914, NWPP.
22. Ibid.
23. Hunter to Paul, 19 October 1914, NWPP; Hunter to Paul, 26 October 1914, NWPP.
24. Pincus to Paul, 4 November 1914, NWPP.
25. Gilson Gardner, "Women a Political Power in Nine States," 14 November 1914, *Suffragist*, 6.
26. Paul to Stevens, 9 November 1914, NWPP.

CHAPTER 9

1. *New York Mail*, 12 January 1915.
2. *New York Tribune*, 15 January 1915.
3. *NYT*, 13 January 1915.
4. Paul to Belmont, 11 March 1915, NWPP.

5. Paul to Gardner, 11 March 1915, NWPP.
6. Paul to Whittemore, 25 January 1915, NWPP.
7. Paul to Whittemore, 23 February 1915, NWPP.
8. Carl Hayden to Ella St. Clair Thompson, 27 September 1915, NWPP.
9. "Connecticut Suffragists See Representative Glynn," *Suffragist*, 24 July 1915, 3.
10. Flexner, *Century of Struggle*, 270.
11. *Trenton Times*, 8 July 1915.
12. *New York Tribune*, 29 July 1915.
13. Paul to Burns, 13 July 1915, NWPP.
14. Thompson to Paul, 25 July 1915; 29 July 1915; 20 June 1915, NWPP.
15. Belmont to Burns, 10 June 1915, NWPP.
16. Paul to Burns, 23 August 1915, NWPP.
17. *Sara Bard Field: Poet and Suffragist*, An Interview Conducted by Amelia R. Fry, Suffragists Oral History Project, The Bancroft Library, University of California at Berkeley, 1979, 249.
18. Alice Huyler Ramsey, *Veil, Duster, and Tire Iron* (Covina, CA: Alice Huyler Ramsey, 1961), 69.
19. *Sara Bard Field*, 303.
20. Ibid.
21. Ibid.
22. Ibid.
23. *Lowell Sun*, 27 February 1937.
24. "Mr. Bryant at the Pacific Panama Exposition," *Suffragist*, 17 July 1915, 5.
25. Quoted in "The Farewell to the Woman Voters' Envoys," *Suffragist*, 2 October 1915, 5.
26. Ibid.
27. *Philadelphia North American*, 15 September 1915.
28. *Sara Bard Field*, 310.
29. Ramsey, *Veil, Duster, and Tire Iron*, 25.
30. Field to Burns, 8 October 1915, NWPP.
31. Field to Burns, 28 September 1915, NWPP.
32. Vernon to Paul, 15 October 1915, NWPP.
33. Vernon to Paul, 16 October 1915; October 1915, NWPP.
34. Vernon to Paul, 23 October 1915, NWPP.
35. Ibid.
36. Vernon to Paul, 24 October 1915, NWPP.
37. Stevens to Paul, 27 October 1915, NWPP.
38. "For the Portland Oregonian," 31 October 1918, NWPP.
39. *Sara Bard Field*, 321.
40. Ibid., 323.
41. Ibid., 324.
42. Field to Paul, 29 October 1915, NWPP.
43. Ibid.
44. Ibid.
45. Ibid.
46. Paul to Vernon, 29 October 1915, NWPP; Field to Paul, 29 October 1915, NWPP.
47. Field to Paul, 29 October 1915, NWPP.
48. "Illinois Greets Women Voters' Envoy," *Suffragist*, 31 November 1915, 3.
49. Quoted in "Women Voters' Envoys Reach the East," *Suffragist*, 20 November 1915, 3.
50. Vernon to Paul, 1 November 1915, NWPP.
51. "From Boston to New York," *Suffragist*, 4 December 1915, 5; Field, report for the *Suffragist*, 21 November 1915, NWPP.
52. "From Boston to New York," *Suffragist*, 4 December 1915, 5.
53. Ibid., 6.

54. Vernon to Paul, 1 November 1915, NWPP.
55. Field to Paul, 29 November 1915, NWPP.
56. *WP,* 7 December 1915.
57. Ibid.
58. Lewis to Paul, 29 December 1915, NWPP.
59. Irwin, *Uphill,* 117–118.

CHAPTER 10

1. Arthurs S. Link, *The New Freedom* (Princeton, NJ: Princeton University Press, 1956), 63.
2. Ibid., 68.
3. Robert S. Byrd, "The Woodrow Wilson Years, 1913–1920," *The Senate 1789–1989, Addresses on the History of the United States Senate* (Washington, D.C.: U.S. Senate Historical Office, 1991), 407.
4. Kathleen L. Wolgemuth, *The Journal of Negro History* (Washington, D.C.: The Association for the Study of Negro Life and History, 1959), 44: 158–171.
5. "The Diary of Nancy Saunders Toy," 6 January 1915, PWW, 32: 21.
6. "Diary of Colonel House," 22 September 1915, PWW, 34: 508.
7. Axson to Wilson, 27 February 1885, PWW, 4: 307; Wilson to Axson, 1 March 1885, *PWW,* 4: 316.
8. Wilson to Richard Heath Dabney, 28 October 1885, PWW, 5: 38; Wilson's Confidential Journal, 20 October 1887, PWW, 5: 619; W.W. Bridges, 16 August 1888, Woodrow Wilson-Robert Bridges Correspondence, Princeton University Library, quoted in Link, *The Road to the White House* (Princeton, NJ: Princeton University Press, 1947), 20.
9. Wilson to Edith Bolling Galt, 9 May 1915, quoted in Edwin Tribble, ed., *A President in Love: The Courtship Letters of Woodrow Wilson and Edith Bolling Galt* (Boston: Houghton Mifflin, 1981), 34.
10. Diary of Colonel House, 22 September 1915, PWW, 34: 508.
11. Ellen Axson Wilson to Wilson, 23 July 1913, PWW, 28: 67.
12. Harper, ed., *Woman Suffrage,* 5: 376.
13. Irwin, *Uphill,* 59–60.
14. John Randolph Thornton to Wilson, 29 June 1914, *PWW,* 30: 225.
15. "Democratic Deputation to the President," *Suffragist,* 9 January 1915, 4.
16. Irwin, *Uphill,* 147.
17. "Remarks in New York to a Suffrage Delegation," 27 January 1916, *PWW,* 36: 3.
18. Vernon to Burns, 3 February 3, 1916, NWPP; *Suffragist,* 12 February 1916, 5.
19. "Hearing Before the House Judiciary Committee," *Suffragist,* 25 December 1915, 5–7.
20. Matilda Hill Gardner, "The Farewell to the Envoys," and "The Washington Press on the Demonstration," *The Suffragist,* 15 April 1916, 7.
21. Belmont to Paul, 12 April 1916, NWPP.
22. Vernon to Burns, 8 April 1916, NWPP; Ross to Paul, 9 April 1916, NWPP; Belmont to Paul, 12 April 1916, NWPP.
23. Mallon to Paul, 15 April 1916, NWPP.
24. Paul to Beard, 18 March 1916, NWPP.
25. Beard to Paul, 20 March 1918, NWPP.
26. Burns to Paul, 15 April 1916, NWPP.
27. Burns to Paul, 29 April 1916, NWPP.
28. Katzenstein to F. F. Forbes, 29 April 1916, NWPP.
29. Paul to Burns, 17 April 1916, NWPP.
30. Winifred Mallon to Paul, 18 April 1916, 1 May 1916, NWPP; Baker to Paul, 19 April 1916, NWPP.
31. Irwin, *Uphill,* 153.

32. Linda J. Lumsden, *Inez: The Life and Times of Inez Milholland* (Bloomington: Indiana University Press, 2004), 146.
33. Ida M. Tarbell, "Woman's Party is Made Up of Voters Wise in Politics," *New York World*, 7 June 1916, quoted in *Suffragist*, 17 June 1916, 8.
34. Irwin, *Uphill*, 61.
35. Merlo J. Pusey, *Charles Evans Hughes*, vol. 1 (New York: The Macmillan Company, 1952), 350.
36. Adamson to Burns, 15 June 1916, NWPP.
37. "Mr. Hughes Hears the Case for the Federal Suffrage Amendment," *Suffragist*, 15 July 1916, 7.
38. "Mr. Hughes Endorses Susan B. Anthony Amendment," *Suffragist*, 5 August 1916, 3.
39. Alison Hopkins to Burns, 1 August 1916, NWPP; Beard to Paul, 7 August 1916, NWPP; *WP,* 2 August 1916.
40. Paul to Lewis, 6 August 1916, NWPP.
41. Unidentified newspaper clipping, 3 August 1916, Alva Belmont Scrapbooks, reel 168, NWPP.
42. *Mabel Vernon*, 63.
43. "President Hears Woman's Protest," *Suffragist*, 8 July 1916, 7.
44. Ibid.
45. *Mabel Vernon*, 63; Paul to Clara S. Boggs, 8 July 1916, NWPP.
46. Thompson to Paul, 7 July 1916, NWPP.
47. Thompson to Burns, 29 August 1916, NWPP.
48. Stevens to Martin, 1 September 1916, NWPP.
49. Stevens to Paul, 22 August 1916, NWPP.
50. Stevens to Martin, 1 September 1916, NWPP.
51. K. Morey to Paul, 8 September 1916, NWPP; Whittemore to Paul, 7 September 1916, NWPP.
52. Agnes Campbell to Paul, 10 September 1916, NWPP.
53. Younger to Paul, 6 September 1916, NWPP.
54. Younger to Paul, 6 September 1916, NWPP; Ross to Paul, 19 September 1916, NWPP.
55. Vivian Pierce to Paul, 23 September 1916, NWPP; Thompson to Paul, 25 September 1916, NWPP.
56. Paul to Lewis, 27 September 1916, NWPP.
57. Paul to Winslow, 23 October 1916, NWPP.
58. Jane Pincus to Paul, 30 September 1916, NWPP.
59. Blatch to Hill, 13 October, NWPP.

CHAPTER 11

1. Milholland to Paul, n.d., 1916, reel 33, NWPP.
2. Paul to Stevens, 25 October 1916, NWPP.
3. Lumsden, *Inez*, 152–153.
4. V. Milholland to Paul, 30 October 1916, NWPP; Paul to I. Milholland, 16 October 1916, NWPP.
5. V. Milholland to Paul, 30 October 1916, NWPP; Hurlburt to Paul, 15 October 1916, NWPP.
6. Ida Finney Macrille to Stevens, 14 October 1916, NWPP.
7. *Chicago Tribune*, 20 October 1916.
8. V. Millholland to Paul, 30 October 1916, NWPP.
9. Ibid.
10. Amidon to Stevens, 24 October 1916, NWPP.
11. Dr. Catherine Lynch to Paul, 25 October 1916, NWPP; Paul to Perry, 26 October 1916, NWPP.

12. Amidon to Paul, 28 October 1919, NWPP; Paul to Perry, 29 October 1916, NWPP.
13. Available at www.archives.gov/federal-register/electoral-college/scores.html#1916.
14. *NYT,* 12 November 1916.
15. Ibid.
16. Paul to Beard, 4 December 1916, NWPP.
17. Martin to Amidon, 14 December 1916, NWPP.
18. Amidon to Martin, 14 December 1916, NWPP.
19. V. Milholland to Paul, 30 October 1916, NWPP.
20. Irwin, *Uphill,* 184.
21. Ibid., 186.
22. *NYT,* 6 December 1917; *Oneonta Daily Star,* 6 December 1917.
23. Paul to Rogers, 17 December 1916, NWPP.
24. Irwin, *Uphill,* 22.
25. Available at http://cyberhymnal.org/htm/f/o/forwardb.htm.
26. "The National Memory Service in Memory of Inez Milholland," *Suffragist,* 30 December 1916, 9.
27. Ibid.
28. Irwin, *Uphill,* 191.

CHAPTER 12

1. Thomas W. Brahany to Wilson, 6 January 1917, PWW, 40: 420–421.
2. Irwin, *Uphill,* 194.
3. Maud Younger, "Revelations of a Female Lobbyist," *McCall's,* part two, 12 October 1919.
4. Ibid.
5. Ibid.
6. Blatch and Lutz, *Challenging Years,* 268.
7. Ibid., 269.
8. Ibid., 276.
9. Ibid.
10. *WP,* 10 January 1917.
11. *NYT,* 11 January 1917.
12. *WP,* 11 January 1917.
13. Ibid.
14. Irwin, *Uphill,* 203.
15. *WP,* 11 January 1917.
16. Hazel Hunkins, "Materials for Autobiography," HHHP, 1: 9.
17. "Suffragists Wait at the White House for Action," *Suffragist,* 17 January 1917, 7. Without citing examples, the *NYT,* 11 January 1917, stated that "The White House has been picketed before, but never until today by hostile suffragists."
18. *NYT,* 11 January 1917.
19. *Lowell Sun,* 11 January 1917; *Fitchburg Daily Sentinel,* 11 January 1917; *Oakland Tribune,* 13 January 1917.
20. Marjory Miller Whittemore to Paul, 10 January 1917, NWPP; Ethel Adamson to Paul, 11 January 1917, NWPP.
21. *NYT,* 17 January 1917.
22. Paul to Belmont, 14 January 1917, NWPP.
23. Tacie Paul to Alice Paul, 13 January 1917, NWPP.
24. Paul to Hilles, 11 January 1917, NWPP; Carolyn Katzenstein to Paul, 15 January 1917, NWPP.
25. *Syracuse Herald,* 15 January 1917.
26. Paul to Mrs. John Dewey, 16 January 1917, NWPP.
27. Carolyn Katzenstein to Vernon, 6 January 1917, NWPP.

28. Paul to Agnes Morey, 13 January 1917, NWPP.
29. Alison Hopkins to Vernon, 22 January 1917, NWPP.
30. *Trenton Evening Times*, 31 January 1917.
31. Irwin, *Uphill*, 204.
32. Ibid.
33. Ibid., 205.
34. *WP*, 13 January 1917.
35. Irwin, *Uphill*, 202.
36. Stevens, *Jailed for Freedom*, 64.
37. Ibid.
38. Ibid., 68.
39. Ibid., 66.
40. Carrie Chapman Catt to Frances M. Lane, 14 February 1917, NWPP.
41. *NYT*, 1 February 1917.
42. *NYT*, 11 February 1917.
43. Mary B. Anthony to Paul, 1 February 1917, NWPP.
44. *Syracuse Herald*, 20 February 1917.
45. *NYT*, 11 February 1917.
46. Alice Paul to Elsie Hill, 2 July 1917, NWPP.
47. Charles Heaslip to Alice Paul, January 1917,NWPP.
48. Heaslip to Joe Platt, 15 January 1917, NWPP.
49. Heaslip to Stevens, 13 February 1917, NWPP.
50. Ibid.
51. Heaslip to Howard Conover, 19 February 1917, NWPP.
52. Heaslip to Joe Platt, 19 February 1917, NWPP.
53. Heaslip letter of resignation, 8 March 1917, NWPP.
54. Baker to Ernestine Evans, 14 March 1917, NWPP.
55. Martin to Burns, 21 February 1917, NWPP; Paul to Burns, 24 February 1917, NWPP.
56. *Oelwein Daily Register*, 20 February 1917.
57. Transcript of the Congressional Union convention, 2 March 1917, 24–25, NWPP.
58. *NYT*, 5 March 1917.
59. Richard V. (signature unclear, possibly Oldham) to Baker, 10 March 1917, NWPP.
60. *NYT*, 5 March 1917. The *NYT* estimated the number of marchers at 400. The *WP* put the number at 500 and the *Suffragist* 1,000.
61. Joseph Tumulty to Baker, 8 February 1917, NWPP.
62. Stevens, *Jailed*, 79.
63. *La Crosse Tribune and Leader-Press*, 6 March 1917.
64. *NYT*, 11 February 1917.
65. *NYT*, 3 April 1917.
66. Ibid.
67. Ibid.

CHAPTER 13

1. *NYT*, 3 April 1917.
2. *Conversations with Alice Paul*, 175.
3. *NYT*, 6 April 1917; *Fitchburg Daily Sentinel*, 6 April, 1917.
4. Virginia Arnold to Paul, 14 June 1917, NWPP.
5. Thompson to Amidon, 22 October 1917, NWPP.
6. Younger, "Revelations," part one, 7.
7. "The Legislative Work," *Suffragist*, 7 February 1917, 8.
8. Interview by Maud Younger, May 1917, NWPP.
9. Interview by Mrs. W. G. Whipple and Mrs. E. St. Clair Thompson, 16 April 1917, NWPP.

10. Interview by Whipple and Thompson, 27 April 1917, NWPP.
11. Beulah Amidon to Mildred Gilbert, n.d., reel 40, NWPP.
12. Ibid.
13. Stevens to Paul, 1 April 1917, NWPP.
14. Stevens to Paul, 4 April 1917, NWPP.
15. Thompson to Needham, 14 June 1917, NWPP.
16. *Vicksburg Herald*, 4 July 1872, available at www.oldcourthouse.org.
17. Ella Thompson, "Report for Suffragist," 1 June 1917, NWPP.
18. Ibid.
19. Catt to Paul, 24 May 1917, NWPP.
20. Thompson to Mrs. R. P. Crump, 9 June 1917, NWPP.
21. *The Spokesman Review*, 15 June 1917, NWPP; Ross to Stevens, 27 May 1917, NWPP.
22. Katzenstein to Paul, 17 May 1917, NWPP.
23. Martin to Paul, 12 June 1917, NWPP.
24. Paul to Ross, 1 June 1917, NWPP; Paul to Whittemore, 5 June 1917, NWPP.
25. Amidon to Needham, 24 May 1917, NWPP.
26. Rebecca Hourwich Reyher, *Working for Women's Equality, 1978*, oral history by Amerilia R. Fry and Fern Ingersoll, Suffragists Oral History Project, The Bancroft Library, University of California at Berkeley, 60.
27. Ibid., 201.
28. Ibid., 104.
29. Ibid., 83.
30. *Diary*, October 8 and September 27, 1901, APP, 1:14.
31. Heffelfinger to Paul, 17 January 1920, NWPP.
32. Mary MacCracken Jones, "Alice Paul: One of the Great Champions of Women's Rights," *The Woman's Viewpoint*, 10 August 1925, APP, 1:2.
33. Alice Paul Interview with Sydney R. Bland, quoted in Sydney R. Bland, "'Never Quite as Committed as We'd Like': The Suffrage Militancy of Lucy Burns," *The Journal of Long Island History*, Summer/Fall 1981, 17.
34. Marion May to Vernon, 29 May 1917, NWPP.

CHAPTER 14

1. *NYT*, 17 June 1917.
2. *NYT*, 21 June 1917.
3. Ibid.
4. Ibid.
5. Paul to Marion May, 21 June 1917, NWPP.
6. Adamson to Baker, 23 June 1917, NWPP.
7. Paul to Ascough, 21 June 1917, NWPP; Burns to Mrs. J. B. Rubles, 20 August 1917, NWPP.
8. *Lincoln Daily Star*, 21 June 1917.
9. *New York Sun*, quoted in *Syracuse Herald*, 21 June 1917. *Reno Evening Gazette*, 21 June 1917.
10. *NYT*, 22 April 1917.
11. *NYT*, 29 April 1917.
12. *NYT*, 11 November 1917; *NYT*, 3 February 1918; *NYT*, 11 November 1917.
13. *NYT*, 12 April 1917.
14. *NYT*, 29 May 1917.
15. *NYT*, 7 April 1917.
16. *NYT*, 2 June 1917.
17. Robert La Follette, address to the U.S Senate, *Congressional Record*, 6 October 1917, 65th Cong., 1st sess., 7878–79. Quoted in Bruno Leone, ed., *World War I: Opposing Viewpoints* (San Diego, CA: Greenhaven Press, Inc., 1998), 150–153.

18. "Introduction to Suffrage Movement: The Summer of 1916," HHHP, 2: 11.
19. *NYT,* 22 June 1917.
20. *Kansas City Star,* 21 June 1917.
21. Hazel Hunkins to "Dear Mother [Anna Isabel Hunkins]," 8 July 1917, HHHP, 61: 9.
22. *Iowa City Citizen,* 21 June 1917; *NYT,* 22 June 1917.
23. Hunkins to "Dear Mother," 8 July 1917, HHHP, 61: 9.
24. Ibid.
25. "Suffrage Sentinels Arraigned by the Government," *Suffragist,* 30 June 1917, 7.
26. Stevens, *Jailed for Freedom,* 95.
27. *Billings Gazette,* 21 June 1917; Hunkins to Ross, 2 July 1917, NWPP.
28. Hunkins to "Dear Little Mother of Mine," 5 July 1917, HHHP, 61: 9.
29. Ibid.
30. "Jack" to Hunkins, n.d., HHHP, 61: 9.
31. Crystal and Max Eastman to Burns, 21 June 1917, NWPP; Bella Neumann-Zilberman to NWP, 21 June 1917, NWPP.
32. Marion May to Paul, 22 June 1917, NWPP.
33. Adamson to Baker, 23 June 1917, NWPP.
34. Abby Roberts to Paul, 25 June 1917, NWPP.
35. Beatrice Castleton to Grace Needham, 25 June 1917, NWPP.
36. *Bismarck Tribune,* 30 June 1917.
37. Maud Wood Park, report on press situation, 5 July 1917, in National American Woman Suffrage Party Papers (hereafter NAWSA), reel 32, LC; Park to J. P. Yoder, July 1917, NAWSA, reel 32, LC. Quoted in Sarah Hunter Graham, *Woman Suffrage and the New Democracy* (New Haven, CT: Yale University Press, 1996), 109. Graham offers a full discussion of this episode.
38. Memorandum by Woodrow Wilson to Joseph P. Tumulty, n.d., PWW, reel 209, Library of Congress, quoted in Graham, *Woman Suffrage and the New Democracy,* 109.
39. *Washington Times,* 22 June 1917.
40. Quoted in "Suffrage Sentinels Arraigned by the Government," *Suffragist,* 30 June 1917, 8.
41. "Six Suffragists Are Tried by the United States Courts," *Suffragist,* 17 July 1917, 5.
42. *NYT,* 18 June 1917.
43. *Dunkirk Evening Observer,* 27 June 1917.
44. *WP,* 28 June 1917.
45. *NYT,* 28 June 1917.
46. Arnold to Younger, 28 June 1917, NWPP.
47. Ibid.
48. *Mansfield News,* 29 June 1917.
49. Available at http://news.google.com/newspapers?nid=2712&dat=19090128&id=n3M9AAAAIBAJ&sjid=ZisMAAAAIBAJ&pg=2562,5446660.
50. *NYT,* 29 June 1917.
51. *NYT,* 5 July 1917.

CHAPTER 15

1. Stevens, *Jailed for Freedom,* 100.
2. Doris Stevens Papers (hereafter DSP), Arthur and Elizabeth Schlesinger Library on the History of Women in America, Radcliffe Institute for Advanced Study, Harvard University, Cambridge, MA, 2: 36.
3. Stevens, *Jailed for Freedom,* 104.
4. "The United States Convicts Eleven More Women for Demanding Democracy," *Suffragist,* 14 July 1917, 4.
5. Matilda Hall Gardener, "Occoquan," *Suffragist,* 28 July 1917, 5.
6. Doris Stevens, "Justice As Seen at Occoquan," *Suffragist,* 11 August 1917, 7.

7. Ibid.
8. *Middletown Times-Press*, 28 July 1917.
9. *WP,* 18 July 1917.
10. Ibid.
11. Margaret Sanger to Anne Martin, 19 July 1917, NWPP.
12. Josephine du Pont to Florence Hilles, 18 July 1917, NWPP.
13. *NYT,* 18 July 1917.
14. Hunkins to Hill, 12 July 1917, NWPP.
15. Elizabeth Stuyvesant to Iris Calderhead, 12 July 1917, NWPP.
16. Stevens, *Jailed for Freedom,* 116.
17. Hunkins to Mrs. Charles Amidon, 23 July 1917, NWPP.
18. Hunkins to Mrs. W. P. Vaughan, 16 July 1917, NWPP.
19. Hunkins to Hill, 21 July 1917, NWPP; unidentified letter writer to Elizabeth Kent, 26 July 1917, NWPP.
20. Ascough to Lucy Burns, 2 August 1917, NWPP; Burns to Mrs. Donald R. Hooker, 3 August 1917, NWPP; Burns to Alice Randolph Purdy, 3 August 1917, NWPP.
21. "Kaiser Wilson," *Suffragist,* 18 August 1917, 6.
22. "President Onlooker at Mob Attack on Suffragists," *Suffragist,* 18 August 1917, 7.
23. *NYT,* 14 August 1917.
24. Young to Paul, 18 August 1917, NWPP.
25. "The Administration Versus the Woman's Party," *Suffragist,* 25 August 1917, 7.
26. Mary Winsor, "Seeing a Jail from the Inside," *Suffragist,* 16 March 1918, 6.
27. "Prayer by Mary Winsor in Occoquan," DSP, 7: 225.
28. Affidavit of Virginia Bovee, August 28, 1917, NWPP.
29. Malone to Wilson, 7 September 1917, NWPP.
30. Ibid.
31. Paul to Malone, 9 September 1917, NWPP.
32. Affidavit of Mary Donohue, n.d., reel 49, NWPP.
33. Affidavit of Susie Washington, 2 October 1917, NWPP.
34. Malone to John Joy Edson, 2 October 1917, NWPP; "Investigation of Occoquan Workhouse," *Suffragist,* 20 October 1917, 5.
35. Alice Paul to Tacie Paul, 22 October 1917, NWPP.

CHAPTER 16

1. Lewis to Alyse Gregory et al., 2 November 1917, NWPP; Paul to Hilles, 17 October 1917, NWPP.
2. *NYT,* 11 November 1917.
3. *NYT,* 12 November 1917.
4. Ibid.
5. Stevens, *Jailed for Freedom,* 224.
6. Ibid., 223.
7. Ibid., 224.
8. *NYT,* 14 November 1917.
9. *NYT,* 15 August 1917.
10. Stevens, *Jailed for Freedom,* 196. The account of events from that night is drawn from prisoners' affidavits in NWPP files, reel 53; Stevens, *Jailed for Freedom,* 192–209; Irwin, 279–290; affidavit of Camilla Whitcomb, 28 November 1917, NWPP.
11. Ibid.
12. Affidavit of Kathryn Lincoln, 28 November 1917, NWPP.
13. Affidavit of Dora Lewis, 28 November 1917, NWPP.
14. Affidavit of Camilla Whitcomb, 28 November 1917, NWPP; affidavit of Kathryn Lincoln, 28 November 1917, NWPP.
15. Affidavit of Camilla Whitcomb, 28 November 1917, NWPP.
16. Affidavit of Dorothy Day, 28 November 1917, NWPP.

17. Affidavit of Minnie Quay, 28 November 1917, NWPP.
18. Affidavit of Phoebe Scott, 28 November 1917, NWPP.
19. Irwin, *Uphill*, 280.
20. Affidavit of Kathryn Lincoln, 28 November 1917, NWPP.
21. Affidavit of Dora Lewis, 28 November 1917, NWPP; affidavit of Mrs. C. T. Robertson, 28 November 1917, NWPP.
22. Affidavit of Dora Lewis, 28 November 1917, NWPP.
23. Affidavit of Dorothy Day, 28 November 1917, NWPP.
24. Dorothy Day, *The Long Loneliness* (San Francisco, CA: Harper & Row, Publishers, 1952), 77.
25. Ibid., 78.
26. Affidavit of Kathryn Lincoln, 28 November 1917, NWPP.
27. Irwin, *Uphill*, 284; ibid., 286.
28. Ibid., 284.
29. Ibid., 286.
30. Stevens, *Jailed for Freedom*, 206.
31. Irwin, *Uphill*, 291–292.
32. *NYT,* 25 November 1917.
33. "Dr. John Winters Brannan on Occoquan Workhouse," *Suffragist*, 8 December 1917, 10.
34. Stevens, *Jailed for Freedom*, 201–202.
35. Day, *Long Loneliness*, 81.
36. Hourwich to Amidon, 6 November 1917, NWPP; Vernon to Pauline Clark, 2 November 1917, NWPP.
37. Vernon to Pauline Clark, 2 November 1917, NWPP.
38. *Nevada State Journal,* 23 November 1917; *Olean Evening Herald,* 30 November 1917.
39. Shaw to Shippen Lewis, 28 November 1917, NWPP.
40. *LaCrosse Tribune and Leader-Press,* 24 November 1917.
41. *WP,* 4 March 1917.
42. Amidon to Vernon, 27 October 1917, NWPP.
43. Irwin, *Uphill*, 291.
44. Irwin, *Uphill*, 288; Stevens, *Jailed for Freedom*, 208–209.
45. Affidavit of Kathryn Lincoln, 28 November 1917, NWPP.
46. *Modesto Evening News,* 23 November 1917; Stevens, *Jailed for Freedom*, 232–240.
47. Irwin, *Uphill*, 290.
48. Stevens, *Jailed for Freedom*, 238.
49. Mullowney to Zinkham, 26 November 1917, NWPP.
50. Zinkham to Mullowney, 27 November 1917, NWPP.
51. Stevens, *Jailed for Freedom*, 241.
52. Ibid.

CHAPTER 17

1. *Oneonta Daily Star,* 10 January 1918.
2. *Chicago Daily Tribune,* 10 January 1918.
3. *New York Herald Tribune,* 10 January 1918.
4. *NYT,* 10 January 1918.
5. Ibid.
6. *New York Herald Tribune,* 11 January 1918.
7. *NYT,* 11 January 1918.
8. Younger, "Revelations," part three, 14.
9. *Hartford Globe,* 13 January 1918, quoted in *Suffragist*, 30 January 1918, 14.
10. "The Pickets' Part," *Farribault [sic] News-Republican*, 11 January 1918, quoted in *Suffragist*, March 16, 1918, 7.

11. *NYT,* 1 January 1918.
12. *NYT,* 17 February 1918.
13. *NYT,* 24 July 1918; *Waukesha Freeman,* 16 January 1919.
14. "A Suffragist Makes Munitions," *Suffragist,* 25 May 1918, 7.
15. Lewis to Paul, 5 February 1918, NWPP; "Join the Furniture Campaign," *Suffragist,* 23 February 1918, 10.
16. Younger, "Revelations," part two, 12.
17. Younger, "Revelations," part three, 14.
18. Ibid.
19. Paul to Hopkins, 24 April 1918, NWPP.
20. Younger, "Revelations," part three, 46.
21. Marian C. McKenna, *Borah* (Ann Arbor: University of Michigan Press, 1961), 89.
22. "Senator Borah Affirmatively Opposes Federal Suffrage Amendment," *Suffragist,* 4 September 1915, 5.
23. Borah to Ruth A. Crapo, 31 August 1918, NWPP.
24. Whittemore to Paul, 11 June 1918, NWPP; Paul to Whittemore, 15 June 1918, NWPP.
25. *New York World,* 14 January 1918, quoted in *Suffragist,* 30 January 1918, 14.
26. Younger, "Revelations," part three, November 1919, 46, 50.
27. *NYT,* 2 March 1919.
28. Hill to Paul, n.d., reel 67, NWPP.
29. "The Court of Appeals on Picketing," *Suffragist,* 16 March 1918, 6.
30. Paul to Alice Henkle, 24 May 1918, NWPP.
31. *Washington Herald,* 2 July 1918, quoted in *Suffragist,* 13 July 1918, 8.
32. "War Workers Will Ask Interview With the President," *Suffragist,* 8 June 1918, 11; *Indianapolis Star,* 25 May 1918.
33. *NYT,* 5 July 1918.
34. Ascough to Paul, 28 July 1918, NWPP.
35. Paul to "Dear Suffragist," 28 July 1918, NWPP.
36. U.S. Army Col. C. S. Ridley to Paul, 6 August 1918, NWPP.
37. Irwin, *Uphill,* 363.
38. "Women's Protest Against Disfranchisement Broken Up by Federal Police," *Suffragist,* 17 August 1918, 5; *NYT,* 7 August 1920.
39. "Women's Protest," *Suffragist,* 5.
40. *NYT,* 8 August 1918; ibid.; *NYT,* 9 August 1918.
41. *NYT,* 13 August 1918.
42. Pauline Clarke, "The Trial," *Suffragist,* 24 August 1918, 6; ibid.
43. Ibid.
44. Louis Brownlow, *A Passion for Anonymity,* vol. 2 (Chicago: University of Chicago Press, 1958), 78–79; Maud Wood Park, *Front Door Lobby* (Boston: Beacon Press, 1960), 162.
45. Brownlow, 80.
46. "President's Words Burned as [*sic*] Suffrage Protest in Front of White House," *Suffragist,* 28 September 1918, 7.
47. *NYT,* 26 September 1918.
48. *NYT,* 28 September 1918.
49. *NYT,* 29 September 1918.
50. *NYT,* 1 October 1918.
51. Ibid.
52. *NYT,* 2 October 1918.

CHAPTER 18

1. Irwin, *Uphill,* 382.
2. "Picketing Continued," *Suffragist,* 2 November 1919, 8.

3. Paul to Lee Meriwether, 1 June 1920, NWPP.
4. Ibid.
5. Paul to Whittemore, 21 October 1918, NWPP.
6. Paul to Whittemore, 29 October 1918, NWPP.
7. Irwin, *Uphill*, 489.
8. Whittemore to Paul, 4 November 1918, NWPP.
9. John Milholland to George Moses, 24 October 1918, NWPP.
10. Paul to Flanagan et al., 23 October 1918, NWPP.
11. *NYT,* 12 November 1918.
12. "Miss Paul Speaks at National Headquarters," *Suffragist,* 16 November 1918, 4.
13. Annie G. Porritt, "The Suffragist Conference at Washington," *Suffragist,* 28 December 1918, 4.
14. Tacie Paul to Alice Paul, 25 December 1917, NWPP.
15. Irwin, *Uphill*, 402.
16. Lewis to Mary Burnham, 4 January 1919, NWPP.
17. Vernon to Olive Richard et al., 6 January 1919, NWPP. Lewis to Katzenstein, 24 January 1919, NWPP.
18. Alice Paul to Tacie Paul, 6 January 1919, NWPP; Helen Paul to Alice Paul, 9 January 1919, NWPP.
19. *WP,* 14 July 1919.
20. Elizabeth Kalb, "The Watch Fire Goes On," *Suffragist,* 8 February 1919, 8.
21. Mildred Morris, "An Impression of the Jail," *Suffragist,* 1 February 1919, 6.
22. Young to Paul, 17 January 1919, NWPP; Paul to Pollitzer, 27 January 1919, NWPP.
23. Burns to Clara Wolfe, 23 January 1919, NWPP.
24. *NYT,* 10 February 1919; Paul to Lavinia Dock, 31 March 1919, NWPP.
25. Park, *Front Door Lobby,* 234–235.
26. *NYT,* 11 February 1919, NWPP.
27. Lewis to Katzenstein, 4 March 1919, NWPP.
28. For a list of women prisoners see Stevens, *Jailed for Freedom,* 354–371.
29. Irwin, *Uphill*, 427–428.
30. *NYT,* 21 May 1919.
31. *NYT,* 23 May 1919.
32. Park, *Front Door Lobby,* 266.
33. Emory to Paul, 6 June 1919, NWPP.
34. Walter Clark to Paul, 4 June 1919, NWPP.
35. Rogers to Paul, 5 June 1919, NWPP.
36. "Suffragists Rejoice," *Suffragist,* 14 June 1919, 9.
37. Howard G. Brownson to Paul, 19 October 1919, NWPP.
38. Frank Stephens to Paul, 18 April 1919, NWPP.
39. "Lobbying and Political Work," *Suffragist,* 10 May 1919, 5.
40. *NYT,* 6 June 1919.

CHAPTER 19

1. Pierce to Paul, 1 July 1919, NWPP.
2. Riegel to Vernon, 7 August 1919, NWPP.
3. *WP,* 6 June 1919; *Waterloo Times-Tribune,* 6 June 1919;
4. Geidel, 623–4; 648.
5. Lewis to Paul, 13 July 1919, NWPP.
6. *Ada Evening News,* 19 January 1920.
7. *Reno Evening Gazette,* 8 January 1920.
8. Kerr to Paul, 26 February 1920, NWPP.
9. *Charleston Daily Mail,* 6 March 1920.
10. Paul to R. J. Caldwell, 6 April 1920, NWPP.
11. "Picketing the Republican Party," *Suffragist,* July 1920, 125.

12. Paul to Winsor, August 1920, NWPP.
13. Mildred Hicks to Paul, July, 1920; Mrs. M.C. Barnard, July 1920; Gertrude Achilles, July 1920, NWPP.
14. Carrie Chapman Catt and Nettie Rogers Shuler, *Woman Suffrage and Politics* (Seattle: University of Washington Press, 1969), 429–30.
15. Ibid., 442.
16. Paul to Pollitzer, Wold to Marion W. Myrick, 16 August 1920, NWPP.
17. Febb Burn to Harry T. Burn, August 1920, Knox County Public Library Calvin M. McClung Digital Collection, http://cmdc.knoxlib.org/cdm4/browse.php?CISO ROOT=%2Fp265301coll8;
18. *NYT,* 27 August 1920
19. Emma Wold to Caroline Spencer, 30 August 1920, NWPP.
20. Ibid.
21. *NYT,* 27 August 1920.
22. *Indianapolis Star,* 3 November 1920.
23. Tacie Paul's scrapbook, APP, 14:211.

EPILOGUE

1. Madelyn Doty, *New York Call,* 19 August 1920.
2. "Minutes of the Monthly Executive Committee Meeting of the National Woman's Party [*sic*]," 10 September 1920, DSP, 7: 225.
3. Alice Paul to Tacie Paul, 5 July 1921, SL, copy in API.
4. Thomas C. Pardo, ed., *National Woman's Party Papers, 1913–1974: The Guide to the Microform Collection* (Sanford, NC: Microfilming Corporation of America, 1979), 1–2.
5. Burns, Eighteenth Annual Bulletin (1931), VULSC, 11.
6. *NYT,* 13 February 1933.
7. "Alice Muller: Alice Paul in Geneva at the Start of World War II," interview conducted by Amelia Roberts Fry, 4 March 1982, 29–30, API.
8. Ibid., 27.
9. Pardo, *National Woman's Party Papers 1913–1974,* 173–174.
10. Ibid., 169.
11. Susan D. Becker, *The Origins of the Equal Rights Amendment: American Feminism Between the Wars* (Westport, CT: Greenwood Press, 1981), 279.
12. Letha Mae Glover, interview with author, 30 June 2009.
13. Ibid.
14. Christopher Hanson, interview with author, 17 September 2008.
15. Glover interview.
16. "Alice Muller," 56.
17. Ibid., 57.
18. *Burlington County Times,* 27 January 1977.
19. Carol Mullin, interview with author, 10 March 2009.
20. Hazel Hunkins-Hallinan, speech delivered 20 July 1977, HHHP, 6: 7.
21. Ibid.

INDEX

CPSIA information can be obtained
at www.ICGtesting.com
Printed in the USA
LVOW08s2026151216
517433LV00003BA/357/P